A B C D E F G H I J K L M N O P Q R S

monday morning®

Reading Connections

by Mary Bannister, Lillian Lieberman & Annalisa Suid
illustrated by Marilynn G. Barr

Cab

Cat's Cab

c c c c C

A B C D E F G H I J K L M N O P Q R S T U V W X Y Z

Dedicated to teachers everywhere

Publisher: Roberta Suid
Editor: Carol Whiteley
Design & Production: MGB Press

Other books in the Connection series:
Alphabet Connections (MM 1969), *Preschool Connections* (MM 1993),
Storybook Connections (MM 1999)

Online address: MMBooks@AOL.com

A B C D E F G H I J K L M N O P Q R S T U V W X Y Z

Contents

a b c d e f g h i j k l m n o p q r s t u v w x y z

A B C D E F G H I J K L M N O P Q R S T U V W X Y Z

Introduction

Introduce young children to beginning reading skills with *Reading Connections*. The creative activities in this book *connect* children to reading through links with the alphabet, art, literature, phonics, sight words, and more.

Exploring the Alphabet

The alphabet connection involves hands-on experiences with the letters of the alphabet. Duplicate and color the large letter cards, hold them up, and name the letters. Give each letter's sound and a key word. Have children echo you.

Draw large models of each letter on the chalkboard and show the proper writing sequence. Have children practice writing the letter in the air while naming the letter. Invite individual children to trace the large chalkboard letter using colored chalk. Guide the fingers and hands of children who have difficulty. For further reinforcement, children can write the letter in trays of fingerpaint, pudding (yum!), or sand. Children may also enjoy forming the letter shape with their bodies!

After introducing the "letter of the week," read the Mother Goose-inspired alphabet poems to the children. Alphabet puzzles with key pictures help children associate the sound for each letter with appropriate words. Children can cut, paste, color, and assemble the alphabet puzzles to build fine motor skills and visual spatial skills. Other delightful alphabet activities foster creativity with dramatic play, crafts, or games.

Learning Through Literature

To make the *literature connection*, read and discuss the suggested storybooks found in each chapter. Reinforce the alphabet letter and its sound with the accompanying activities. What better way to learn about letter "C" than to collect camping gear to label, examine, and pretend with at the camping corner? (*Curious George Goes Camping*). Or, for the letter "B," make bear beanbags with blue, black, or brown fabric for use with the story *The Berenstain Bears and the Bad Dream*.

In the "resources" section, you will find listings of additional books and materials such as video- and audiotapes.

Learning to Read with Mini-Books

For the *phonics and reading connection*, children move on to more formal reading skills with mini-books involving sound-symbol association, beginning sight words, short vowel patterns, and reading in context. The mini-book pages may be duplicated, colored, cut, and assembled by the teacher or by the children. (See the "How to Make" and "How to Use" sections on pp. 241-242.)

Have children make their own book for each letter and then work on mini-books matching initial letter and sounds to key pictures. Next, they can work on mini-books with short vowel word patterns with picture reinforcement. Simple sight words are also included. Finally, the children can work on illustrated mini-books with the short vowel word patterns. More sight words are also included. Pictures for each story support decoding of word patterns not previously covered.

Children will have fun reading the mini-books. Encourage your students to take the books home to share with family, friends, and relatives.

Reading Connections is geared toward engaging the "whole" child. Through the use of these activities, teachers or parents can ensure a balanced approach toward reading success.

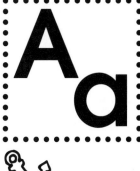

EXPLORE LETTER A

Discuss upper- and lower-case A's and read literature links featuring starts-with-A characters such as Alexander.

⚓ FIND THE "LETTER OF THE WEEK"

• Use a permanent marker to write a letter "A" on the lid of a clear plastic deli tub. Place as many items for letter "A" in the tub as you can find, including plastic ants and animals, acorns, toy autos, an atomizer, pictures of animals, a picture of an anchor, and so on.

• On a cardboard cutout of the letter "A," paste pictures of starts-with-A items cut from magazines. These could include airplanes, alligators, ants, apples, an astronaut, and so on. Other "A" items to glue onto the cardboard: an ace from a deck of cards, real acorns, your autograph, etc.

• Bring in an atlas for children to look through. Have them find places that begin with the letter "A."

• Have the children help you make a list of as many fruits and vegetables as you can think of that start with the letter "A," including almonds, apples, apricots, artichokes, asparagus, avocados, and so on. Consider bringing in one or two items from the list for children to taste.

ASTOUNDING "A" ACTIVITIES

• ALPHABET GAME: Play a lap-slap-clap circle game. Clap your hands and slap your thighs in time as a group. Have each child in turn say a word that starts with letter "A" as the group slaps and claps. If a child cannot think of a word within three slap-clap sets, the next child takes a turn. Continue for as long as the game remains fun for the group. "A" words to use: ant, art, act, about, apple, accordion, astound, anchor, ax, ask, and so on. Repeat this activity through the year as the children learn each letter.

• ACROBATICS: Show the pictures of children doing acrobatics (see next page). Have children practice their own acrobatic activities, such as somersaults and jumping jacks.

 Reading Connections © 1996 Monday Morning Books, Inc.

Aa
Acrobat Patterns

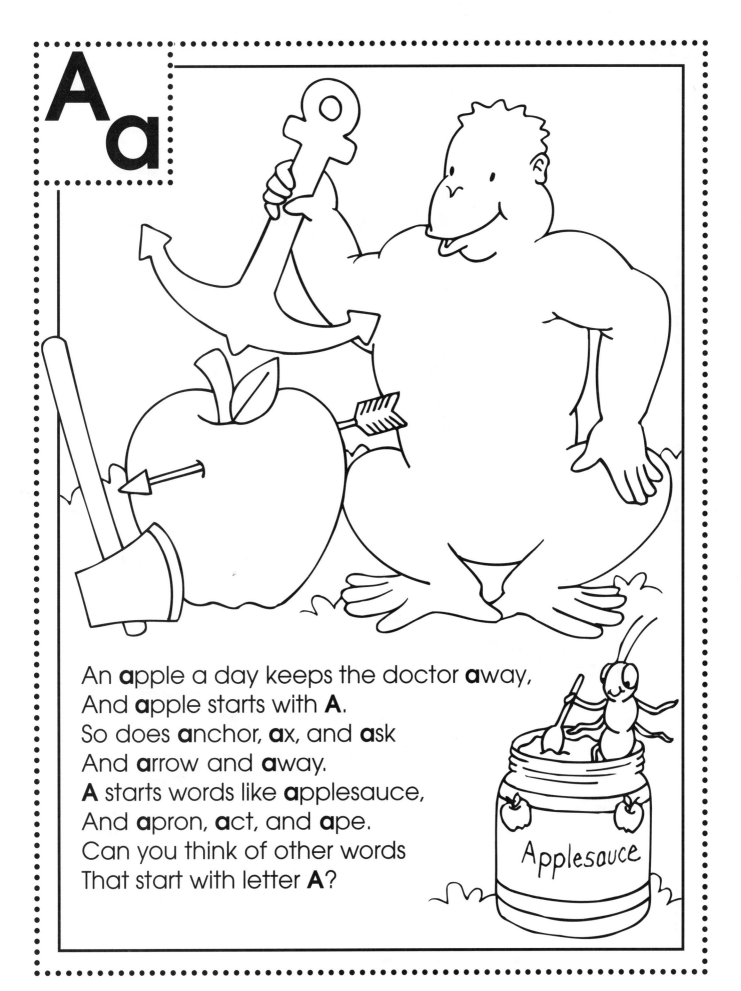

A a

An **a**pple a day keeps the doctor **a**way,
And **a**pple starts with **A**.
So does **a**nchor, **a**x, and **a**sk
And **a**rrow and **a**way.
A starts words like **a**pplesauce,
And **a**pron, **a**ct, and **a**pe.
Can you think of other words
That start with letter **A**?

Applesauce

9

Aa
Upper- and Lower-case A

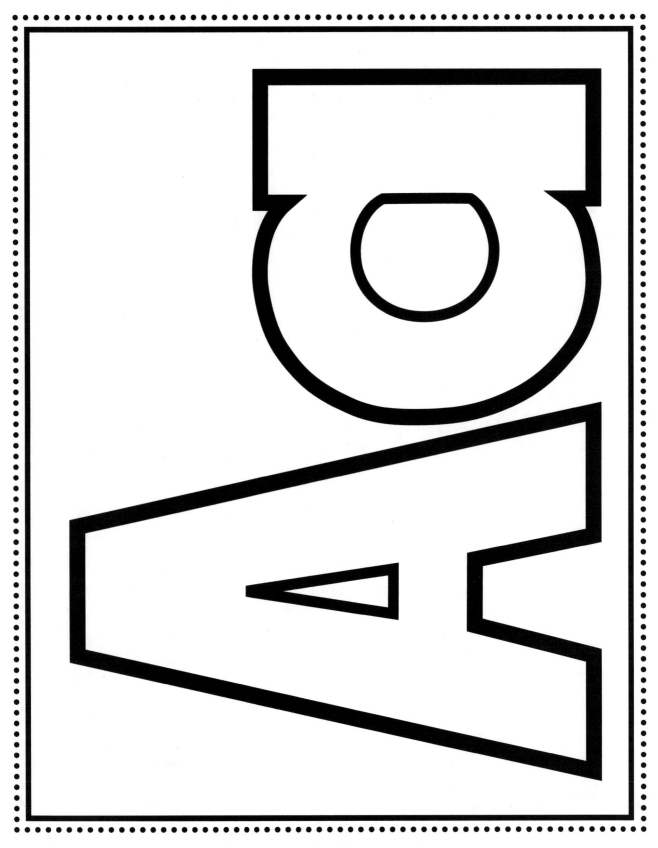

Aa
Alphabet Puzzle

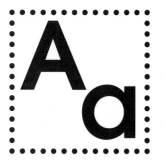

Literature Connection

ALEXANDER

The main character for this unit is Alexander, the star of three books by Judith Viorst. Alexander is best remembered for having a terrible, horrible, no good, very bad day.

READ A BOOK

• *Alexander and the Terrible, Horrible, No Good, Very Bad Day* by Judith Viorst, illustrated by Ray Cruz (Atheneum, 1972). All day long things go wrong for Alexander. But when he complains, no one even answers him! Finally, he decides that life must be easier in Australia.

• *Alexander, Who Used to Be Rich Last Sunday* by Judith Viorst, illustrated by Ray Cruz (Atheneum, 1978). As Alexander quickly finds out, there are many things that can be done with one dollar.

• *Alexander, Who's Not (Do You Hear Me? I Mean It!) Going to Move* by Judith Viorst, illustrated by Robin Preiss Glasser (Atheneum, 1995). Alexander does not want to move with his family. He says, "Never. Not ever. No way. Uh uh. N.O." Ultimately, he decides that the *next* time his family relocates he is "Not—DO YOU HEAR ME? I MEAN IT!—going to move."

ALEXANDER ACTIVITIES

• AMAZING AUSTRALIA: Decorate a corner of the room in honor of Australia. Send away for some travel posters, or bring in a stuffed koala or kangaroo. Set out atlases open to Australia. (Be sure to set out a toy telephone, just in case Alexander decides to call Australia.)

• AN AWFUL/AMAZING DAY: Have students write or dictate personal stories about an awful day. Then have them tell or write a story about an amazing, astounding, awesome day. Once the awful/awesome story sets are illustrated, post them back to back and suspend from fishing line around the room.

• ANGRY ALEXANDER: Brainstorm and chart a list of the moments in each book when Alexander was angry.

Art Connection

THE VISIBLE CASTLE

Mrs. Dickens, Alexander's teacher, liked Paul's picture of the sailboat better than Alexander's picture of the invisible castle. Challenge your students to draw *visible* castles in this activity.

Materials:

Castle pattern (next page), crayons and markers (both thin and thick), silver glitter, glue, aluminum foil, small triangles of colored construction paper, blue cellophane or blue tempera paint and paintbrushes

Directions:

1. Duplicate one castle pattern for each child.
2. Provide assorted colors of crayons and markers for children to use to decorate the castles.
3. For added sparkle, children can glue on silver glitter or bits of aluminum foil.
4. Colored construction paper triangles can be glued on for flags at the tops of turrets. Children can draw flagpoles using thin markers.
5. Provide blue cellophane or blue tempera paint and paintbrushes for children to use to create a moat around their castles.
6. Post the completed castles on a "Visible Castle" bulletin board.

Aa
Castle Pattern

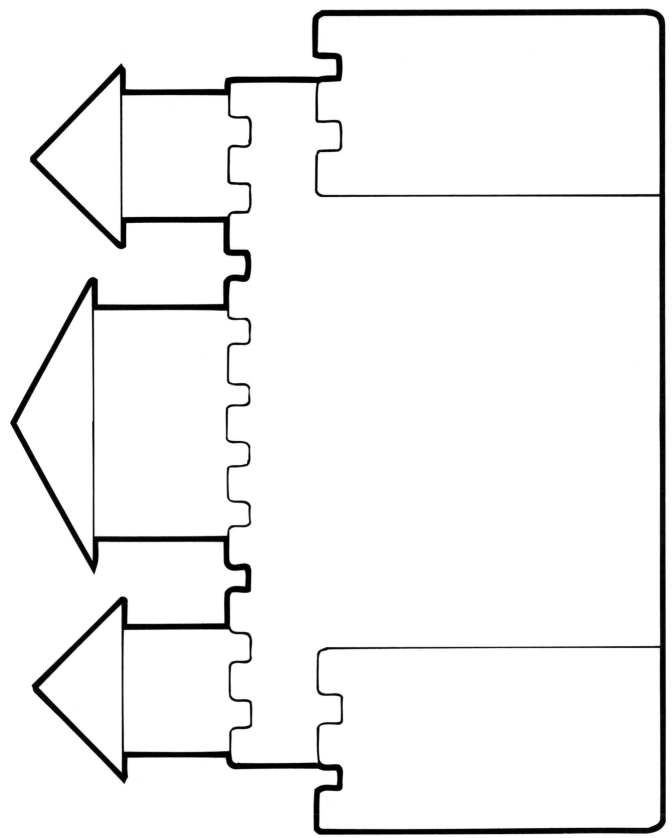

Game Connection

ALEXANDER, MAY I?

After reading *Alexander and the Terrible, Horrible, No Good, Very Bad Day*, play "Alexander, May I?" (a new version of "Mother, May I?"). Choose one child to be Alexander. The other students will ask questions related to the story, for example, "Alexander, may I take five sneaker steps to Australia?" Or "Alexander, may I take two elevator door steps to Australia?" (Children can make up steps to fit the scenes in the book. "Elevator door steps" might be hops because Alexander got his foot caught in the door!) The chosen Alexander will answer with a "yes" or "no."

THE AIRPLANE GAME

For this game, you need an airplane model or game piece and a flat world map. Locate your town or city, then use the plane to fly to: Australia, America (Arkansas, Anchorage, Alaska), Antarctica, Asia, or Africa. Challenge your students to find as many "A" locations as they can within 10 minutes.

ACTING OUT

Have your student actors and actresses play different characters from different "A" stories. On index cards write the name of a character and a setting from the book. Students can act or pantomime the scene until their classmates guess what it is. For example, from *Alexander and the Terrible, Horrible, No Good, Very Bad Day* children can act out the roles of a shoe salesperson, carpool driver, teacher, dentist, father at office, child with gum in his/her hair, and so on.

There's Australia!

Reading Connections © 1996 Monday Morning Books, Inc.

Aa
Resources

Other Alexanders
- *Alexander and the Dragon*
  by Katharine Holabird
  (Clarkson Potter, 1988).
- *Alexander and the Magic Boat*
  by Katharine Holabird
  (Clarkson Potter, 1990).

One afternoon Alexander takes his mother on an imaginary adventure in his magic (armchair) boat.

Other "A" Books
- *Albert's Alphabet*
  by Leslie Tryon
  (Atheneum, 1991).

Albert, the school janitor (who is also a duck), creates an alphabet from bits and pieces of materials.

- *Albert's Play*
  by Leslie Tryon
  (Atheneum, 1992).

Albert and the children in the elementary school (all animals) put on "The Owl and the Pussycat."

- *Alicia Has A Bad Day*
  by Lisa Jahn-Clough
  (Houghton, 1994).

Alicia has a very bad day and may find it better to simply stay in bed.

Australia Books
- *Bossyboots*
  by David Cox
  (Crown, 1987).

Abigail's bossiness is irritating, but her habit helps when her stagecoach is held up by an outlaw.

- *Dial-a-Croc*
  by Mike Dumbleton
  (Orchard, 1991).

Vanessa tries to put her crocodile to work for her.

- *Farmer Schultz's Ducks*
  by Colin Thiele
  (Harper and Row, 1988).

How will the ducks cross the busy freeway daily?

- *Possum Magic*
  by Mem Fox
  (Abingdon, 1987).

In this delightful story, a protective possum turns her charge invisible to protect him from predators.

- *One Wooly Wombat*
  by Rod Trinca and Kerry Argent
  (Kane Miller Books, 1985).

Teach numbers from 1-14 with these Australian animals.

- *Waltzing Matillda*
  by A. B. Paterson
  (Holt, 1970).

An illustrated version of the song.

- *Where the Forest Meets the Sea*
  by Jeannie Baker
  (Greenwillow, 1988).

This story is set during a camping trip in the Australian rainforest.

- *Wombat Stew*
  by Marcia Vaughan
  (Silver Burdett, 1986).

The Australian animals give the dingo interesting suggestions in making his wombat stew.

Additional Resources

Alexander and the Terrible, Horrible, No Good, Very Bad Day puzzle. Order from JTG, 800-327-5113 ($6.95).

EXPLORE LETTER B

Discuss upper-and lower-case B's and read literature links featuring starts-with-B characters such as the Berenstain Bears.

FIND THE "LETTER OF THE WEEK"

• Use a permanent marker to write a letter "B" on the lid of a clear plastic deli tub. Place as many items that begin with the letter "B" in the tub as you can find, including a little ball, a balloon, a box, a bag, a bead, a plastic beetle, a birthday candle, etc.

• On a cardboard cutout of the letter "B," paste buttons and bows.

• Have children help you make a list of as many foods as you can think of that start with the letter "B," including bananas, bamboo shoots, barley, broccoli, blackberries, boysenberries, blueberries, bacon, etc.

• Brainstorm begins-with-B occupations: baker, ballerina, banker, barber, boxer, broker, butcher.

• Play recordings of musical instruments that start with "B," including bagpipe, banjo, bass, bassoon, bongo drum, and so on.

BEAUTIFUL "B" ACTIVITIES

• BUBBLE, BUBBLE: Blow bubbles outside.

• BUTTONS AND BOWS: Count and sort buttons and yarn bows into bowls.

• BEES BUZZ: Duplicate the bee patterns (see next page) to use to create a "Bb" bulletin board. Cut out a construction paper tree to pin to the board and duplicate the letters to make the word B-U-Z-Z!

• B IS FOR BEDTIME: Bring a favorite *bedtime book* such as *The Berenstain Bears Say Good Night* to share with the class.

Reading Connections © 1996 Monday Morning Books, Inc.

Bb
Bee Patterns

BEES BUZZ

B b

Poor **B**o Peep has lost her sheep,
And **B**o begins with **B**.
So does **b**ear and **b**oat and **b**ox
And **b**utterfly and **b**ee.
B begins **b**alloon and **b**all,
Banana, **b**lue, and **b**east.
Can you think of other words
That start with letter **B**?

Bb
Upper- and Lower-case B

Bb
Alphabet Puzzle

Literature Connection

BERENSTAIN BEARS

The main characters for this unit are the Berenstain Bears from the books by Jan and Stan Berenstain. There are many books to choose from in this series. They come in reading levels ranging from the "Bright and Early" series to the new "Big Chapter Books."

READ A BOOK

• *The Berenstain Bears and the Missing Dinosaur Bone* by Stan and Jan Berenstain (Random House, 1980).
When the Bear Museum is missing a bone, the Bear Detectives rush to solve the case.

• *The Berenstain Bears Blaze a Trail* by Stan and Jan Berenstain (Random House, 1987).
The Bear Scouts try to earn merit badges in spite of bumbling Papa Bear.

• *The Berenstain Bears Forget Their Manners* by Stan and Jan Berenstain (Random House, 1985).
The Bear family's behavior is getting rude, so Mama comes up with a plan to change their ways.

• *The Berenstain Bears and Mama's New Job* by Stan and Jan Berenstain (Random House, 1984).
The family members pitch in when Mama turns her hobby into a new job!

BEAR ACTIVITIES

• "B" SCAVENGER HUNT: Challenge students to find begins-with-B words in any Berenstain Bear book.

• BEAR BADGES: Your class can invent merit badges for skills the students are currently working on. Set out the blank badges (see next page) and let students design them. (*The Berenstain Bears Blaze a Trail*)

• BEAR MUSEUM: Set up a classroom museum. Have each child bring an item to display. (*The Berenstain Bears and the Missing Dinosaur Bone*)

• BEAR QUILTS: Have children make paper quilts (see patterns next page) with construction paper and crayons. (*The Berenstain Bears and Mama's New Job*)

Bb
Bear Badges

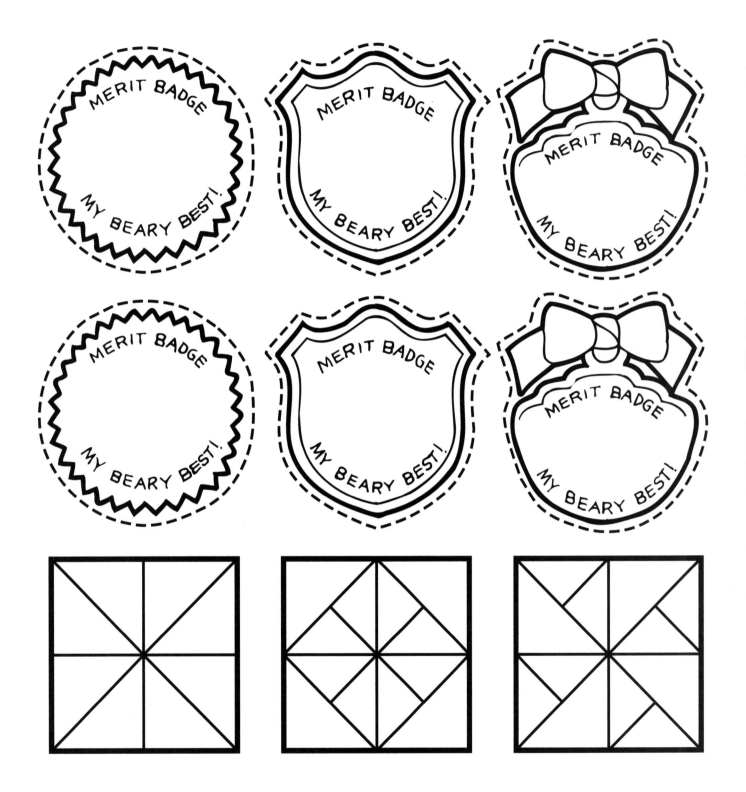

MERIT BADGE
MY BEARY BEST!

MERIT BADGE
MY BEARY BEST!

MERIT BADGE
MY BEARY BEST!

MERIT BADGE
MY BEARY BEST!

MERIT BADGE
MY BEARY BEST!

MERIT BADGE
MY BEARY BEST!

Art Connection

DEM BONES

In *The Berenstain Bears and the Missing Dinosaur Bone*, the Bear Museum is missing a bone and the Bear Detectives rush to solve the case. This bones-into-beasts activity would be a very good one for Halloween.

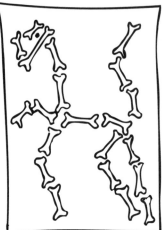

Materials:

Washed and boiled chicken bones, stiff black paper or card stock, glue

Directions:

1. Provide chicken bones, black paper, and glue for children to use to create their own skeleton creatures.
2. Students can glue the boiled bones onto the paper or card stock and then name their beast!

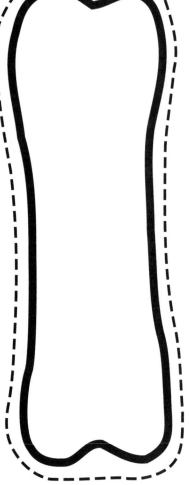

Note:

Advanced preparation is important for this activity. Notify families ahead of time so that they can start saving their bones for you. If possible, get a parent volunteer to do the washing and boiling of bones.

Art Connection
BEAR BEANBAGS

Materials:

Bear beanbag pattern (next page), construction paper (brown or black), stapler (or tape), dried beans, scissors

Directions:

1. Duplicate the bear beanbag pattern onto brown or black construction paper. Make two copies per child.
2. Have the children cut out the patterns.
3. Show children how to staple or tape the edges of the patterns together, leaving a small hole open.
4. Have children place a handful of beans into their bears.
5. Show children how to seal their patterns with the stapler or tape.

Note:

These bags can also be made from fake fur, with sewn-on button eyes, noses, and mouths.

Bb
Beanbag Pattern

Bb
Resources

More Berenstain Bear Books

- *The Berenstain Bears and the Bad Dream*
  by Stan and Jan Berenstain
  (Random House, 1988).
Brother Bear has a bad dream after watching a scary movie.

- *The Berenstain Bears and the Bad Habit*
  by Stan and Jan Berenstain
  (Random House, 1986).
Sister Bear bites her fingernails, but her family helps her to break this bad habit.

- *The Berenstain Bears and the Double Dare*
  by Stan and Jan Berenstain
  (Random House, 1988).
Brother Bear tries to get Sister Bear's jump rope back from Too-Tall and the gang and learns an important lesson.

- *The Berenstain Bears and the In-Crowd*
  by Stan and Jan Berenstain
  (Random House, 1989).

- *The Berenstain Bears and the Messy Room*
  by Stan and Jan Berenstain
  (Random House, 1983).

- *The Berenstain Bears and the Missing Honey*
  by Stan and Jan Berenstain
  (Random House, 1987).
The Berenstain Bears and their dog, Snuff, locate the thief who took Papa Bear's blackberry honey.

- *The Berenstain Bears and the Trouble with Money*
  by Stan and Jan Berenstain
  (Random House, 1983).

- *The Berenstain Bears and the Wild, Wild Honey*
  by Stan and Jan Berenstain
  (Random House, 1983).

- *The Berenstain Bears Are a Family*
  by Stan and Jan Berenstain
  (Random House, 1991).

- *The Berenstain Bears at the Super-Duper Market*
  by Stan and Jan Berenstain
  (Random House, 1991).

- *The Berenstain Bears' Four Seasons*
  by Stan and Jan Berenstain
  (Random House, 1991).

- *The Berenstain Bears Get Stage Fright*
  by Stan and Jan Berenstain
  (Random House, 1986).

- *The Berenstain Bears Go Out for the Team*
  by Stan and Jan Berenstain
  (Random House, 1986).

- *The Berenstain Bears Go to Camp*
  by Stan and Jan Berenstain
  (Random House, 1982).

 Reading Connections © 1996 Monday Morning Books, Inc.

Bb
Resources

More Berenstain Bear Books

- *The Berenstain Bears Go to the Doctor*
  by Stan and Jan Berenstain
  (Random House, 1981).

- *The Berenstain Bears Go to School*
  by Stan and Jan Berenstain
  (Random House, 1978).

- *The Berenstain Bears in the Dark*
  by Stan and Jan Berenstain
  (Random House, 1982).

- *The Berenstain Bears Media Madness*
  by Stan and Jan Berenstain
  (Random House, 1995).

Will the new TV station bring the Bears
fame or trouble?

- *The Berenstain Bears' Moving Day*
  by Stan and Jan Berenstain
  (Random House, 1981).

- *The Berenstain Bears No Girls Allowed*
  by Stan and Jan Berenstain
  (Random House, 1986).

- *The Berenstain Bears on the Moon*
  by Stan and Jan Berenstain
  (Random House, 1985).

Brother and Sister Bear take their dog to
the moon.

- *The Berenstain Bears Say Good Night*
  by Stan and Jan Berenstain
  (Random House, 1991).

- *He Bear, She Bear*
  by Stan and Jan Berenstain
  (Random House, 1974).

Part of the Bright and Early Books for
BEGINNING Beginners series.

- *Inside, Outside, Upside Down*
  by Stan and Jan Berenstain
  (Random House, 1968).

This brief Bright and Early Book describes
a bear cub going to town in a box.

- *Old Hat, New Hat*
  by Stan and Jan Berenstain
  (Random House, 1970).

A Bright and Early Book focusing on
repetitive vocabulary in a hat shop.

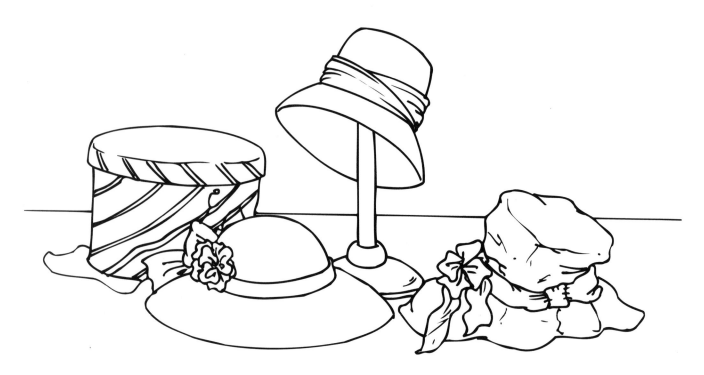

EXPLORE LETTER C

Discuss upper- and lower-case C's and read literature links featuring starts-with-C characters such as Curious George.

FIND THE "LETTER OF THE WEEK"

• Use a permanent marker to write a letter "C" on the lid of a clear plastic deli tub. Place as many items for letter "C" in the tub as you can find, including pieces of white and colored chalk, a picture of a cat, a plastic toy crab, a miniature car, and so on.

• On a cardboard cutout of the letter "C" paint fluffy clouds. Have children help you glue white cotton onto the cloud outlines.

• Challenge children to brainstorm names of animals that start with letter "C," including cats, chickens, Chihuahuas, collies, coyotes, crabs, and so on.

• Have children help you make a list of as many foods as they can think of that begin with the letter "C," including cake, cookies, candy, chocolate, cream, cheese, corn, cotton candy, carrots, cauliflower, cantaloupe, cabbage, cherries, and so on. Consider bringing in one or two items from the list for children to taste.

• Sing "C Is for Cookie" as a class. (This is a favorite song of *Sesame Street*'s Cookie Monster.)

CREATIVE "C" ACTIVITIES

• C IS FOR CLAPPING: Play a clapping game. Have children turn to each other and play pattycake, slapping their hands on their thighs, then together, and then against each other's open hands. As they clap, have children say as many words that begin with "C" as they can think of. Start them off with some of the "C" words in the C Alphabet Rhyme.

• "C" IS FOR ME!: Have children think of as many "C" words as they can to describe their personalities. Start them off with a few adjectives, including cute, cheerful, curious, careful, cool, and so on. Duplicate the "C" cards (see next page) for children to choose from, decorate, and wear (pinned to their shirt with a safety pin).

Cc
"C" Cards

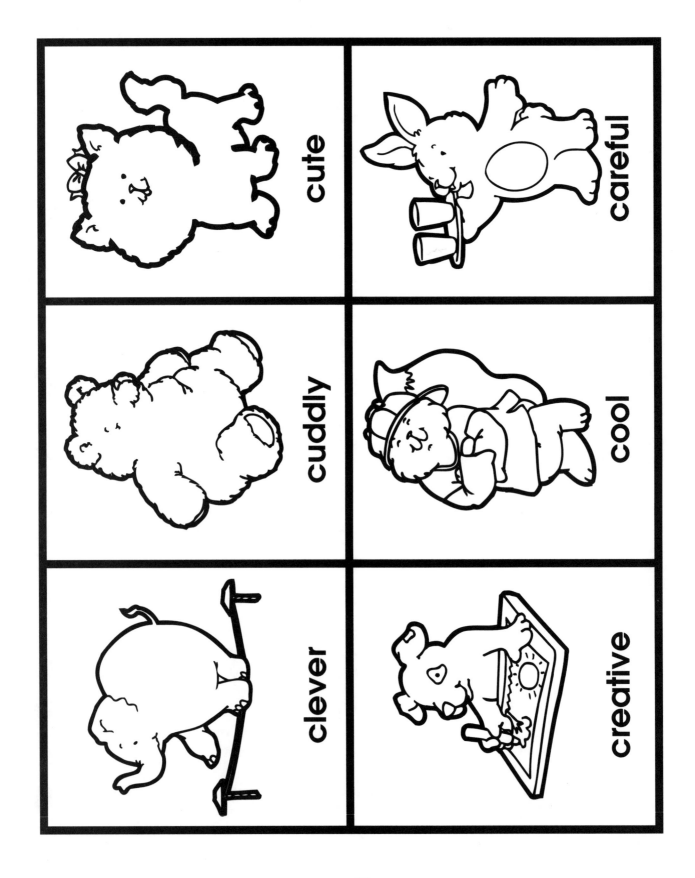

cute

careful

cuddly

cool

clever

creative

C c

Cobbler, cobbler, mend my shoe,
And cobbler starts with C.
So do words like cat and cow
And cottage, comb, and cream.
C starts words like calendar
And car and cup and creep.
Can you think of other words
That start with letter C?

Cc

Upper- and Lower-case C

Cc
Alphabet Puzzle

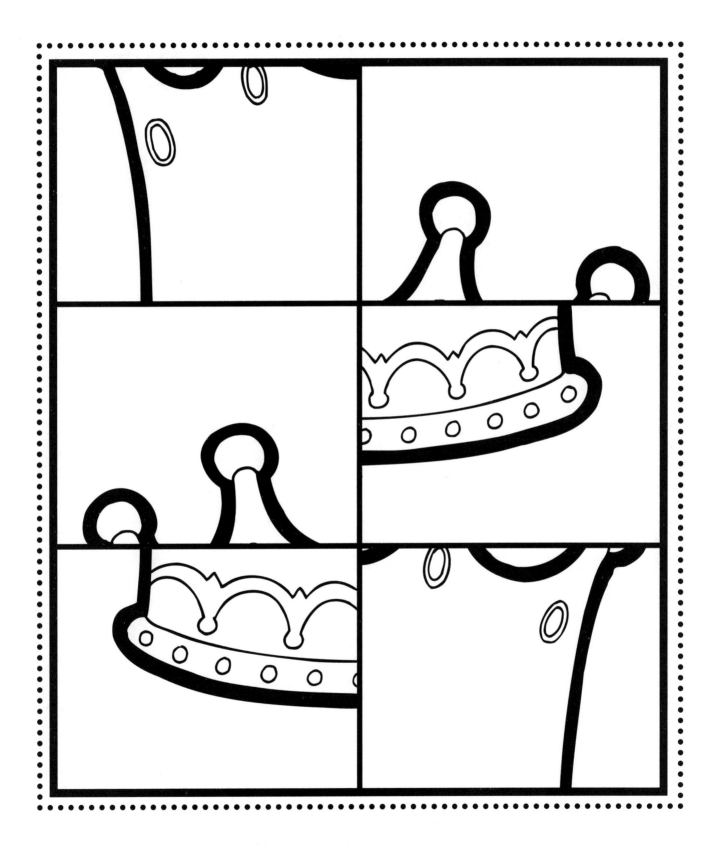

Literature Connection
CURIOUS GEORGE

The following books detail the adventures and misadventures of Curious George as he hops from trouble and tragedy to triumph. . .all due to his insatiable CURIOSITY!

READ A BOOK

• *Curious George* by H. A. Rey (Houghton Mifflin, 1969).
The curiosity of the newly captured George gets him into constant trouble!

• *Curious George at the Laundromat* by Margret Rey (Houghton Mifflin, 1987).
Taking the clothes to the laundromat to be cleaned is quite an adventure with Curious George along.

• *Curious George Bakes a Cake* by Margret Rey (Houghton Mifflin, 1990).
Curious George gets in and out of trouble when he helps a friend bake a cake.

• *Curious George Gets a Medal* by H. A. Rey (Houghton Mifflin, 1957).
Curious George makes a disaster at home, but earns a medal for bravery in his assistance to space research.

• *Curious George Goes Camping* edited by Margret Rey (Houghton Mifflin, 1990).
While the man with the yellow hat prepares to cook at the campsite, Curious George gets into a bit of trouble.

CURIOUS GEORGE ACTIVITIES

• CURIOUS ABOUT CAMPING?: Collect camping gear to pretend with at a camping corner. (*Curious George Goes Camping*)

• CURIOUS ABOUT CLEANING?: Set up a laundry center in one corner of the room. Provide plastic dishtubs, doll clothes, and warm soapy water. Have children wash and rinse the clothes. They can use clothespins to hang the clothes on a line to dry. (*Curious George at the Laundromat*)

• COUNTING DOWN!: Have children count backwards from 5 as Curious George sits at the controls of the spaceship. (*Curious George Gets a Medal*)

• CURIOUS CHART: Make a chart of the times Curious George was curious in each story you read.

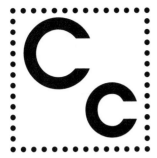

Art Connection
CURIOUS GEORGE BAKES A CAKE

Materials:

Cake pattern (see next page), crayons or markers, colorful glitter, glue

Directions:

1. Duplicate the cake pattern for each child.
2. Provide crayons, markers, glitter, and glue for children to use to decorate the cake patterns however they'd like.
3. Have children draw on as many birthday candles as their age.
4. Post the completed cakes on a "Creative Cake" bulletin board.

Creative Cake

Option:

Cover the bulletin board ahead of time with colorful wrapping paper.

Note:

Cover the work area with newsprint to catch extra glitter.

Other Art Ideas:

• Make cardboard cutouts of jungle animals like the ones Curious George painted. (*Curious George Takes a Job*)

Cc
Cake Pattern

Cc
Resources

More Curious George Books

- *Curious George Goes to a Costume Party*
  by Margret Rey
  (Houghton Mifflin, 1986).
Curious George finds lots of interesting things up in the attic, including a party costume that earns him first prize.

- *Curious George Goes to the Circus*
  by Margret Rey
  (Houghton Mifflin, 1984).
Curious George becomes the hit of the circus when he gets into the acrobat's act.

- *Curious George Goes Fishing*
  by Margret Rey
  (Houghton Mifflin, 1987).

- *Curious George Goes to an Ice Cream Shop*
  by Margret Rey
  (Houghton Mifflin, 1989).

- *Curious George Goes to the Dentist*
  by Margret Rey
  (Houghton Mifflin, 1989).
Curious George helps a friend see that a trip to the dentist is not something to cry about!

- *Curious George Goes Hiking*
  by Margret Rey
  (Houghton Mifflin, 1985).
Curious George has a few accidents along the trail following the cardinal and deer, but he knows how to find the way back when the children go off the trail.

- *Curious George Goes to the Hospital*
  by Margret Rey
  (Houghton Mifflin, 1966).
Poor Curious George gets a stomachache when he swallows a piece of his puzzle. He gets into mischief in the hospital, but makes everyone smile at the end of his stay.

- *Curious George Goes to a Restaurant*
  by Margret Rey
  (Houghton Mifflin, 1988).

- *Curious George Goes to School*
  by Margret Rey
  (Houghton Mifflin, 1989).

- *Curious George Goes Skiing*
  by Margret Rey
  (Houghton Mifflin, 1975).

- *Curious George Goes Sledding*
  by Margret Rey
  (Houghton Mifflin, 1984).

- *Curious George Goes to a Toy Store*
  by Margret Rey
  (Houghton Mifflin, 1990).
The new customers are delighted by Curious George's help at the grand opening of the toy store.

- *Curious George Learns the Alphabet*
  by H. A. Rey
  (Houghton Mifflin, 1963).
Curious George uses his new spelling skills to change an order from one dozen donuts to ten dozen!

- *Curious George Plays Baseball*
  by Margret Rey
  (Houghton Mifflin, 1986).
Curious George has a remarkable ability to catch, but will he get caught when he plays baseball at the wrong time?

- *Curious George Rides a Bike*
  by H. A. Rey
  (Houghton Mifflin, 1952).

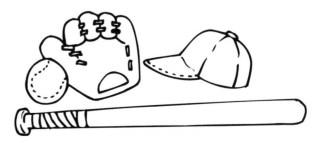

Cc
Resources

More Curious George Books

- *Curious George Gets a Job*
  by H. A. Rey
  (Houghton Mifflin, 1947).
This is an adventure-packed story as
Curious George escapes from the zoo,
rides to town, gets a job, breaks his leg,
and ends up starring in a movie.

- *Curious George Visits an Amusement Park*
  by Margret Rey
  (Houghton Mifflin, 1988).

- *Curious George Visits the Police Station*
  by Margret Rey
  (Houghton Mifflin, 1987).

- *Curious George Visits the Zoo*
  by Margret Rey
  (Houghton Mifflin, 1985).
Curious George solves a problem at the
monkey cage and keeps a young boy from
crying.

Filmstrips

- *Curious George Gets a Job*
  (Random House, 1982).

- *Curious George Gets a Medal*
  (Random House).

- *Curious George Goes to the Amusement Park*
  (Random House).

- *Curious George Goes to the Dentist*
  (Random House, 1984).

- *Curious George Goes to the Hospital*
  (Random House, 1983).

Sound Recordings

- *Curious George Rides a Bike*
  (Weston Woods).

Videotapes

- *The Adventures of Curious George*
  (Churchill Films, 1984).

- *Curious George*
  (Churchill Films, 1984).

- *Curious George Goes to the Hospital*
  (Churchill Films, 1983).

- *Dr. De Soto and Other Stories*
  (Weston Woods, 1985).
This video includes "Curious George Rides
a Bike."

EXPLORE LETTER D

Discuss upper- and lower-case D's and read literature links featuring starts-with-D characters such as Danny's dinosaur and other delightful dinos!

FIND THE "LETTER OF THE WEEK"

• Use a permanent marker to write a letter "D" on the lid of a clear plastic deli tub. Place as many items for letter "D" in the tub as you can find, including a domino, a dime, dice, a doll, a plastic dog, and so on.

• On a cardboard cutout of the letter "D," paste pictures of dresses cut from magazines or catalogs.

• In a picture dictionary, have children look at different items that start with letter "D."

• Describe different jobs that start with "D," including dressmaker, driver, dancer, doorman, and diver.

DARING "D" ACTIVITIES

• DINOSAUR DATA: Read books about dinosaurs (see the "Resources" section at the end of this chapter). Keep a dinosaur data chart (see next page). Each day as children gain more knowledge of dinosaurs, they can help you add to the chart.

• DINOSAUR DICTIONARIES: In a dinosaur dictionary (see "Dinosaur Dictionaries" in the "Resources" section at the end of this chapter), have children count how many dinosaurs start with the letter "D." They can choose their favorite dinosaur and discover three new facts about it.

39   Reading Connections © 1996 Monday Morning Books, Inc.

Dd
Dinosaur Data Chart

Dinosaur Name	Description

D d

We're **d**own in the **d**umps because
   diamonds are trumps,
And **d**iamonds starts with **D**.
So do words like **d**oor and **d**oll
And **d**rum and **d**uck and **d**eep.
D starts words like **d**inosaur
And **d**ragon, **d**og, and **d**ice.
Do you know some more **D** words
You think are rather nice?

Dd
Upper- and Lower-case D

Dd
Alphabet Puzzle

Literature Connection
DINOSAURS

Since dinosaurs are a popular topic with children, dozens of dinosaur books are listed for this unit, here and on the "Resources" pages. But *Danny and the Dinosaur* is one of the classics.

READ A BOOK

• *Danny and the Dinosaur* by Syd Hoff (Harper and Row, 1958).
Danny visits the museum and brings home a dinosaur for a day!

• *Dazzle the Dinosaur* by Marcus Pfister, translated by J. Alison James (North-South Books, 1994).
Dazzle starts as a beautiful dinosaur egg, then hatches into a sparkling dinosaur!

• *Dinosaur Dances* by Jane Yolen, illustrated by Bruce Degen (Putnam, 1990).
This whimsical, delightfully illustrated book contains 17 poems about dinosaur activities.

• *I'm Tyrannosaurus!* A Book of Dinosaur Rhymes by Jean Marzollo, illustrated by Hans Wilhelm (Scholastic, 1993).
These very short poems are about an assortment of dinosaurs.

• *Tyrannosaurus Was a Beast: Dinosaur Poems* by Jack Prelutsky, illustrated by Arnold Lobel (Greenwillow, 1988).
These silly poems are a bit longer than those in *I'm Tyrannosaurus!*

 **DINOSAUR ACTIVITIES**

• DINO-DANCE: Hold a dinosaur dance and play some disco music! You can put on one of the many available dinosaur tapes or CDs, such as *Dinosaur Rock* by Michele Valeri (Caedmon, 1984). (*Dinosaur Dances*)

• DO A DINO A DAY: Write a dinosaur poem on the board every day during your dinosaur unit. (*Tyrannosaurus Was a Beast: Dinosaur Poems* or *I'm Tyrannosaurus!*)

Art Connection
DINOSAUR DIORAMAS

Dd

Materials:

Shoe box (one per child—have children bring them from home), glue, crayons and markers, sand, small pebbles, twigs, grass, tinfoil (or blue plastic wrap), dinosaur patterns (next page), scissors, modeling clay, heavy paper or card stock

Directions:

1. Help children write their names across the back of their boxes.
2. Show children how to set their boxes inside the lid as shown and glue the two pieces together.
3. Provide crayons and markers for children to use to draw and color the backdrop for the diorama, filling in the ground, the sky, and any large vegetation.
4. Children can glue sand, small pebbles, twigs, and grass inside their dioramas to create a habitat for dinosaurs. Tinfoil or blue plastic wrap can be added for water.
5. Duplicate the dinosaur patterns onto heavy paper or card stock for children to color, cut out and place in their dioramas. They can use balls of modeling clay to form stands for the patterns.
6. Display the dioramas in a trophy case for the school community to enjoy.

Option:

If children want to draw their own dinosaurs for the dioramas, set out *Dinosaurs!* by Ed Emberley (Little, Brown, 1983) at a drawing station.

Reading Connections © 1996 Monday Morning Books, Inc.

Dd
Dinosaur Patterns

Art Connection
DAZZLING DINOSAURS

Read *Dazzle the Dinosaur* by Marcus Pfister before doing this activity.

Materials:

Dinosaur patterns (p. 46), silver foil, silver glitter, glue, crayons or markers, plastic eggs (optional), scissors

Directions:

1. Duplicate the dinosaur patterns.
2. Let children choose a dinosaur pattern to cut out and decorate.
3. Give the children silver foil to use to make their dinosaurs dazzling.
4. Provide crayons or markers and silver glitter for additional decoration.
5. If available, give each child a plastic egg for dinosaur pattern storage.

This is my dazzling dinosaur Mr. Triceratops.

Game Connection
DINOSAUR DETECTIVES GAME
Dinosaur Time by Peggy Parish is a perfect starting source for this game.

Materials:

Dinosaur patterns (p. 8), crayons or markers, scissors

Directions:

1. Put up a colored pattern of an unnamed dinosaur in the room daily.
2. Ask students to write down their guesses of the dinosaur's name, or write down guesses for them.
3. If any student guesses the name of the dinosaur correctly, ask him or her to help choose a dinosaur for another day.

Dd
Resources

More Dinosaur Books

- *A Boy Wants A Dinosaur*
  by Hiawyn Oram & Satoshi Kitamura
  (Scholastic, 1990).
  A boy wants a dinosaur for a pet, but when he actually gets one will it be a disaster?

- *Can I Please Have A Stegosaurus, Mom? Can I? Please?*
  by Lois Grambling
  (BridgeWater, 1995).
  A boy tries to convince his mother to let him keep a stegosaurus for a pet.

- *A Dinosaur Named After Me*
  by Bernard Most
  (Harcourt, 1991).
  Children's names are incorporated into the renaming of dinosaurs as information is presented about each type of dinosaur.

- *The Dinosaur Alphabet Book*
  by Jerry Pallotta
  (Children's Press, 1991).
  Lesser-known dinosaurs are presented in this dinosaur ABC.

- *Dinosaur Babies*
  by Lucille Recht Penner
  (Random House, 1991).
  This book has large type and large dinosaur pictures on each page.

- *Dinosaur Bones*
  by Aliki
  (Harper, 1988).
  This book explains how scientists learn from dinosaur bones.

- *Dinosaur Day*
  by Liza Donnelly
  (Scholastic, 1987).
  Includes a great glossary.

- *Dinosaur Dream*
  by Dennis Nolan
  (Macmillan, 1990).
  Wilbur, a dinosaur fan, is startled one night to find a dinosaur outside his bedroom window.

- *Dinosaur Garden*
  by Liza Donnelly
  (Scholastic, 1990).
  A boy accompanied by his dog, Bones, creates a garden that the plant-eaters would have enjoyed. Includes a glossary.

- *Dinosaur Hunt*
  by Philip Hood
  (Putnam, 1995).
  As you open the book, a 3-D skeleton of a tyrannosaurus is revealed.

- *Dinosaur Time*
  by Peggy Parish
  (Scholastic, 1974).
  This easy-to-read book includes 11 dinosaur descriptions.

- *Dinosaurs*
  by Gail Gibbons
  (Scholastic, 1987).
  Great introductory book for very young audiences.

- *Dinosaurs: A First Discovery Book*
  by Jean Marzollo
  (Scholastic, 1991).
  Beautiful illustrations make this book unique.

- *Dinotopia: A Land Apart from Time*
  by James Gurney
  (Turner, 1992).
  Join Professor Dennison and his son as they land on Dinotopia, an island where humans and dinosaurs live in peace.

- *Dougal Dixon's Dinosaurs*
  (Boyd Mills Press, 1993).
  Interesting illustrations and photos focus on dinosaurs.

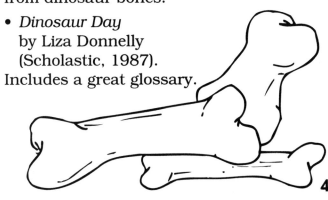

Dd
Resources

More Dinosaur Books

- *How I Captured A Dinosaur*
  by Henry Schwartz
  (Orchard, 1989).
  Liz finds a dinosaur on a camping trip and convinces her parents to bring it home.

- *Let's Go Dinosaur Tracking!*
  by Miriam Schlein
  (HarperCollins, 1991).
  This book explores many types of dinosaur tracks.

- *The Littlest Dinosaur*
  by Bernard Most
  (Harcourt, 1989).
  Small dinosaurs (under 14 feet) are described both fictitiously and factually.

- *The Magic School Bus in the Time of the Dinosaur*
  by Joanna Cole
  (Scholastic, 1994).
  Ms. Frizzle's class goes on a dinosaur dig.

- *My Visit to the Dinosaurs*
  by Aliki
  (Harper, 1969).
  This is a Let's Read and Find Out Science Book about a visit to a museum of natural history, with information on 14 dinosaurs.

- *New Questions and Answers About Dinosaurs*
  by Seymour Simon
  (Trumpet, 1990).
  This is a great reference.

- *Time Flies*
  by Eric Rohmann
  (Crown, 1994).
  This Caldecott Honor Book wordlessly draws the connection between dinosaurs and birds.

- *What Happened to Patrick's Dinosaurs?*
  by Carol Carrick
  (Clarion, 1986).
  Patrick combines his imagination and his fascination with dinosaurs to come up with his own theory about why they are extinct. Also available: *Patrick's Dinosaurs* (Clarion, 1983).

- *Whatever Happened to the Dinosaurs?*
  by Bernard Most
  (HBJ, 1984).
  A very humorous look at possible, but improbable, extinction theories.

- *ZOOBOOKS: Dinosaurs*
  by John Bonnett Wexo
  (Wildlife Education, 1992).
  This magazine is fact-filled.

Dinosaur Dictionaries

- *Dictionary of Dinosaurs*
  by Joseph Rosenbloom
  (Messner, 1980).

- *The New Dinosaur Dictionary*
  by Donald Glut
  (Citadel, 1982).

- *The Illustrated Dinosaur Dictionary*
  by Helen Roney Sattler
  (Lothrop, Lee, and Shepard, 1983).

Videotapes

- *The Dinosaurs*
  Available from PBS Home Video, P.O. Box 25675, West Los Angeles, CA 90025, 1-800-PLAY-PBS.

- *Bill Nye, The Science Guy's Dinosaurs: Those Big Bone Heads and Lifestyles of the Large and Extinct*
  (Walt Disney Home Video, 1994), 49 minutes.

- *Reading Rainbow's Digging Up Dinosaurs*
  with Levar Burton
  (Lancit Media Productions, 1983).

EXPLORE LETTER E

Discuss upper- and lower-case E's and read literature links featuring elephants.

FIND THE "LETTER OF THE WEEK"

• Use a permanent marker to write a letter "E" on the lid of a clear plastic deli tub. Place as many items for letter "E" in the tub as you can find, including a small envelope, a picture of an ear, a plastic egg, a drawing of an elephant, and so on.

• On a cardboard cutout of the letter "E," have children draw eggs or eyes.

• Focus on numbers eight and eleven during this unit.

• Have the children help you make a list of as many animals as they can think of that start with the letter "E," including eagles, eels, elephants, elks, emus, and ermines. Are any endangered?

EXCITING "E" ACTIVITIES

• EGGS, EGGS, EGGS: Bring in eggs for children to decorate. Hard-boil the eggs ahead of time and provide colored dyes (available at Easter) for children to use to create exciting egg masterpieces. Display the finished products in baskets around the room.

• I ONLY HAVE EYES FOR YOU: Duplicate the face patterns (see next page) and have children color in the facial features that start with letter "E": eyes, ears, earlobes, eyelids, eyelashes, eyebrows.

Ee
Face patterns

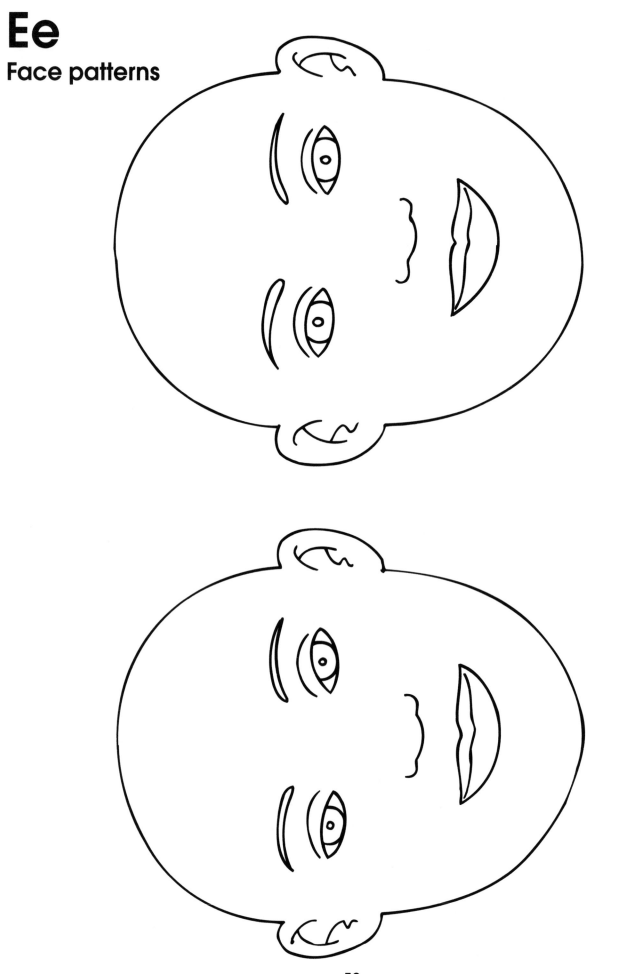

E e

The **e**ency weency spider
Knows **e**ency starts with **E**.
So do words like **e**gg and **e**ar
And **e**lephant and **e**el.
E starts words like **e**agle, **e**yes,
And **e**asel, **e**lf, and **e**at.
Can you think of other words
That start with letter **E**?

Ee
Upper- and Lower-case E

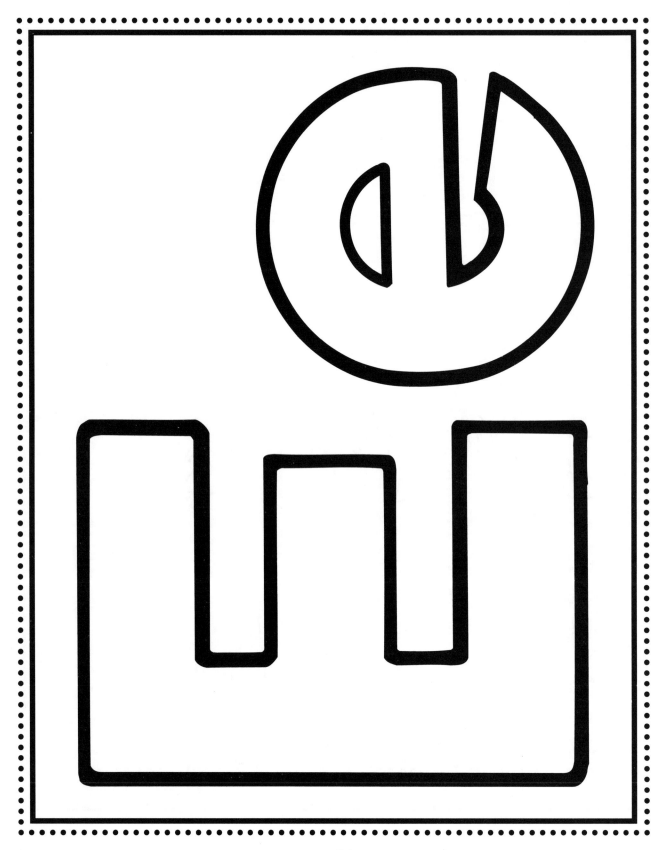

Ee
Alphabet Puzzle

Reading Connections © 1996 Monday Morning Books, Inc.

Literature Connection

ELEPHANTS

Excite your students about reading with these enjoyable elephant books!

READ A BOOK

• *Babar's Anniversary Album* by Jean de Brunhoff (Random House, 1981).
This anthology includes "The Story of Babar," "The Travels of Babar," "Babar's Birthday Surprise," "Babar's Mystery."

• *Elephant Buttons* by Noriko Ueno (Harper, 1973).
Young readers will love this wordless book: an elephant's skin is unbuttoned to expose a horse, which unbuttons to a lion, and on through a series of animals.

• *Encore for Eleanor* by Bill Peet (Houghton, 1981).
Eleanor is a retired circus elephant who finds a new job as an artist in the zoo.

• *Five Minutes Peace* by Jill Murphy (Scholastic, 1986).
All this elephant mother desires is to be left alone for five minutes, but with young children in the family, this is impossible.

• *Horton Hatches the Egg* by Dr. Seuss (Random House, 1940). (Also: *Horton Hears a Who*.)
Horton is a friendly elephant who agrees to "egg-sit" for an irresponsible bird.

ELEPHANT ACTIVITIES

• EGG-CITING EGG-SITTING: Provide shredded newspaper for children to use to make small nests. Give each child a plastic egg to set in a nest. Children can pretend to be Horton watching over Maisie's egg. (*Horton Hatches an Egg*)

• DRESS-UP DAY: Provide a variety of colored dress-up clothes for children to use to layer their attire. Gray clothes can be used for an elephant's hide, yellow for a lion, and so on. Children can peel off the layers as they recreate the story. (*Elephant Buttons*)

• FIVE-MINUTE FUN: Set up timers in the classroom to go off every five minutes. Have children move from station to station at five-minute intervals. (*Five Minutes Peace*)

Art Connection

ELEPHANT BUTTONS

Do this activity after reading *Elephant Buttons* by Noriko Ueno.

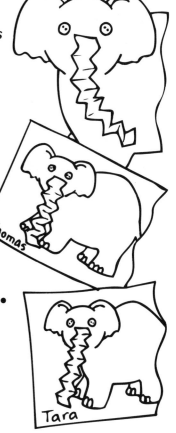

Materials:

Elephant pattern (next page), buttons, glue, crayons or markers, strips of construction paper, tape

Directions:

1. Duplicate the elephant pattern for each child.
2. Provide crayons or markers for children to use to decorate the pattern.
3. Give each child two buttons to glue on for the elephant's eyes.
4. Show children how to make "accordion" strips of construction paper for the trunks.
5. Children can attach the trunks to the elephants using a strip of tape at the base.
6. Post the 3-D elephant pictures in the classroom or in a hallway.

Option:

Display elephant books on a table below the "Elephant Buttons" pictures.

Ee
Elephant Pattern

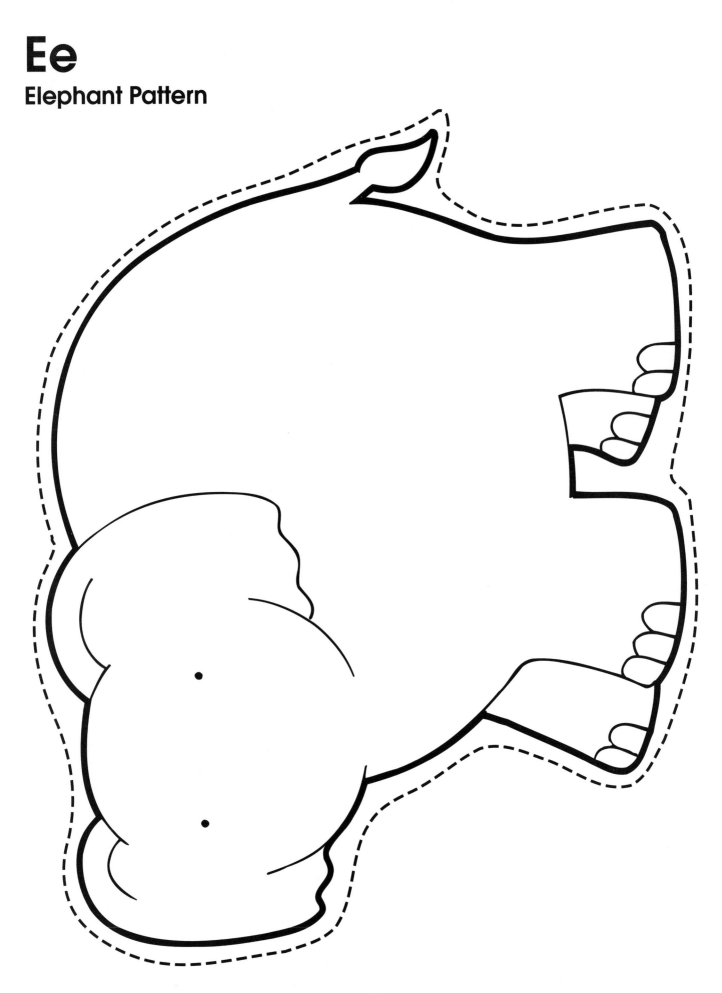

Ee
Resources

More Elephant Books

- *African Elephants*
  by Dorothy Hinshaw Patent
  (Holiday House, 1991).
This book describes the physical characteristics, behavior, feeding, and habitat of African elephants.

- *Alexander's Midnight Snack: A Little Elephant's ABC*
  by Catherine Stock
  (Clarion, 1988).
A little elephant's midnight snack becomes a feast composed of a different food for each letter of the alphabet.

- *America's First Elephant*
  by Robert M. McClung
  (Morrow, 1991).
Recounts the tale of the first elephant that arrived in the U.S. in 1795.

- *Elephant Crossing*
  by Toshi Yoshida
  (Philomel, 1989).
The book follows a gentle African elephant herd.

- *Elephant Families*
  by Arthur Dorros
  (HarperCollins, 1994).
This book has illustrations and text designed for the primary reader.

- *The Elephant's Wrestling Match*
  by Judy Sierra
  (Dutton, 1992).
Several animals accept the boastful elephant's challenge to wrestle him, but the tiny bat alone is the only contestant to defeat him.

- *Never Ride Your Elephant to School*
  by Doug Johnson
  (Holt, 1995).
This book treats pet elephants as if they were perfectly ordinary! Delightful pictures accompany a list of at-school elephant activities.

- *A Piece of Cake*
  by Jill Murphy
  (Putnam, 1989).
Mother puts her elephant family on a diet with exercise. Their will power is great until Granny sends a cake.

- *17 Kings and 42 Elephants*
  by Margaret Mahy
  (Dial, 1987).
This rhyme tells the story of 17 kings and 42 elephants as they romp through the jungle and rollick noisily with the animals one wet night.

- *Stand Back," Said the Elephant, "I'm Going to Sneeze!"*
  by Patricia Thomas
  (Lothrop, 1990).
While it may not be a laughing matter to the other animals when the elephant is about to sneeze, the reader will giggle with every page turned.

Ee
Resources

More "E" Books

- *Bravo, Ernest and Celestine*
  by Gabrielle Vincent
  (Greenwillow, 1982).
Ernest, a bear, and Celestine, a mouse,
come up with a plan to earn money to
mend the roof.

- *Ernest and Celestine*
  by Gabrielle Vincent
  (Greenwillow, 1982).
Celestine and Ernest lose Celestine's
stuffed bird in the snow, but a wonderful
solution is found to make Celestine and
many other little friends happy.

- *Ernest and Celestine at the Circus*
  by Gabrielle Vincent
  (Greenwillow, 1989).
Ernest and Celestine visit the circus.

- *Feel Better, Ernest*
  by Gabrielle Vincent
  (Greenwillow, 1988).
Celestine entertains and takes care of
Ernest while he is ill.

- *Merry Christmas, Ernest and Celestine*
  by Gabrielle Vincent
  (William Morrow, 1984).
Even without money, Ernest and Celestine
manage to put on a wonderful Christmas
party.

Audiotapes

- *Babar the King*
  (Caedmon, 1976).
This children's favorite is read by Louis
Jourdan.

- *Ernest and Celestine*
  (Weston Woods, 1983).

- *Ernest and Celestine's Picnic*
  (Weston Woods, 1984).

Videotapes

- *Dumbo*
  (Walt Disney Home Video, 1990).

- *The Elephant's Child*
  (Random House Home Video, 1986).
This Rabbit Ears Production story is read
by Jack Nicholson and has music by
Bobby McFerrin.

- *Horton Hatches the Egg*
  (Random House Home Video, 1992).
Billy Crystal narrates this Dr. Seuss
classic.

- *Horton Hears a Who!*
  (MGM/UA Home Video, 1986).

EXPLORE LETTER F

Discuss upper- and lower-case F's and read literature links featuring starts-with-F characters such as everyone's favorite badger: Frances.

FIND THE "LETTER OF THE WEEK"

• Use a permanent marker to write a letter "F" on the lid of a clear plastic deli tub. Place as many items for letter "F" in the tub as you can find, including a feather, plastic fangs (available at Halloween), a piece of foil, a dried flower, and so on.

• On a cardboard cutout of the letter "F," let children print their fingerprints!

• Create a "Friends and Family" photo display. Have children bring in pictures from home (well-labeled) and post on a bulletin board.

• Have the children help you brainstorm a list of occupations that start with "F," including firefighter, fisherman, flight attendant, furniture maker, fruit seller, fast-food chef, and so on.

FABULOUS "F" ACTIVITIES

• VERY FISHY: Have children practice making fish faces in a mirror by sucking in their cheeks and pouting out their lips.

• FOOD, FANTASTIC FOOD: Duplicate the food pyramid chart (see next page). Children can make their own charts and draw the food options in the appropriate spaces or cut out pictures from grocery store ads and paste them on the pattern. (Note: This activity could also be done as a festive mural by enlarging the pattern onto butcher paper and using colorful ads from magazines to cover the food icons.)

Ff
Food Pyramid Pattern

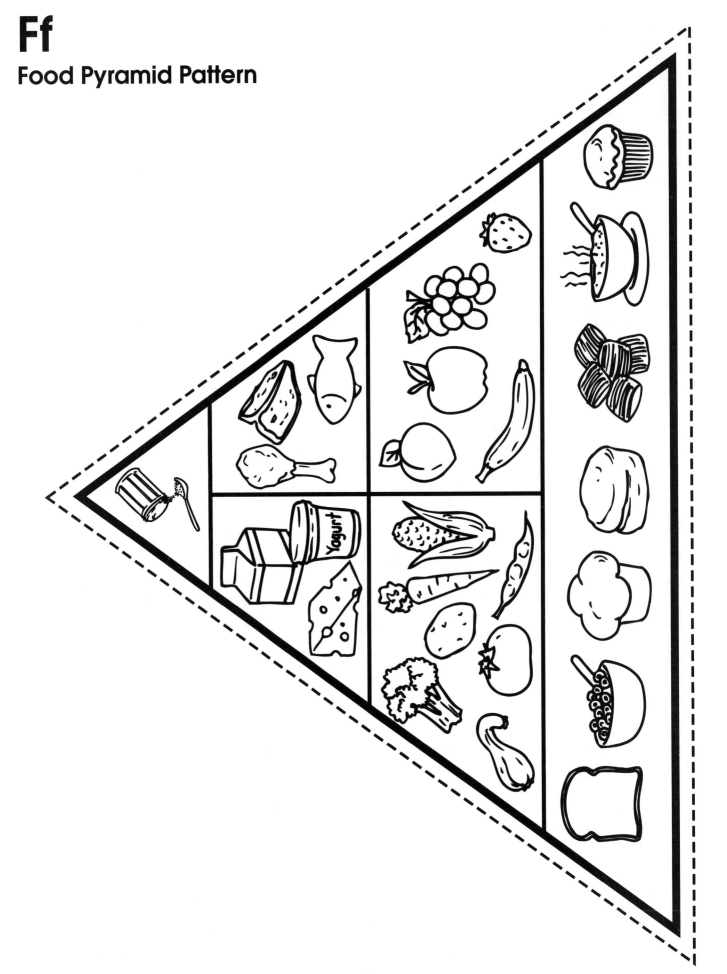

F f

Fiddle de dee, fiddle de dee,
Fiddle starts with **F**.
So do words like **f**urniture
And **f**ish and **f**lag and **f**luff.
F starts words like **f**an and **f**ly
And **f**lower, **f**rog, and **f**in.
Can you think of other words
That letter **F** begins?

Reading Connections © 1996 Monday Morning Books, Inc.

Ff
Upper- and Lower-case F

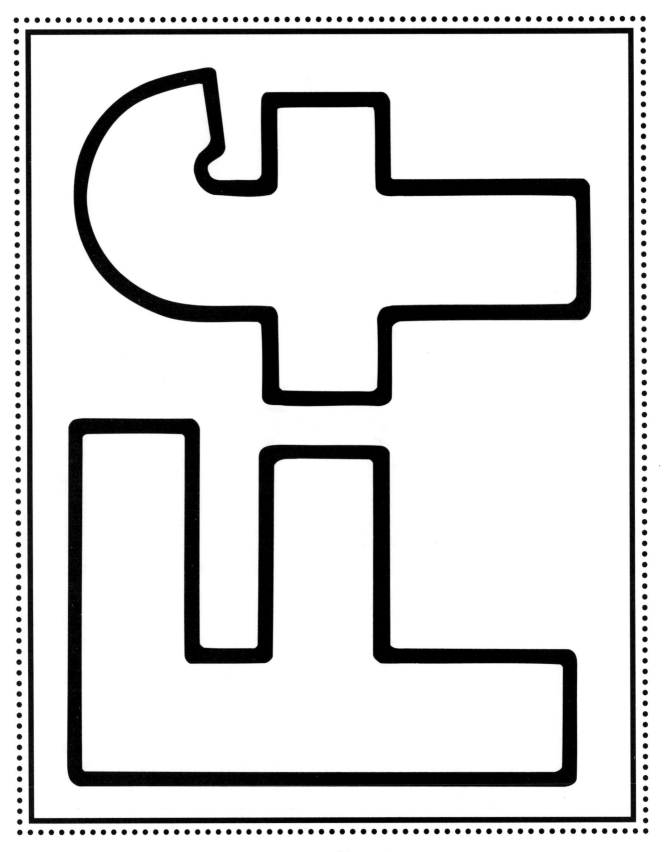

Ff
Alphabet Puzzle

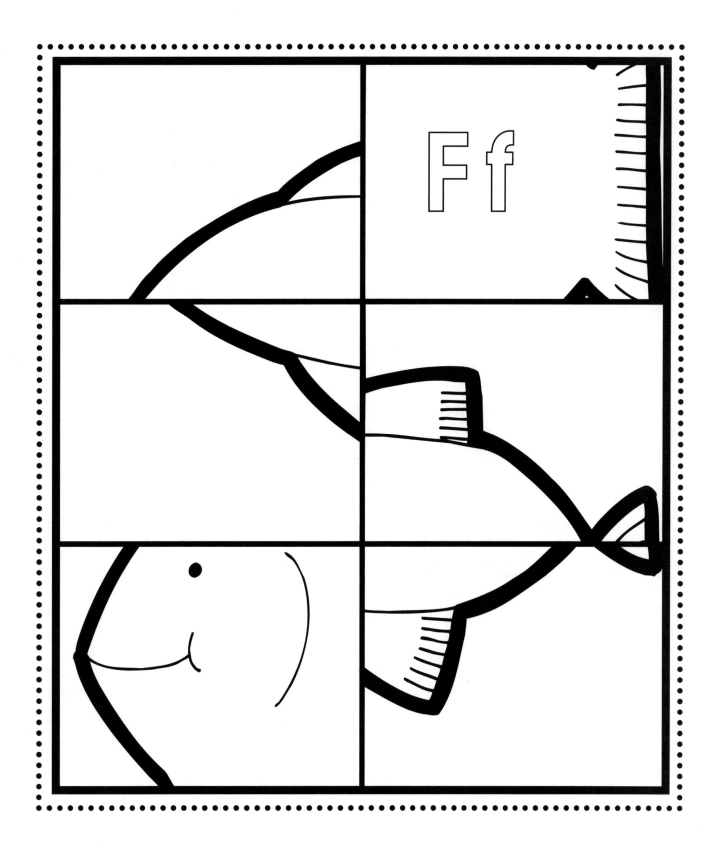

Reading Connections © 1996 Monday Morning Books, Inc.

Literature Connection
FRANCES

The main character for this unit is Frances from the series by Russell and Lillian Hoban. This fiesty, friendly badger has fun and a few fights with family and friends.

READ A BOOK

• *A Baby Sister for Frances* by Russell Hoban, illustrated by Lillian Hoban (Harper, 1964).
Frances runs away (to a hiding place under the dining room table) when her life is disrupted by the arrival of a baby sister.

• *A Bargain for Frances* by Russell Hoban, illustrated by Lillian Hoban (Harper, 1970).
Is it better to break a bargain or lose a friend? Frances and Thelma are faced with this dilemma.

• *A Birthday for Frances* by Russell Hoban, illustrated by Lillian Hoban (Harper, 1968).
Frances finally gets in the party spirit and buys her sister a present. But can she bring herself to part with the gift?

• *Bread and Jam for Frances* by Russell and Lillian Hoban (Harper, 1964).
Frances likes to stick with a sure thing: bread and jam. Ultimately, she learns that variety can make meals more interesting.

 **FRANCES ACTIVITIES**

• FAVORITE FOODS: Frances has strong feelings about food. Make a classroom chart listing your students' favorite foods. (*Bread and Jam for Frances*)

• FRANCES' FUNDS: Put out coins for students to practice counting. (*A Baby Sister for Frances* and *A Birthday for Frances*)

•FRIENDS TEA P ARTY: Have a friendly tea party and serve ice tea and cookies. (*A Bargain for Frances*) Make place cards for family and friends for the feast. (*A Birthday for Frances*)

F f

Art Connection

FUNNY, FRIENDLY BIRTHDAY CARDS

After reading *A Birthday for Frances*, children can make birthday cards for each other. Ask if they agree with Frances' statement, "Your birthday is always the one that is not now."

Materials:

Sunday comics, construction paper, crayons or markers, scissors, glue or paste

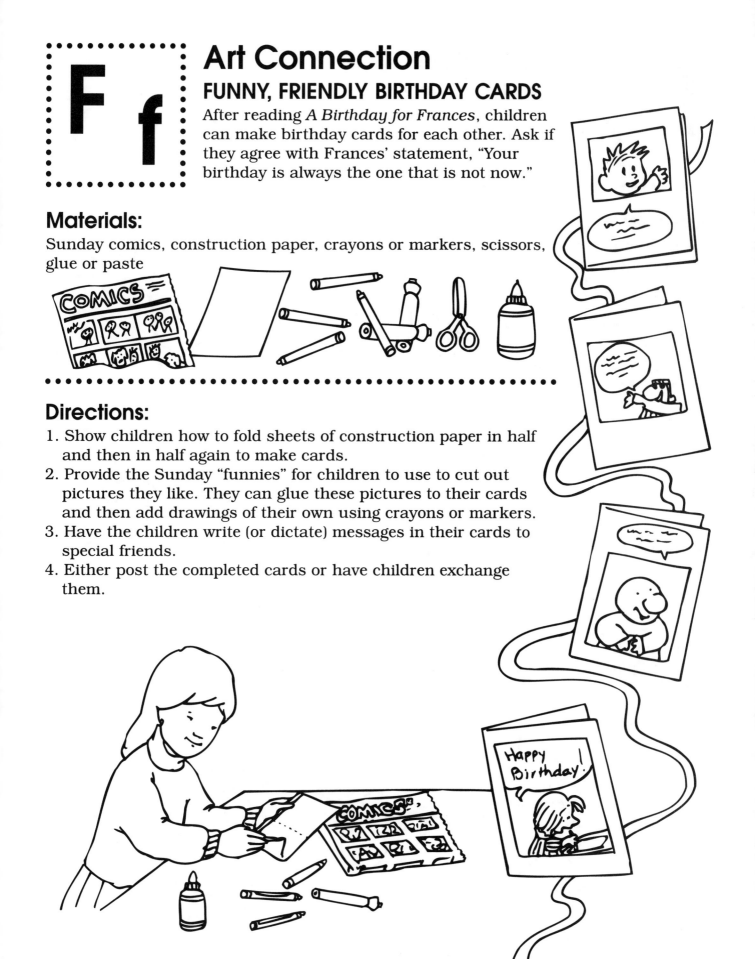

Directions:

1. Show children how to fold sheets of construction paper in half and then in half again to make cards.
2. Provide the Sunday "funnies" for children to use to cut out pictures they like. They can glue these pictures to their cards and then add drawings of their own using crayons or markers.
3. Have the children write (or dictate) messages in their cards to special friends.
4. Either post the completed cards or have children exchange them.

Reading Connections © 1996 Monday Morning Books, Inc.

Art Connection

FAVORITE FLOWERS

Decorate the room with these friends-and-family flowers.

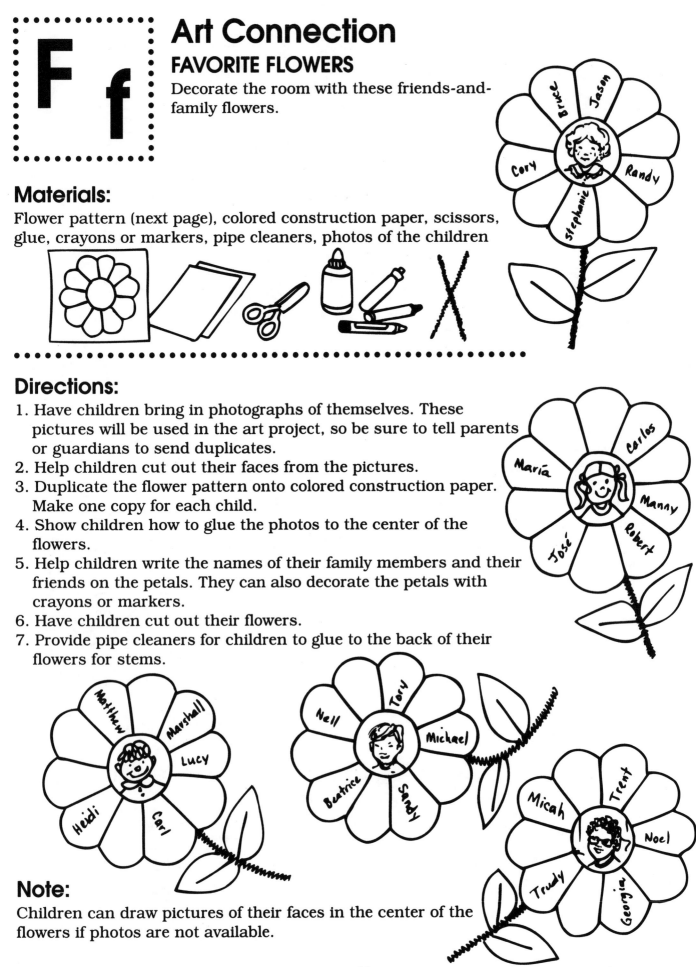

Materials:

Flower pattern (next page), colored construction paper, scissors, glue, crayons or markers, pipe cleaners, photos of the children

Directions:

1. Have children bring in photographs of themselves. These pictures will be used in the art project, so be sure to tell parents or guardians to send duplicates.
2. Help children cut out their faces from the pictures.
3. Duplicate the flower pattern onto colored construction paper. Make one copy for each child.
4. Show children how to glue the photos to the center of the flowers.
5. Help children write the names of their family members and their friends on the petals. They can also decorate the petals with crayons or markers.
6. Have children cut out their flowers.
7. Provide pipe cleaners for children to glue to the back of their flowers for stems.

Note:

Children can draw pictures of their faces in the center of the flowers if photos are not available.

Ff
Flower Pattern

Ff
Resources

More Frances Books

- *Bedtime for Frances*
  by Russell Hoban
  (Harper, 1960).
  Frances is frightened by many fearsome things when she tries to go to bed.

- *Best Friends for Frances*
  by Russell Hoban
  (Harper, 1969).
  Frances and Gloria learn to get along with the boys on a Best Friends Outing and at the baseball field.

- *Egg Thoughts and Other Frances Songs*
  by Russell Hoban
  (Harper, 1972).
  Twenty-two of Frances' songs and poems are compiled in this book.

Family Books

- *Chuckie*
  by Nikki Weiss
  (Greenwillow, 1982).
  Lucy isn't too pleased about the new baby in the house.

- *Fathers, Mothers, Sisters, Brothers: A Collection of Family Poems*
  by Mary Ann Hoberman
  (Scholastic, 1991).
  These humorous poems celebrate every kind of family member, including cats!

- *Julius: The Baby of the World*
  by Kevin Henkes
  (Greenwillow, 1990).
  Lilly isn't too pleased with the arrival of Julius. But when her cousin Garland insults Julius, Lilly rushes to her baby brother's defense.

- *Little Rabbit's Baby Brother*
  created by Lucy Bate
  by Fran Manushkin
  (Scholastic, 1986).
  It can be hard to be a big sister sometimes.

- *Love You, Forever*
  by Robert Munsch
  (Firefly, 1986).
  As this boy moves through childhood, his mother's love never falters.

- *My Mama Says There Aren't Any Zombies, Ghosts, Vampires, Creatures, Demons, Monsters, Fiends, Goblins, or Things*
  by Judith Viorst
  (Atheneum, 1973).
  Nick's mother tells him that there are no scary creatures. But he's not sure if he can believe her, because sometimes she makes mistakes. Luckily, his mama is right about the important things.

- *The Relatives Came* by Cynthia Rylant
  (Bradbury, 1985).
  A Caldecott Honor Book with rollicking pictures and text. Also available as an audiocassette.

Audiotapes

- *A Baby Sister for Frances*
  (HarperCollins, 1995).
  Read by Glynis Johns.

- *A Bargain for Frances and Other Frances Stories*
  (Caedmon, 1977).
  This audiotape includes "Best Friends" and "Egg Thoughts and Other Frances Songs."

EXPLORE LETTER G

Discuss upper- and lower-case G's and read literature links featuring starts-with-G characters such as the Golly sisters.

FIND THE "LETTER OF THE WEEK"

• Use a permanent marker to write a letter "G" on the lid of a clear plastic deli tub. Place as many items for letter "G" in the tub as you can find, including something green, a piece of gum, a blade of grass, a pair of glasses, a game piece, and so on.

• Use gold spray-paint to cover a cardboard cutout of the letter "G." (Do this when there are no children present.) Or decorate with gold glitter after covering the cardboard with gold Contac paper.

• Have the children help you brainstorm a list of as many foods as they can think of that start with the letter "G," including grapes, grapefruits, garbanzo beans, green beans, gravy, etc.

• Bring in a globe and have children find as many locations that start with "G" as they can.

• Ask children to help you think of as many animals that start with "G" as they can, including a gazelle, gerbil, giraffe, goat, goose, gopher, gorilla, grasshopper, greyhound, grizzly bear, and guppy.

GROOVY "G" ACTIVITIES

• GOLD, GOLD, GOLD: Have children pretend to pan for gold, with pre-painted pebbles scattered in with other rocks. Set up the rocks and pebbles (along with an old foil pie pan) at the water or sand table. For larger pieces of gold, spray-paint plastic poker chips.

• GOOSEY, GOOSEY GANDER: Read Mother Goose poems, such as "Goosey, goosey gander, whither dost thou wander? Upstairs, downstairs, in my lady's chamber." Then duplicate the Mother Goose pattern (see next page) to use to create a "Mother Goose" bulletin board. Add your favorite Mother Goose rhymes.

Gg
Mother Goose Patterns

G g

Georgie Porgie, pudding and pie,
Knows Georgie starts with G.
So do words like grapes and grand
And glasses, goose, and grease.
G starts words like ghost and gasp
And goat and gray and grin.
Can you think of other words
That letter G begins?

Gg
Upper- and Lower-case G

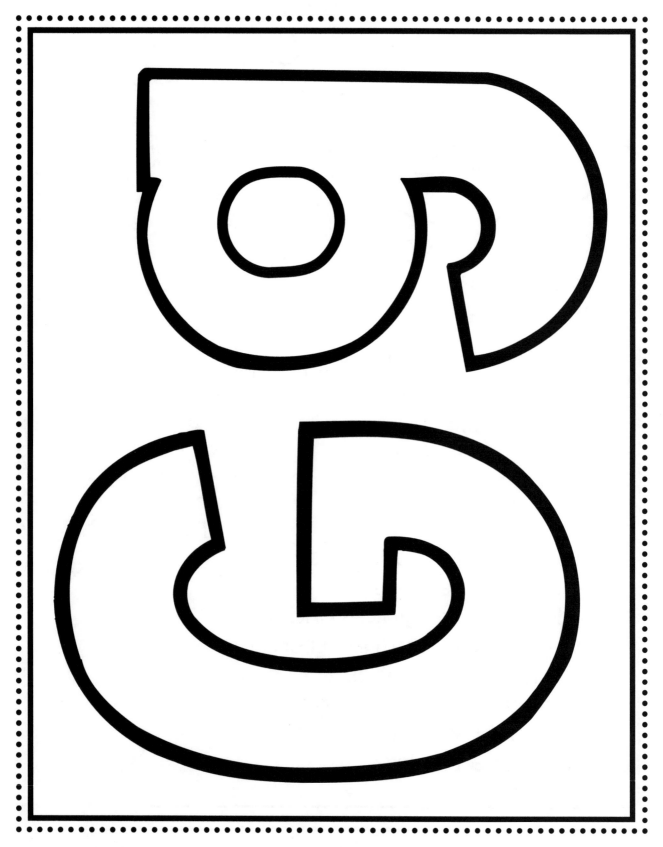

Gg
Alphabet Puzzle

Literature Connection
GOLLY SISTERS

The Golly sisters are famous in the west for their goofy yet glamorous stage productions. While they were seeking fame there, others were looking for their fortunes in gold! Enjoy this selection of Golly sisters books, as well as other "Gold Rush" selections.

READ A BOOK

• *The Golly Sisters Go West* by Betsy Byars, illustrated by Sue Truesdell (Harper, 1985).
The Golly sisters GO, GIVE, and GET in six short fun-filled chapters! An I Can Read Book intended for ages 4-8.

• *The Golly Sisters Ride Again* by Betsy Byars, illustrated by Sue Truesdell (HarperCollins, 1994).
Those goofy Golly sisters are up to mischief again in five more adventures in this short chapter book.

• *Hooray for the Golly Sisters* by Betsy Byars, illustrated by Sue Truesdell (Harper, 1990).
More adventures and misadventures of the Golly sisters' road show. How can they perform if the goat in the audience is going to bring them bad luck?

 GOLLY ACTIVITIES

•A NA TIONAL "GOLLIDAY": When the Golly sisters were going to have a holiday, they called it a "Golliday." Have your students brainstorm what kind of "Golliday" they would like to celebrate. (*The Golly Sisters Ride Again*)

• GLITTERY STARS: Students can write their names with gold glitter and glue on white paper stars. Add student photos if possible for added glamour! Display the stars on a glittery bulletin board. (*The Golly Sisters Ride Again*)

• GOLLY GLOVES: Have the students notice the Golly sisters' gloves. Place a collection of gloves in your dress-up area. (*Hooray for the Golly Sisters*)

Art Connection
GOLD GLITTER GLUE STARS

Materials:

Star pattern (next page), heavy paper, scissors, waxed paper, white glue, gold glitter, gold ribbon

Directions:

1. For each child, duplicate the star pattern onto heavy paper and cut out.
2. Give each child a sheet of waxed paper.
3. Show children how to use the star as a template and trace it with white glue onto the waxed paper. (They can either use squeeze bottles of glue, or dip cotton swabs in small containers of glue and use this to "paint" around the template. Then they will remove the template.)
4. Have children sprinkle the glue with gold glitter.
5. Let the star outlines dry for about four hours. Then, starting at each point, peel the star off the waxed paper.
6. Hang the stars from windows in the classroom by threading a length of ribbon through one point and tying.

Reading Connections © 1996 Monday Morning Books, Inc.

Gg
Resources

More Going West Books

- *Araminta's Paint Box*
  by Karen Ackerman
  (Atheneum, 1990).
Araminta and her paint box get separated on their journey westward, but through a series of new owners the paint box ends up in California with Araminta.

- *Beats Me, Claude*
  by Joan Lowery Nixon
  (Viking Kestrel, 1986).
There is plenty of excitement at this homestead each time Shirley tries to make an apple pie. Luckily for her, Tom knows how to make one!

- *Chang's Paper Pony*
  by Eleanor Coerr
  (Harper & Row, 1988).
During the San Francisco Gold Rush, Chang wants to buy a horse but cannot afford one until he is helped by Big Pete.

- *The Dakota Dugout*
  by Ann Warren Turner
  (Macmillan, 1985).
A woman wistfully describes her experiences living in a Dakota dugout with her husband on the prairie.

- *Fat Chance, Claude*
  by Joan Lowery Nixon
  (Viking Kestrel, 1987).
This story starts where the west begins and continues as Shirley and Claude grow up in Texas and meet when gold mining.

- *Going West*
  by Jean Van Leeuwen
  (Dial, 1992).
Lovely illustrations and a brief text tell the story of a family moving west in a prairie schooner. Told from a seven-year-old's point of view.

- *Little Sure Shot: The Story of Annie Oakley*
  by Stephanie Spinner
  (Random House, 1993).
This is the story of Annie Oakley from age nine until her death in 1926.

- *Long Way Westward*
  by Joan Sandin
  (Harper, 1989).
This story follows the immigration of two Swedish brothers and their families through New York to Minnesota.

- *My Prairie Year*
  based on the diary of Elenore Plaisted
  by Brett Harvey
  (Holiday House, 1986).
A paragraph of story accompanies each double-page spread of wonderful pencil sketches.

- *Pecos Bill*
  by Brian Gleeson
  (Rabbit Ears, 1988).
The talents of a storyteller and an artist are combined to create this legendary work. Also available as a cassette tape and as a video.

- *Songs of the Wild West*
  by Metropolitan Museum of Art in association with the Buffalo Bill Historical Center, commentary by Alan Axelrod with arrangements by Dan Fox
  (Simon and Schuster, 1991).
These are songs for voice with chordal or melody instruments.

- *Wagon Wheels*
  by Barbara Brenner
  (Harper, 1978).
An I Can Read Book which depicts a black family moving west to take advantage of the Homestead Act.

Gg
Resources

More Going West Books

• *You Bet Your Britches, Claude*
  by Joan Lowery Nixon
  (Viking Kestrel, 1989).
Shirley grows into the job of being a
deputy as she catches crooks in a western
town. The language use in this series is
delightful and the illustrations enhance
the story line.

Mother Goose Books

• *The Annotated Mother Goose*
  arranged and explained by William S.
  Baring-Gould and Ceil Baring-Gould
  (Bramhall House, 1962).

• *The Glorious Mother Goose*
  selected by Cooper Edens
  (Atheneum, 1988).

• *Marguerite de Angeli's Book of Nursery
  and Mother Goose Rhymes*
  (Doubleday, 1953).

• *Mother Goose: The Classic Volland
  Edition*
  rearranged and edited by Eulalie Osgood
  Grover
  (Rand McNally, 1971).

• *The Mother Goose Book*
  (Random House, 1976).

• *The Real Mother Goose*
  (Rand McNally, 1944).

Audiotapes

• *Wagon Wheels*
  by Barbara Brenner
  performed by Darrell Carey
  (Harper Children's Audio, 1995).

Videotapes

• *Pecos Bill*
  (Sony Video, 1988).
A Rabbit Ears production.

EXPLORE LETTER H

Discuss upper- and lower-case H's and read literature links featuring starts-with-H characters such as Harold, from Crockett Johnson's classic *Harold and the Purple Crayon.*

FIND THE "LETTER OF THE WEEK"

• Use a permanent marker to write a letter "H" on the lid of a clear plastic deli tub. Place as many items for letter "H" in the tub as you can find, including a paper heart, a plastic house and hotel (from a game of *Monopoly*), and a happy face.

• Cover a cardboard cutout of the letter "H" with drawings of hearts, and happy faces!

• Bring in assorted hats for children to try on in the dress-up corner.

• Have children help you brainstorm as many animals as they can think of that start with the letter "H," including a hare, hedgehog, heron, hippo, horse, housefly, hummingbird, and so on.

HELPFUL "H" ACTIVITIES

• HELPERS OF THE WEEK: Duplicate the "helper of the week" patterns (see next page) and award one to children to decorate and wear when they help around the classroom. Badges can be worn as necklaces by punching a hole in the top, threading through with yarn or ribbon, and tying.

• A HOME IS A HOME FOR ME: Children can create their own homes using small milk cartons and a variety of decorative items: construction paper, clear cellophane, wrapping paper, glue, markers, and crayons.

• HIEROGLYPHICS: Hieroglyphics are symbols used in the picture writing of ancient Europe. Your students can make their own pictures to symbolize themselves and items in nature.

Reading Connections © 1996 Monday Morning Books, Inc.

Hh

Helpers of the Week Patterns

HELPER OF THE WEEK

HELPER OF THE WEEK

HELPER OF THE WEEK

HELPER OF THE WEEK

H h

Humpty Dumpty sat on a wall,
And **H**umpty starts with **H**.
So do words like **h**at and **h**orse
And **h**ammer, **h**ope, and **h**aste.
H starts words like **h**ummingbird
And **h**orseshoe, **h**orn, and **h**en.
Can you think of other words
That letter **H** begins?

Reading Connections © 1996 Monday Morning Books, Inc.

Hh
Upper- and Lower-case H

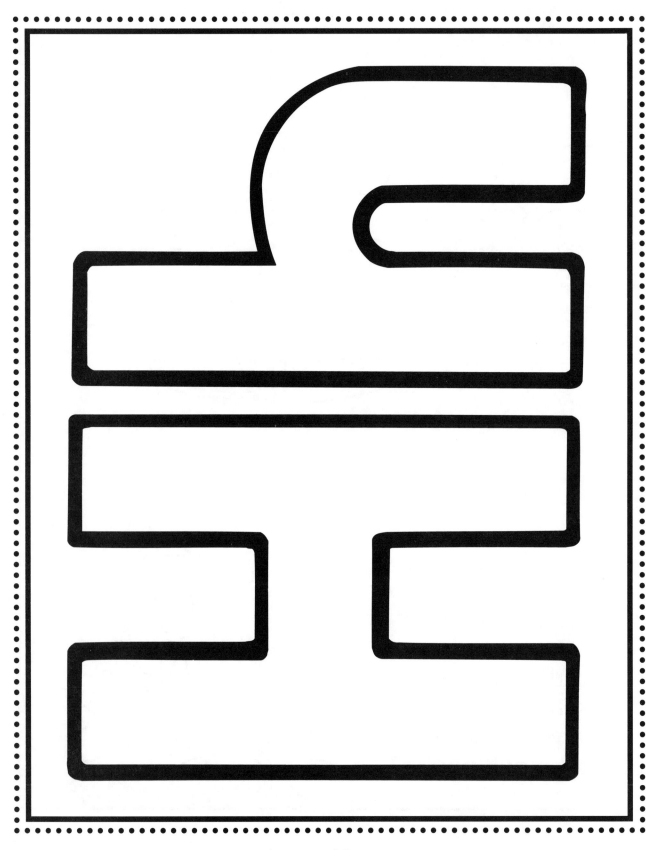

Hh
Alphabet Puzzle

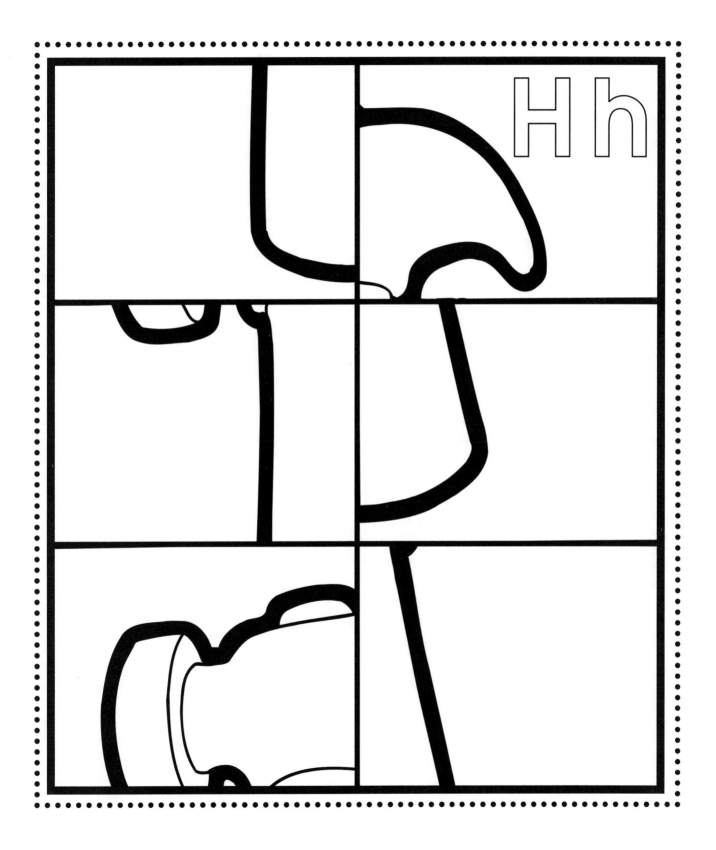

Literature Connection
HAROLD

Harold is a happy, adventurous artist who draws as he wanders, creating his own solutions to problems with a wave of his purple crayon.

READ A BOOK

• *Harold and the Purple Crayon* by Crockett Johnson (HarperTrophy, 1955).
Harold is a creative young boy who has a wonderful purple crayon. With it, he is able to make a moon, a long straight path, a forest, and much more.

• *Harold at the North Pole: A Christmas Journey with the Purple Crayon* by Crockett Johnson (Reader's Digest, 1958).
Harold sets off in his woolen hat and mittens to visit the North Pole.

• *Harold's Circus: An Astounding, Colossal, Purple Crayon Event!* by Crockett Johnson (Scholastic, 1959).
Harold creates a circus with his amazing crayon.

• *A Picture for Harold's Room* by Crockett Johnson (Scholastic, 1960).
Harold wants a picture for his room and starts with a house. Then he enters his picture to draw more and more houses. Finally, he arrives back in his own room to draw a picture for the wall.

HAROLD ACTIVITIES

• HANDSOME HANDPRINTS: Each student can make reindeer antlers. Show children how to dip their hands in tins of brown paint and then make two handprints overlapping at the center (thumbs in) on sheets of white paper. On strips of brown construction paper, have children glue jingle bells for the reindeer harnesses. (*Harold at the North Pole*)

• HAROLD'S HAT: Have children draw Harold's clown hat! Purple-outlined, of course! (*Harold's Circus*)

• HAROLD'S PICTURES: Provide purple crayons and sheets of white drawing paper for children to draw pictures for their bedrooms. Glue the pictures onto different colored sheets of construction paper for borders. (*A Picture for Harold's Room*)

Art Connection

HALLWAY HAROLD MURAL

This hallway mural could be an on-going project.

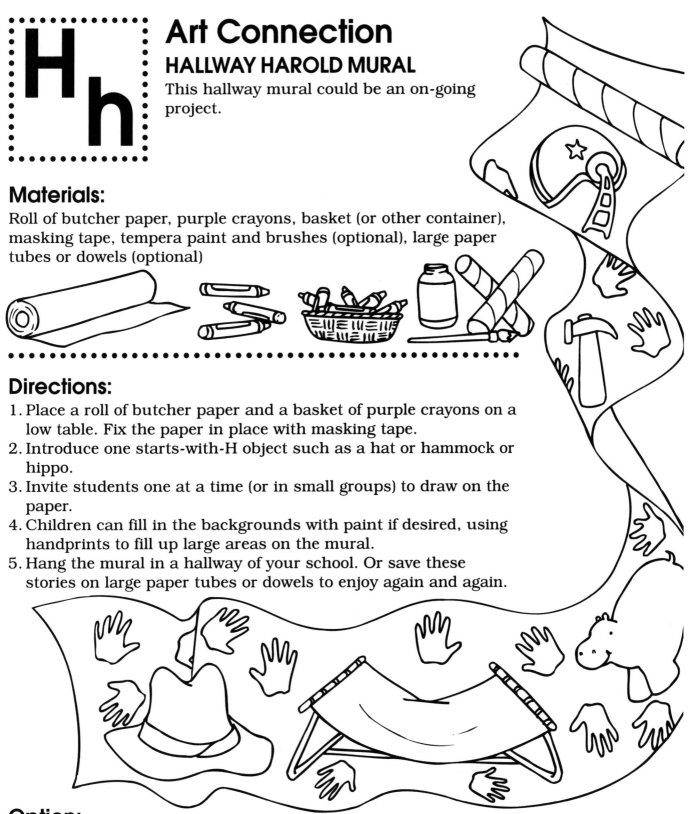

Materials:

Roll of butcher paper, purple crayons, basket (or other container), masking tape, tempera paint and brushes (optional), large paper tubes or dowels (optional)

Directions:

1. Place a roll of butcher paper and a basket of purple crayons on a low table. Fix the paper in place with masking tape.
2. Introduce one starts-with-H object such as a hat or hammock or hippo.
3. Invite students one at a time (or in small groups) to draw on the paper.
4. Children can fill in the backgrounds with paint if desired, using handprints to fill up large areas on the mural.
5. Hang the mural in a hallway of your school. Or save these stories on large paper tubes or dowels to enjoy again and again.

Option:

Set up a station with rolls of adding machine tape for students to draw their own Harold stories. Leave about two inches of blank space between each story so students can attach these strips to dowel handles to take home. Tape each end of the story to a piece of dowel (longer than the story tape is wide). Students hold one handle in each hand as they roll and tell their story.

Reading Connections © 1996 Monday Morning Books, Inc.

Hh
Resources

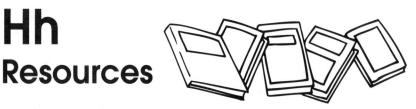

More Harold Books

- *Harold's ABC*
  by Crockett Johnson
  (Harper & Row, 1963).

- *Harold's Fairy Tale*
  by Crockett Johnson
  (Harper, 1956).
  Harold takes a walk in an enchanted garden where he has many imaginative adventures.

- *Harold's Trip to the Sky*
  by Crockett Johnson
  (HarperCollins, 1957).

Home Books

- *Always Room for One More*
  by Leclaire G. Alger
  (Holt, 1965).
  A kind farmer and his wife have plenty of room in their house for visitors—until too many friends stop by and the house falls down!

- *Hillel Builds a House*
  by Soshana Lepon
  (Kar-Ben Copies, 1993).
  Hillel is a little boy who loves to build houses. He creates cardboard houses, pillow houses, a tree house, and more. Then, for the Jewish holiday called Sukkot, Hillel builds the best house of all!

- *A House for Hermit Crab*
  by Eric Carle
  (Picture Book Studio, 1987).
  Poor Hermit Crab keeps outgrowing his shell houses. When he finally finds a shell that's big enough, he decorates it to protect it from sea anemones, urchins, and other ocean dwellers.

- *A House Is a House for Me*
  by Mary Ann Hoberman
  (Penguin, 1987).
  This book shows houses for various animals and objects. A chicken's house is a coop, a hand's "house" is a glove, an ant's house is a hill, and a potato's "house" is a pot.

- *How We Live*
  by Anita Harper
  (Harper, 1977).
  People live in many different types of places, including boats, trailers, houses, apartments, and rooms.

- *The Little House*
  by Virginia Lee Burton
  (Houghton Mifflin, 1942).
  When people begin building around the Little House, she suddenly finds herself living in the middle of a city. Luckily, a relative of the original owner finds the Little House and brings her back to the country.

- *The Old House*
  by Hans Christian Andersen
  adapted by Anthea Bell
  (North-South, 1984).
  A little boy makes friends with an elderly man who lives in an old, magical house across a busy city street.

Videotapes

- *Harold and the Purple Crayon*
  by Crockett Johnson
  (Weston Woods, 1993),
  30 minutes.

- *Harold's Fairy Tale*
  by Crockett Johnson
  (Weston Woods, 1993), 8 minutes.

EXPLORE LETTER I

Discuss upper- and lower-case I's and read literature links featuring starts-with-I books such as *If You Give a Mouse a Cookie* and *If You Give a Moose a Muffin*.

FIND THE "LETTER-OF-THE-WEEK"

• Use a permanent marker to write a letter "I" on the lid of a clear plastic deli tub. Place as many items for letter "I" in the tub as you can find, including a picture of an igloo, a picture of an ice skate, a plastic insect, an ink pen, and so on.

• Decorate a cardboard cutout of the letter "I" with ink blots or pictures of ice cream cones, or drawings of islands.

• Practice positions such as in, into, and inside. Check out *Inside, Outside, Upside Down* by Stan and Jan Berenstain (Random House, 1970).

• Discuss illusions and images after reading *An Illusionary Tale: OPT* by Arlene and Joseph Baum (Puffin, 1987). This is a magical book of optical illusions in which objects seem to shift color and size while images appear and disappear.

INTERESTING "I" ACTIVITIES

• IMAGINE THAT: Have children draw pictures of their imaginary friends—if they have them. Otherwise, have them draw pictures of places that they've dreamed about or seen in their imaginations.

• I AM A ROCK, I AM AN ISLAND: Duplicate the island pattern (see next page) to use to create an "I" bulletin board. Color the palm tree and ocean. Surround with other "I" images cut from colored construction paper.

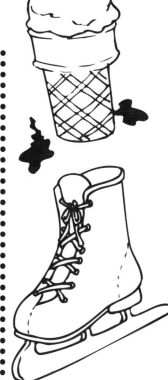

Ii

Island Pattern

I i

In a cottage in Fife lived a man
    and his wife,
And in begins with I.
So do words like icicle
And igloo, ink, and ice.
I starts words like ironing,
Iguana, if, and ill.
Can you think of more I words
Or have you had your fill?

Reading Connections © 1996 Monday Morning Books, Inc.

Ii

Upper- and Lower-case I

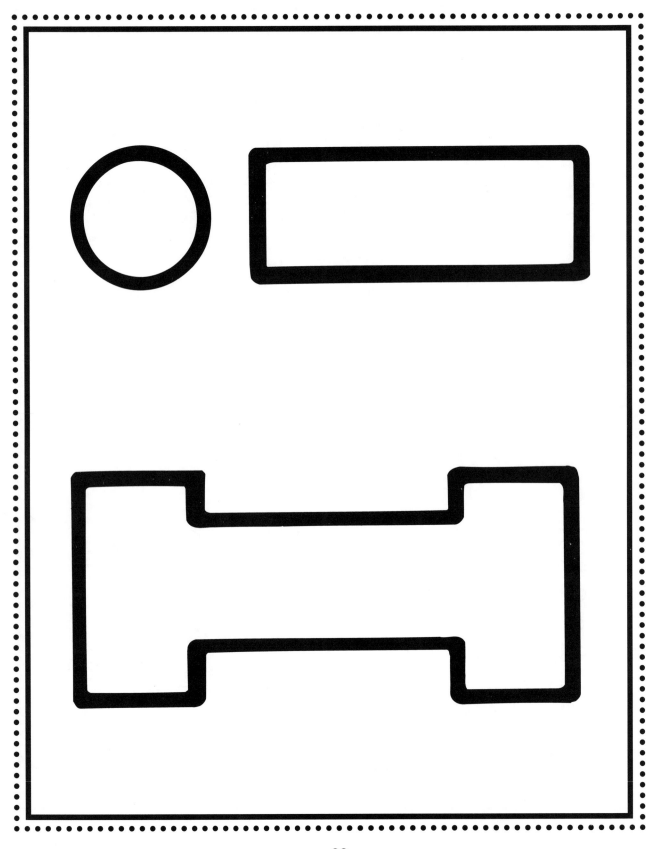

Ii

Alphabet Puzzle

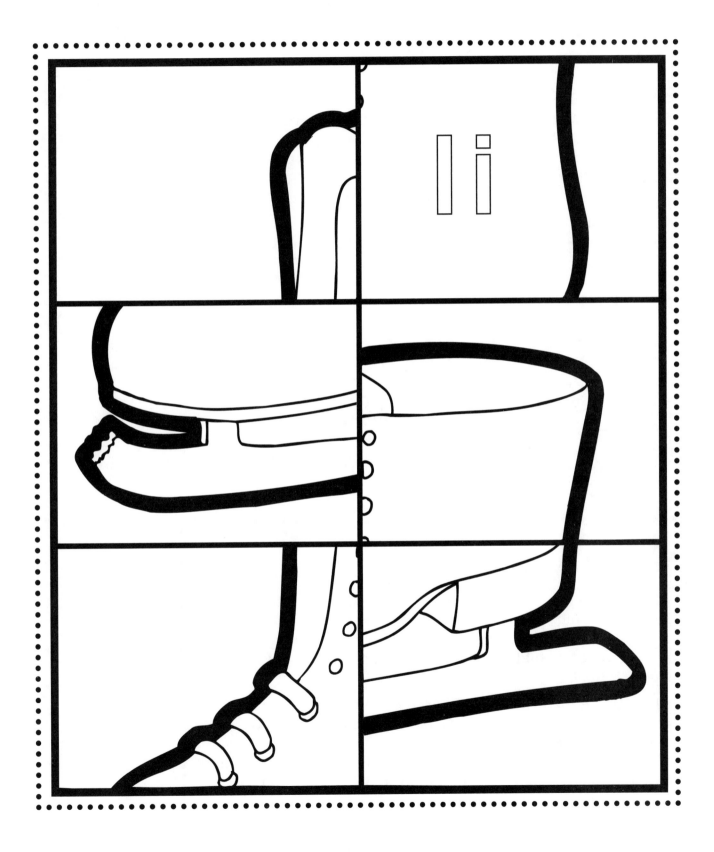

Literature Connection

IF...

The primary books for this unit include "If" in the titles. The "Resources" section notes additional "If" books, as well as books to use to spark the "imagination."

READ A BOOK

• *If You Give a Mouse a Cookie* by Laura Joffe Numeroff, illustrated by Felicia Bond (Scholastic, 1985).
A cookie triggers an amazing chain of events in this delightful, imaginative story.

• *If You Give a Moose a Muffin* by Laura Joffe Numeroff, illustrated by Felicia Bond (Scholastic, 1991).
A boy and a moose have quite an active afternoon together.

 "IF" ACTIVITIES

• IF MICE COULD DRAW: Open this book to the picture of the mouse coloring. Then set out brown, yellow, blue, gray, and orange crayons with a stack of white drawing paper at your art station, and let children draw their own pictures. (*If You Give a Mouse a Cookie*)

• IF I HAD A MOUSE: Give children cotton balls to use to create mini-mice. They can use black markers to dot on eyes and circles of felt to glue on for ears. Provide small boxes for children to use to make homes for their little mice. The mouse in *If You Give a Mouse...* slept in a little powder puff box. (*If You Give a Mouse a Cookie*)

Art Connection

IMAGINATIVE "IF" CLASS BOOK

Children can be artists "imagining if." Their pictures can be anything their imaginations desire.

Materials:

Large white paper, crayons or markers, tempera paint, paintbrushes, hole punch, yarn, scissors

Directions:

1. Give each student a blank piece of paper (large enough to cover the top of the desk).
2. Show children how to fold the paper into eight large squares.
3. Have children draw an illustration in each of the eight squares. When they turn the papers over, there is room for eight more pictures! From these 16 illustrations, students can choose one of their ideas to improve upon for the "Imagine If" book.
4. For the next illustration session, pass out quality art paper.
5. Have students expand upon their ideas and paint or draw their illustration for a cooperative book.
6. If possible, laminate the artwork and then bind the pictures by punching holes in the side and threading through with yarn or ribbon.
7. Donate the book to the school library.

Extension:

In your art station, set out a copy of *The Very Best of Children's Book Illustration*. Encourage students to decide what makes the illustrations interesting, ingenious, or imaginative.

I i

Art Connection
IMAGINARY ISLANDS

Materials:

Paper plates, aluminum foil, tempera paint, paintbrushes, glue, yarn, sand, twigs, plastic flowers, blue cellophane, scissors

Directions:

1. Give each child a paper plate to use to create an island.
2. Children can use aluminum foil to cover their islands, or they can paint their islands using tempera paints.
3. Provide assorted odds and ends for children to use to decorate their islands (yarn, sand, twigs, plastic flowers, and so on).
4. Cut sheets of blue cellophane "oceans" or "seas" for children to set their islands in.
5. Have children invent a title and story to go with their "Imaginary Islands."

This is my "Wish Island." On my island you can wish for anything. You can wish for a baseball glove, a truck, rollerblades, and more.

Ii
Resources

More "If" Books

- *If You Ever Meet A Whale*
  poems selected by Myra Cohn Livingston
  (Holiday House, 1992).

- *If You Look Around You*
  by Fulvio Testa
  (Dial, 1983).
  Children discover geometric shapes in this
  delightfully illustrated book.

- *If You Made A Million*
  by David M. Schwartz
  (Scholastic 1989).
  A sure-fire hit since it combines Kellogg's
  humorous illustrations with something
  that appeals to most kids—MONEY!

- *If You Take a Paintbrush: A Book of Colors*
  by Fulvio Testa
  (Dial, 1982).
  Testa's unique illustrations allow
  instruction to be interesting and fun.

- *If You Take a Pencil*
  by Fulvio Testa
  (Dial, 1982).
  An imaginative journey while counting
  items in the paintings.

Imagination-Starters

- *Flamboyan*
  by Arnold Adoff
  (Harcourt, 1988).
  One afternoon, a girl with hair as red as
  the Flamboyan tree, for which she is
  named, dreams of flying over her island
  home.

- *Free Fall*
  by David Weisner
  (Lothrop, 1988).
  In this wordless Caldecott Honor book, a
  boy dreams of a daring adventure in the
  company of imaginary creatures inspired
  by the items in his room.

- *Going Home*
  by Margaret Wild
  (Scholastic, 1993).
  Hugo wants to leave the hospital. While he
  waits, he imagines adventures with exotic
  animals in faraway lands.

- *Harvey Potter's Balloon Farm*
  by Jerdine Nolen
  (Lothrop, 1989).
  An imaginative tale about a farmer who
  grows balloons.

- *Hey, Al*
  by Arthur Yorinks
  (Farrar, 1986).
  A janitor and his dog escape a small
  apartment to live on an island, only to
  discover that they are turning into birds.
  Also available in a puzzle from JTG of
  Nashville, 1034C 18th Avenue South,
  Nashville, TN 37212, (615) 329-3036.

- *Hurricane*
  by David Wiesner
  (Clarion, 1990).
  When a hurricane downs a tree in the
  neighborhood, Dave and George use it
  as the setting for many imaginary
  adventures.

- *Imogene's Antlers*
  by David Small
  (Crown, 1985).
  How would you feel if you awoke to find
  you had grown antlers? This book
  describes Imogene's family's reaction.

- *June 29, 1999*
  by David Wiesner
  (Clarion, 1992).
  This book includes some great "I" words,
  such as intends, ionosphere, innovative,
  and Iowa.

 Reading Connections © 1996 Monday Morning Books, Inc.

Ii
Resources

More Imagination-Starters

- *Moe the Dog in Tropical Paradise*
  by Diane Stanley
  (Putnam's, 1992).
Moe and his friend Arlene can't afford a vacation, but Moe's imagination and artistic abilities land them in Tropical Paradise.

- *The Mysteries of Harris Burdick*
  by Chris Van Allsburg
  (Houghton, 1984).
The premise of the book is that 14 captioned pictures were left with a publisher and that Harris Burdick promised to return the next day with their stories. He never was seen or heard from again. The pictures grip one's imagination.

- *No Jumping on the Bed*
  by Tedd Arnold
  (Dial, 1987).
Walter cannot resist jumping on his bed. One night, his bed crashes through the floor and he gains neighbors and their activities as they all descend to the basement.

- *That's Good! That's Bad!*
  by Margery Cuyler
  (Scholastic, 1991).
A little boy's trip to the zoo becomes an adventure when he flies away with his red balloon.

- *The Trek*
  by Ann Jonas
  (Mulberry Books, 1985).
An imaginative little girl crosses a desert and a jungle on her way to school.

- *Tuesday*
  by David Wiesner
  (Clarion, 1991).
Looking skyward some Tuesday around 8 p.m., would you expect to see low-flying frogs upon lily pads?

- *The Very Best of Children's Book Illustration*
  compiled by the Society of Illustrators
  (North Light Books, 1993).
One hundred and seventy-five pieces of illustration—artwork from the exhibition held Oct. 21-Nov. 27, 1992. A great opportunity for students to compare and contrast favorite illustrators.

- *Would You Rather...*
  by John Burningham
  (Harper, 1978).
A child's wandering mind explores a series of improbable options.

EXPLORE LETTER J

Discuss upper- and lower-case J's and read literature links featuring starts-with-J characters such as Jesse Bear.

FIND THE "LETTER-OF-THE-WEEK"

• Use a permanent marker to write a letter "J" on the lid of a clear plastic deli tub. Place as many items for letter "J" in the tub as you can find, including a jellybean, a jack (from a game of jacks), a Jack (from a deck of cards), an empty package of Jell-O, and so on.

• On a cardboard cutout of the letter "J" glue multicolored jellybeans.

• Fill a jar with jellybeans and bring it to school. Let the class estimate the number of each color jellybean.

• Teach students to play jacks.

• Have students help you brainstorm types of clothing that start with "J," including jackets, jumpers, jeans, jerseys, and so on.

JOYFUL "J" ACTIVITIES

• JOKING JESTER: Duplicate the jester pattern (see next page) to use to create a "J Is for Joking" bulletin board. Color the pattern and add bells to the hat. Surround the jester with jokes dictated by your students or copied from the resources listed at the end of this unit.

• JUMPING FOR JOY: Have your students write down (or dictate) one thing that makes them happy. Post these reasons for being joyful on a "Jumping for Joy" bulletin board (featuring a yarn jump rope with two tagboard handles with the "joyful" reasons posted above and below it).

Jj
Jester Pattern

J j

Jack and Jill went up the hill,
And J starts both their names.
J starts words like jeep and jar,
And jacket, jacks, and Jane.
J starts words like January,
Juggler and July.
Help me think of more J words,
At least give it a try!

Jj
Upper- and Lower-case J

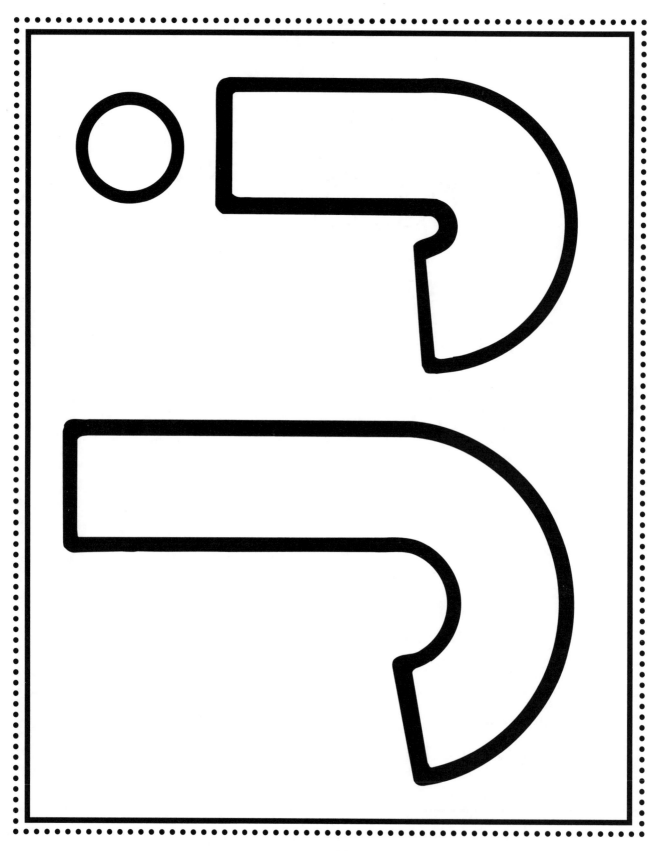

Jj
Alphabet Puzzle

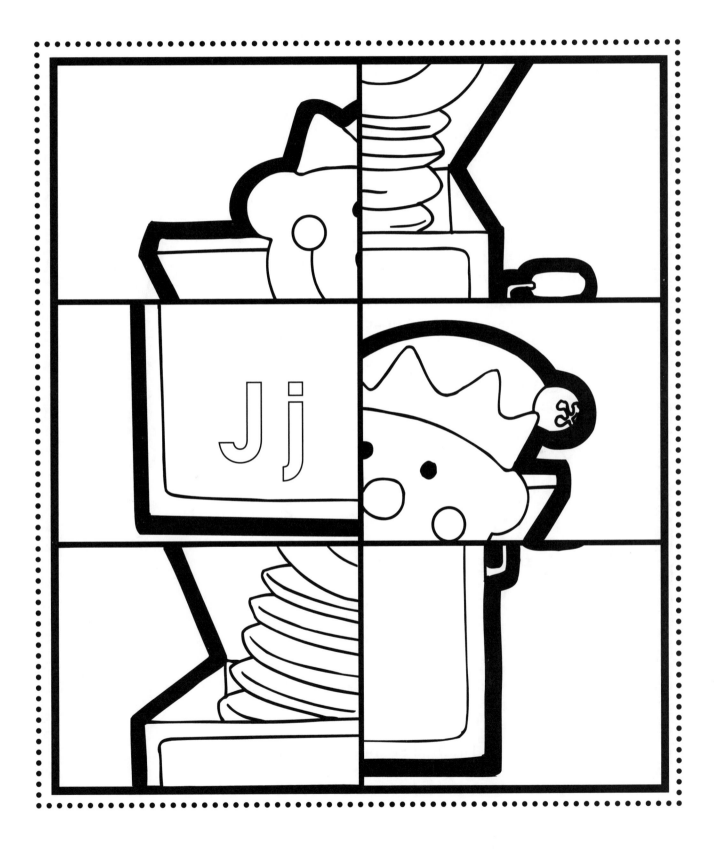

Literature Connection

JESSE BEAR

Jesse Bear is the focus of this literature unit. The Jesse Bear series is written by Nancy White Carlstrom and illustrated by Bruce Degen.

READ A BOOK

• *Better Not Get Wet, Jesse Bear* by Nancy White Carlstrom, illustrated by Bruce Degen (Macmillan, 1988).
Jesse Bear has to wait all day before it's okay for him to get wet in his wading pool!

• *Happy Birthday, Jesse Bear!* by Nancy White Carlstrom, illustrated by Bruce Degen (Macmillan, 1994).
From Jesse's invitations through pre-party impatience, guest arrival, party games and treats, and his parents' exhausted collapse into their chairs—Jesse Bear fans will be entertained.

• *How Do You Say It Today, Jesse Bear?* by Nancy White Carlstrom, illustrated by Bruce Degen (Macmillan, 1992).
Follow the months with Jesse Bear.

• *Jesse Bear, What Will You Wear?* by Nancy White Carlstrom, illustrated by Bruce Degen (Macmillan, 1986).
The rhyming text details Jesse's day from morning until evening.

JESSE ACTIVITIES

• JESSE BEAR'S BIRTHDAY: Look up students' birthdays and mark them on the calendar. Play Musical Chairs and Pin the Tail on the Clown. Host a treasure hunt with clues and prizes. (*Happy Birthday, Jesse Bear!*)

• JUST GET A LITTLE WET: Water play is a must after reading this book. Put out water play supplies at your water table or sink. (*Better Not Get Wet, Jesse Bear*)

• JESSE BEAR, HELP US DRESS!: Set out dolls and dress-up clothes for children to use to practice dressing in layers. You can suggest that they dress the dolls according to the weather outside. (*Jesse Bear, What Will You Wear?*)

Art Connection

J j

JESSE'S JACK-O'-LANTERNS

Make these jack-o'-lanterns after reading *How Do You Say It Today, Jesse Bear?*

Materials:

Jack-o'-lantern pattern (see next page), heavy paper, scissors, orange construction paper, black crayons, green felt, glue

Directions:

1. Duplicate the jack-o'-lantern pattern onto heavy paper for children to use for templates.
2. Have children trace the templates onto orange construction paper.
3. Provide black crayons for children to use to add eyes, nose, and a mouth to their pumpkins.
4. Provide green felt for children to cut out and glue to their pictures for leaves.
5. Post the completed pictures on a "Jesse's Jack-o'-lanterns" bulletin board.

Option:

If the season permits, carve real jack-o'-lanterns.

Jj
Jack-o'-lantern Pattern

Jj Resources

More Jesse Bear Books

- *It's About Time, Jesse Bear and Other Rhymes*
  by Nancy White Carlstrom
  (Scholastic, 1990).

This book includes 13 poems featuring Jesse Bear, including "It's About Time!," "Dressing Myself Today," "Cubby Crunchies," "Boxes Are Best," "Favorite Flower," and "Nitty Gritty Sand Song."

For younger audiences, four "Jesse Bear'" board books are available:

- *Jesse Bear's Tra-La Tub*
  by Nancy White Carlstrom
  (Simon and Schuster, 1994).

- *Jesse Bear's Tum Tum Tickle*
  by Nancy White Carlstrom
  (Simon and Schuster, 1994).

- *Wiggle-Jiggle Jump Up*
  by Nancy White Carlstrom
  (Simon and Schuster, 1994).

- *Yum-Yum Crumble*
  by Nancy White Carlstrom
  (Simon and Schuster, 1994).

Joke Books

- *The Cut-Ups*
  by James Marshall
  (Viking, 1984).

Practical jokers get away with every trick in the book until they meet a little girl.

- *The Cut-Ups Carry On*
  by James Marshall
  (Viking, 1990).

Spud and Joe continue their antics as they are forced to take ballroom dancing lessons.

- *Fozzie's Funnies: A Book of Silly Jokes and Riddles*
  (Muppet Press, 1993).

Muppet fans will be delighted with this collection featuring Fozzie Bear.

- *Funnyman's First Case*
  by Stephen Mooser
  (Franklin Watts, 1981).

A wise-cracking waiter uses some of his best jokes to foil a robbery.

- *Haunted House Jokes*
  by Louis Phillips
  (Viking Kestrel, 1987).

From Dracula hanging out in the attic to mummies in the basement, this seven-chapter book provides ghoulish entertainment.

- *The Joke Book*
  by Roy McKie
  (Random House, 1979).

This book targets young readers with easy-to-read jokes that will appeal to primary-age humor.

- *Llama Beans*
  by Charles Keller
  (Prentice, Hall, 1979).

Collection of animal jokes.

- *Look Out It's April Fools' Day*
  by Frank Modell
  (Greenwillow, 1985).

Marvin just loves to play jokes on his friend Milton. But on April Fools' Day, Milton just won't be fooled.

- *Monster Knock Knocks*
  by William Cole and Mike Thaler
  (Minstrel, 1982).

Crazy Thaler illustrations accompany knock-knock jokes with a monster theme.

107

Jj
Resources

More Joke Books

- *101 Bossy Cow Jokes*
  by Katy Hall and Lisa Eisenberg
  (Scholastic, 1989).

- *101 Cat and Dog Jokes*
  by Katy Hall and Lisa Eisenberg
  (Scholastic, 1989).

- *101 Hamburger Jokes: Meaty Jokes to Be Devoured with Relish*
  by Phil Hirsch
  (Scholastic, 1978).

- *101 Pet Jokes*
  by Phil Hirsch with Hope Hirsch
  (Scholastic, 1980).

- *101 Silly Monster Jokes*
  by Jovial Bob Stine
  (Scholastic, 1986).

- *101 Silly Summertime Jokes*
  by Stephanie Calmenson
  (Scholastic, 1989).

- *101 Sports Jokes: Guaranteed to Make You A Winner*
  by Sam Schultz
  (Lerner, 1982).

- *101 Vacation Jokes*
  by Jovial Bob Stine
  (Scholastic, 1990).

- *150 Gross Monster Jokes*
  by Micheal J. Pellowski
  (Dell, 1991).

- *The Silliest Joke Book Ever*
  by Victoria Hartman
  (Lothrop, 1993).
The jokes are divided into chapters—Food, Funnies, Animal Snickers, Wacky Workers, Techie Ticklers, Journey Jests, and Gruesome Giggles—in a multiple-jokes-per-page format.

- *The Silly Joke Book*
  by Victoria Hartman
  (Scholastic, 1987).
This book includes chapters of Animal Warm-ups, Jokes You'll Eat Up, Ghouly Giggles, Ridiculous Tales, Utter Nonsense, Computer Comics, and Last Laughs.

EXPLORE LETTER K

Discuss upper- and lower-case K's and read literature links featuring starts-with-K characters such as Katie Morag.

FIND THE "LETTER-OF-THE-WEEK"

• Use a permanent marker to write a letter "K" on the lid of a clear plastic deli tub. Place as many items for letter "K" in the tub as you can find, including a picture of a kitten, a kazoo, a cutout of a kite, a key, a kerchief, and so on.

• Cover a cardboard cutout of the letter "K" with rubbings of keys.

• Collect as many extra keys as you can find. Have children sort them by size, shape, and color.

• Bring in a kaleidoscope for children to observe.

• Bring in items that show measurement in kilograms. Explain that in much of the world, this is the standard system of measurement.

• Bring in a kilt for children to observe and try on.

• Have children brainstorm as many animals that start with "K" as they can think of, including katydids (insects), kittens, kangaroos, kookaburras, and koalas.

KINDHEARTED "K" ACTIVITIES

• KINSHIP: On lined tagboard, write the words "kin" and "kinship." As a class, discuss what these words mean. Explain that kin means one's relatives or family. Then have each child draw a picture of some of his or her kin.

• KEYS OF KINDNESS: Copy and cut out the key patterns (see next page). As students notice classmates doing kind acts for each other, they can fill in a key and add it to a "Keys of Kindness" bulletin board.

 Reading Connections © 1996 Monday Morning Books, Inc.

Kk
Key Patterns

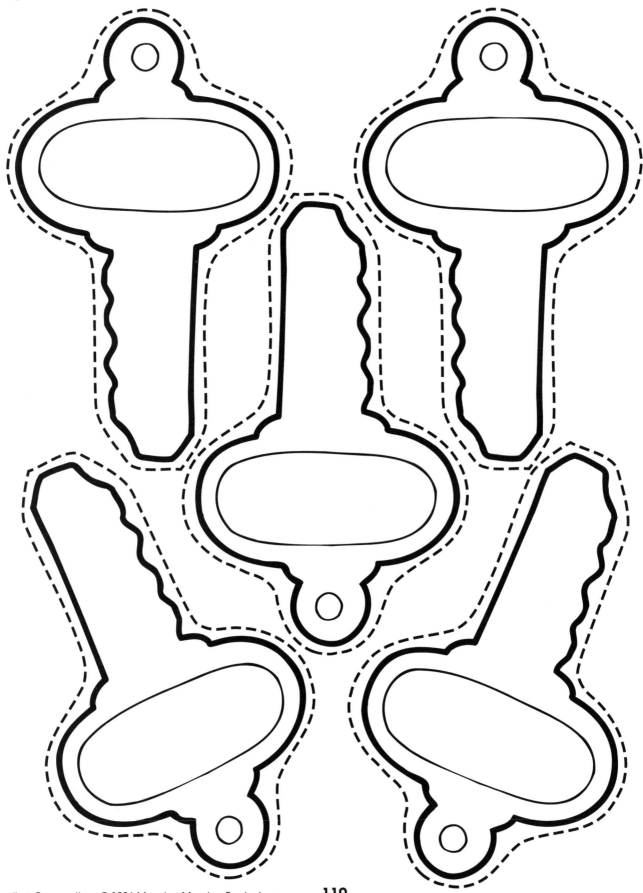

K k

Polly put the **k**ettle on,
And **k**ettle starts with **K**.
So do words like **k**ite and **k**ing
And **k**angaroo and **k**ey.
K starts words like **k**ettledrum
And **k**itten, **k**ick, and **k**iss.
Can you think of more **K** words
To add onto this list?

111

Kk

Upper- and Lower-case K

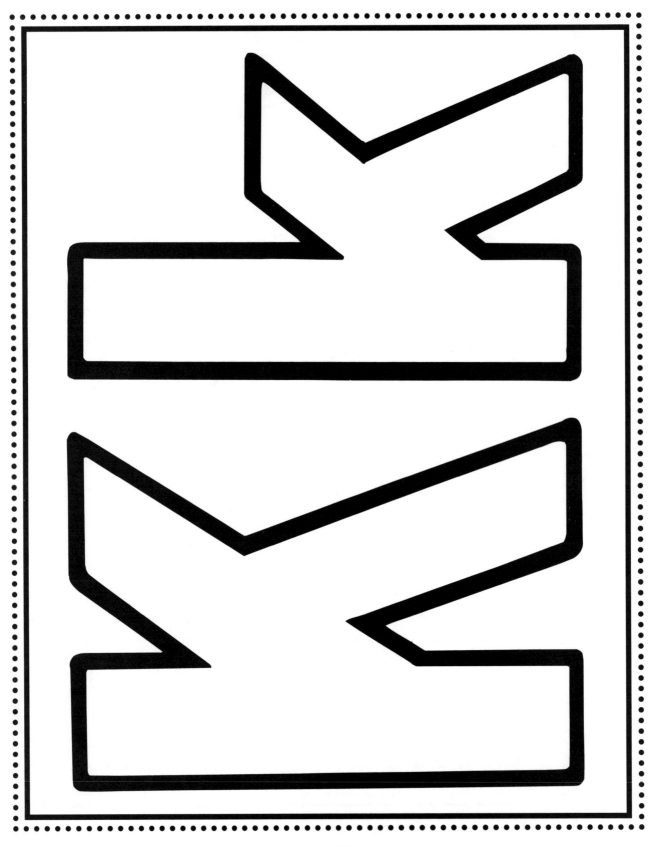

Kk
Alphabet Puzzle

Literature Connection

KATIE MORAG

The main character for this unit is Katie Morag, a Scottish lass. Katie has adventures with a number of her kin.

READ A BOOK

• *Katie Morag and the Big Boy Cousins* by Mairi Hedderwick (Little, Brown, 1987).
Katie loves her wild and unruly cousins. She daringly takes part in their shenanigans until Granny gets them to pitch in with the chores.

• *Katie Morag and the Two Grandmothers* by Mairi Hedderwick (Little, Brown, 1985).
Katie's grandmothers don't seem to have much in common, but Katie brings their ideas closer together in time for Grannie Island's prize sheep to win on Show Day.

• *Katie Morag and the Tiresome Ted* by Mairi Hedderwick (Little, Brown, 1986).
Irritated at the arrival of her baby sister, Katie throws her bear into the sea. She restores her good humor as she restores her bear.

 KATIE ACTIVITIES

• A RIBBON FOR KATIE: Have children make construction paper prize ribbons for their own Show Day. (*Katie Morag and the Two Grandmothers*)

• "KATIE'S KERCHIEF": Play this game as you would "Drop the Hankie." Students sit in a circle. One student holds a kerchief and runs around the outside of the circle. The runner drops the kerchief behind another student. The second student must pick up the kerchief and try to tag the runner before he or she returns to the vacated spot in the circle. If the runner can sit down without being tagged, then the second student becomes the runner. If the second student tags the runner, then the runner tries again.

Art Connection
KATIE MORAG'S KILT KEEPSAKE

Materials:

Heavy paper, colored construction paper, scissors, ruler, marker

Directions:

1. On a large square of heavy paper, measure lines one inch apart beginning one inch away from the outside edge.
2. Help students cut across these lines to form the base for their weaving.
3. Using colorful construction paper strips of varying widths, show children how to weave. They'll begin with their first strip in an under-over pattern. Then they'll alternate between over-under and under-over as they form their kilt-pattern keepsake.

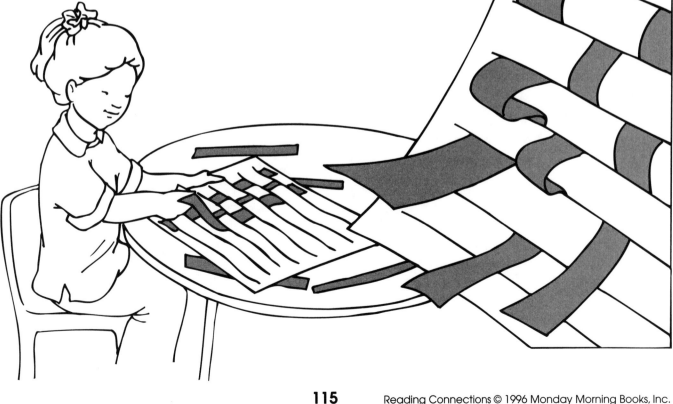

Kk
Resources

More Katie Morag Books

• *Katie Morag Delivers the Mail*
  by Mairi Hedderwick
  (Little, Brown, 1984).
On her way to deliver the local mail, Katie slips in the water and the addresses on the parcels wash away. She visits her grandmother and together the two sort out the problem.

Scottish Books

• *Argyle*
  by Barbara Brooks Wallace
  (Abingdon, 1987).
An unusual sheep with his multicolored wool brings fortune to his owners.

• *The Magic Bagpipe*
  by Gerry and George Armstrong
  (Whitman, 1964).
A Scottish lad receives a bagpipe from a fairy and wins a piping contest.

• *Wee Gillis*
  by Munro Leaf
  (Puffin, 1985).
Wee Gillis, actually named Alastair Roderic Craigellachie Dalhousie Gowan Donnybristle MacMac, visits his kin in the Highlands and Lowlands of Scotland, trying to decide where he best belongs.

Scottish Tartans

• *Tartans* by Christian Hesketh
  (Putnam, 1961).

• *Tartans, Their Art and History*
  by Ann Sutton and Richard Carr
  (Arco, 1984).

Videotapes

• *Wee Gills*
  (Churchill Films, 1985).

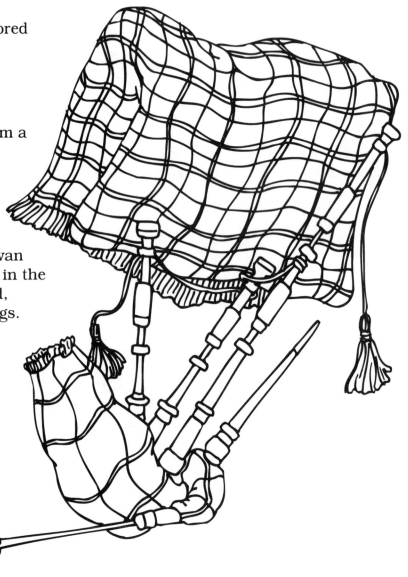

EXPLORE LETTER L

Discuss upper- and lower-case L's and read literature links featuring starts-with-L characters such as Lyle Crocodile.

💡 FIND THE "LETTER-OF-THE-WEEK"

• Use a permanent marker to write a letter "L" on the lid of a clear plastic deli tub. Place as many items for letter "L" in the tub as you can find, including a picture of a ladybug, a leaf, a picture of the Liberty Bell, a light bulb (a small one), a plastic lion, and so on.

• Decorate a cardboard cutout of the letter "L" with leaf rubbings.

• Light up the classroom with twinkling Christmas lights. Turn off the overhead lights and let children watch the little lights twinkle.

• Challenge children to brainstorm as many animals as they can think of that start with "L," including lions, lobsters, lizards, lightning bugs, longhorns (type of cattle), and so on.

• Brainstorm a list with your students of foods that start with "L," including lasagna, leeks, lima beans, and so on.

✉ LOVABLE "L" ACTIVITIES

• DELIVER THE LETTER: Make a letter box from a cardboard box. Students can "mail" letters to each other. Pair children off so that each child writes and receives a letter.

• LETTER BULLETIN BOARD: Duplicate the letter and stamp patterns (see next page) to use to create a "Lovable Letters" bulletin board. As children write letters to each other, add the letters to the bulletin board.

Ll

Letter and Stamp Patterns

Fold

Place stamp here.

L l

London Bridge is falling down
And **L**ondon starts with **L**.
So do words like **l**amb and **l**eash
And **l**adder, **l**amp, and **l**ull.
L starts words like **l**icorice
And **l**ion, **l**ight, and **l**ime.
Can you think of more **L** words
To add onto this rhyme?

119

Ll

Upper- and Lower-case L

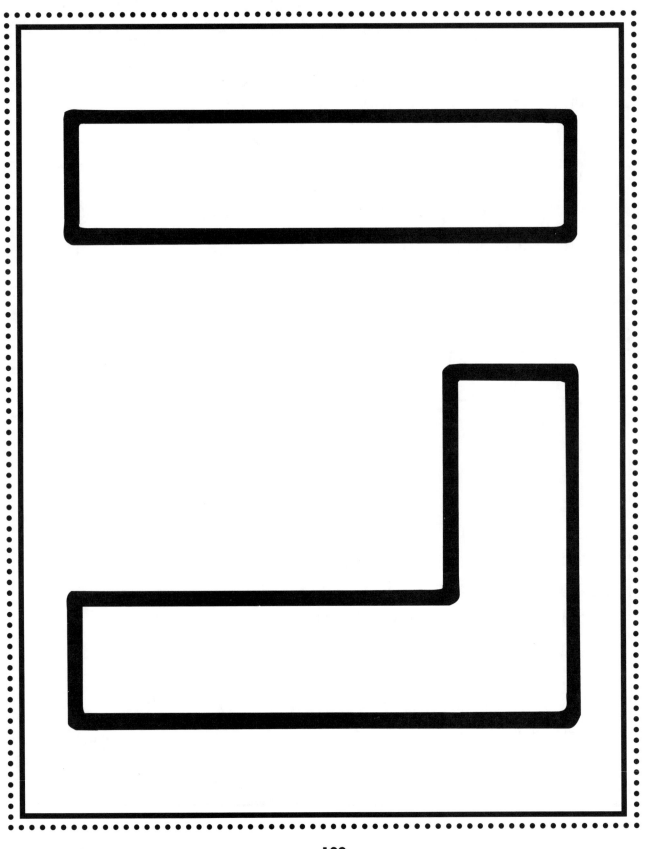

Ll

Alphabet Puzzle

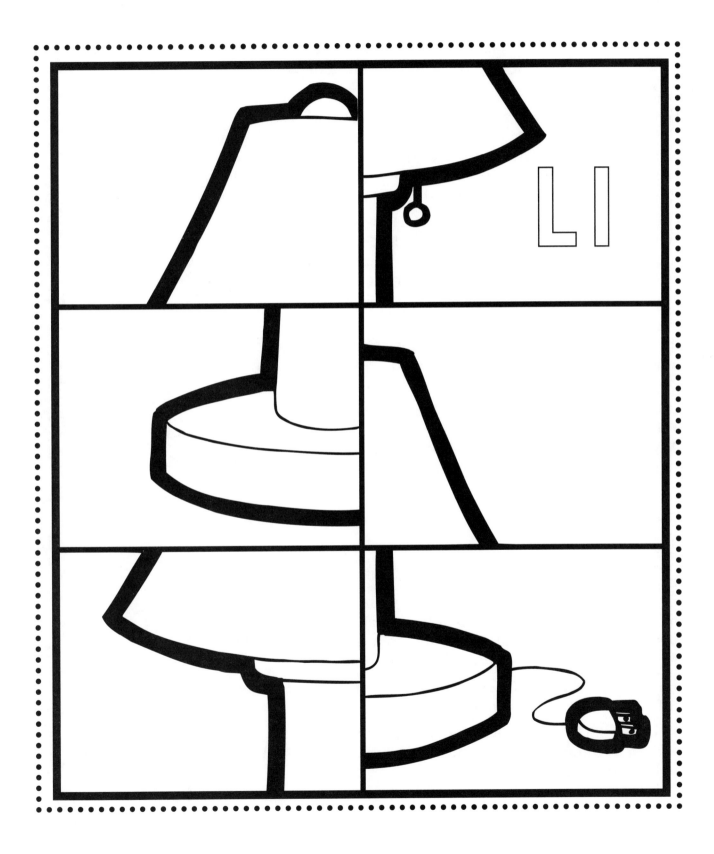

Reading Connections © 1996 Monday Morning Books, Inc.

Literature Connection

LYLE CROCODILE

This unit's main character is lovable Lyle, star of the series by Bernard Waber. Whether Lyle is at the office, on stage, or at the house on East 88th Street, he will likely be loved by you and your students.

READ A BOOK

• *Lovable Lyle* by Bernard Waber (Houghton Mifflin, 1969).
Lyle is loved by family and neighbors, so he is shocked when he starts receiving hate letters. He tries his best to amuse and delight everyone, but the letters continue, until he manages to save the day and make a new friend.

• *Lyle at the Office* by Bernard Waber (Houghton Mifflin, 1994).
Lyle is likeable and popular in the building when he goes to work at Mr. Primm's office, but life gets interesting when he doesn't want to appear in the Krispie Krunchie Krackles ads.

• *Lyle Finds His Mother* by Bernard Waber (Houghton Mifflin, 1974).
In this Lyle adventure, the crocodile goes off in search of his mother at the urging of Hector P. Valenti, leaving his happy home on East 88th Street.

• *Lyle, Lyle, Crocodile* by Bernard Waber (Houghton Mifflin, 1965).
Lyle is not well liked by the neighbors until one evening when he has the opportunity to do them a favor.

LYLE ACTIVITIES

• LETTERS TO LYLE: Have students write letters to Lyle. Ask older student buddies to write letters back from Lyle. Place boxes labeled "Lyle" and "Students" on a table with a large sign: Lyle Loves Letters. (*Lyle Finds His Mother*)

• LIKED LIKE LYLE: Discuss how it feels to be liked, and how it feels to have an enemy. (*Lovable Lyle*)

• SMILE LIKE LYLE: Have students draw pictures of themselves smiling under a heading which states "Smile Like Lyle." (*Lyle at the Office*)

Art Connection
LYLE'S LOVELY LOCKET

Students can make a lovely locket that holds their picture for their own mothers.

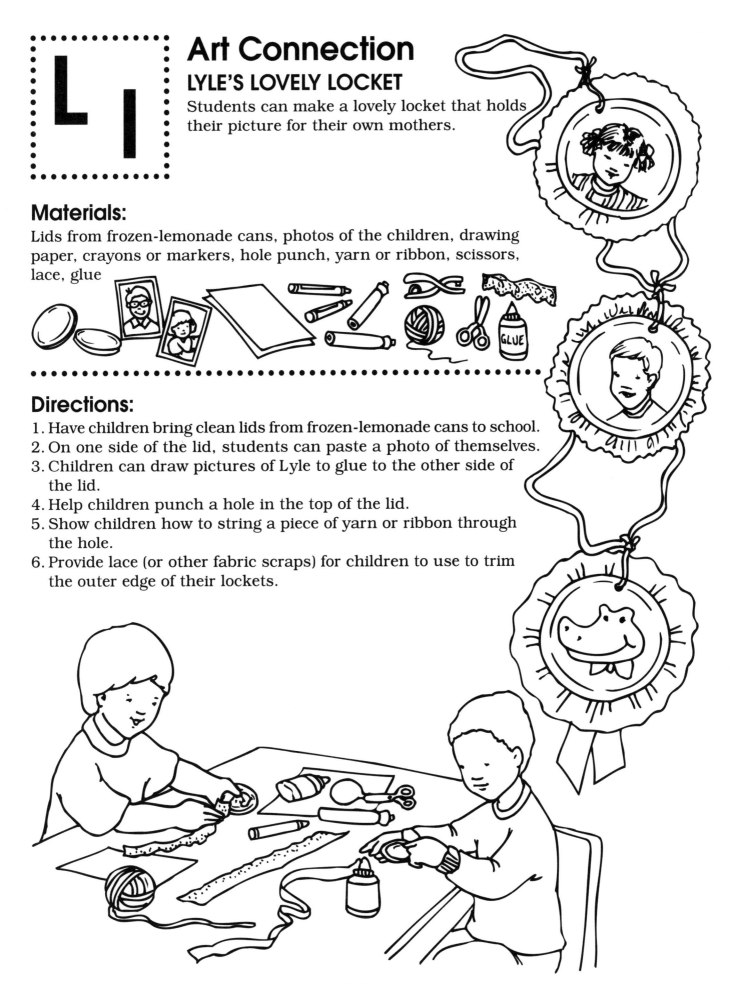

Materials:

Lids from frozen-lemonade cans, photos of the children, drawing paper, crayons or markers, hole punch, yarn or ribbon, scissors, lace, glue

Directions:

1. Have children bring clean lids from frozen-lemonade cans to school.
2. On one side of the lid, students can paste a photo of themselves.
3. Children can draw pictures of Lyle to glue to the other side of the lid.
4. Help children punch a hole in the top of the lid.
5. Show children how to string a piece of yarn or ribbon through the hole.
6. Provide lace (or other fabric scraps) for children to use to trim the outer edge of their lockets.

LI
Resources

More Lyle Books

- *Funny, Funny Lyle*
  by Bernard Waber
  (Houghton Mifflin, 1987).
  Life changes at the Primm household
  when Lyle's mother moves in.

- *The House on East 88th Street*
  by Bernard Waber
  (Houghton Mifflin, 1962).
  When the Primm family moves in, they
  discover Lyle the Crocodile in their tub.

- *Lyle and the Birthday Party*
  by Bernard Waber
  (Houghton Mifflin, 1966).
  When Lyle gets a strong case of jealousy
  at Joshua's birthday party, everyone is
  puzzled by his unusual behavior.

Letter Books

- *Dear Annie*
  by Judith Caseley
  (Greenwillow, 1991).
  The book displays part of a series of letters
  sent between Annie and her grandfather.

- *Dear Bear*
  by Joanna Harrison
  (Carolrhoda Books, 1994).
  Katie is frightened by the bear in the
  closet under the stairs, until they start
  exchanging letters.

- *Dear Brother*
  by Frank Asch and Vladimir Vagin
  (Scholastic, 1992).
  Two mice find some old family letters in
  the attic and read them to each other.

- *Dear Mr. Blueberry*
  by Simon James
  (Margaret McElderry Books, 1991).
  Emily and her teacher, Mr. Blueberry,
  exchange letters during vacation.

- *Dear Peter Rabbit*
  by Alma Flor Ada
  (Atheneum, 1994).
  Delightful letters between fairy tale
  characters accompany lovely illustrations.

- *Don't Forget to Write*
  by Martin Selway
  (Ideals, 1992).
  Rosie's letters home relay that she is
  reluctant about her visit to Grandad's
  farm, but by the time she's supposed to
  return home, she begs to stay longer.

- *The Dove's Letter*
  by Keith Baker
  (Harcourt, 1988).
  A dove finds an unaddressed letter and
  spreads joy as she tries to deliver it.

- *Here Comes the Mail*
  by Gloria Skurynski
  (Bradbury Press, 1992).
  Stephanie in Santa Fe wants to mail
  something to her cousin in Salt Lake City.

- *The Jolly Christmas Postman*
  by Janet and Allan Ahlberg
  (Little, Brown, 1991).
  The nursery rhyme characters are
  corresponding at Christmas.

- *The Jolly Postman and Other People's
  Letters*
  by Janet and Allan Ahlberg
  (Little, Brown, 1986).
  Take the letters out of the envelopes in
  this book and see which fairy tale
  characters have written to each other.

EXPLORE LETTER M

Discuss upper- and lower-case M's and read literature links featuring starts-with-M characters such as Madeline.

FIND THE "LETTER-OF-THE-WEEK"

• Use a permanent marker to write a letter "M" on the lid of a clear plastic deli tub. Place as many items for letter "M" in the tub as you can find, including a plastic man, a marshmallow, a picture of a monkey, a marble, a marker, a plastic moose, and so on.

• On a cardboard cutout of the letter "M," glue M & M's.

• Listen to music during this unit. (French music would be appropriate for the Madeline theme. See "Resources" for suggestions.)

• Have children brainstorm as many foods as they can think of that start with "M," including mozzarella and Muenster cheese, macaroni, mustard, marshmallows, and so on.

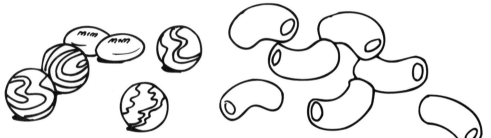

MARVELOUS "M" ACTIVITIES

• MAGICAL MASTERPIECE: Make a "Magical Masterpiece" bulletin board by duplicating, coloring, and posting the magic hat and wand (see next page). Surround the magic hat with glittery stars for extra sparkle.

• MOBILE MAGIC: Make a few cooperative mobiles with your students. Duplicate the patterns (see next page), let children color them in, punch a hole in each pattern, and fasten to a hanger with yarn. Cover the hanger with felt ahead of time, if desired.

Mm
Magic Patterns

M m

Mary had a little lamb,
And **M**ary starts with **M**.
So do **m**itten, **m**ouse, and **m**aze,
And **m**ilk and **m**agazine.
M starts words like **m**ulberry,
And **m**ask, and **m**oon, and **m**a'am.
Can you think of other words
That start with letter **M**?

Mm

Upper- and Lower-case M

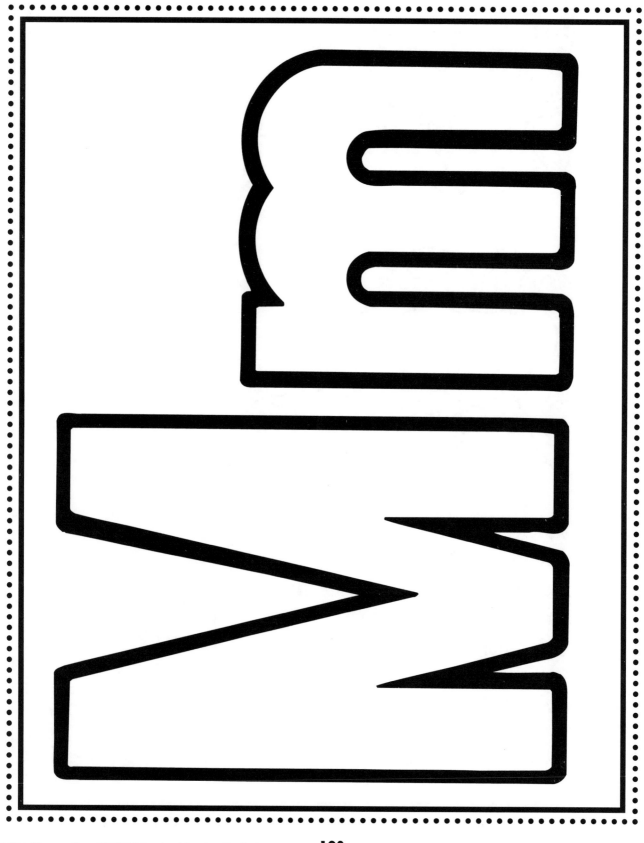

Mm
Alphabet Puzzle

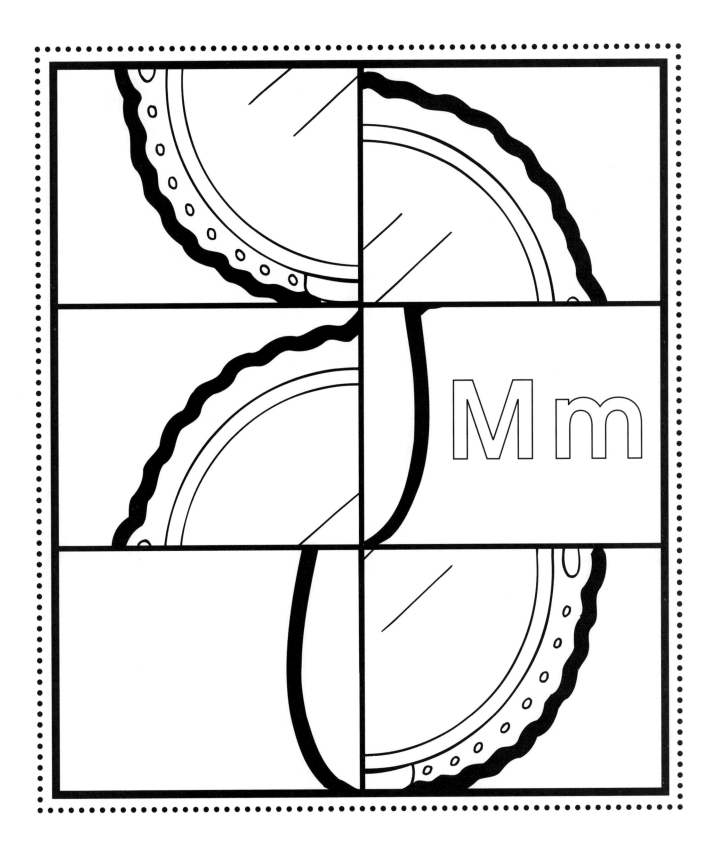

Literature Connection
MADELINE

Madeline is the star of this series by Ludwig Bemelmans. She is sure to be a favorite with your students.

READ A BOOK

• *Madeline* by Ludwig Bemelmans (Viking, 1985).
The first in the series of Madeline adventures involving the 12 charges of Miss Clavel. In this episode, Madeline has her appendix removed.

• *Madeline and the Bad Hat* by Ludwig Bemelmans (Viking, 1957).
Madeline and her friends positively influence the boy next door.

• *Madeline's Christmas* (Viking, 1985).
No one is stirring in the house on Christmas Eve except Madeline and a magician. With the magician's help, Madeline runs the school that night when everyone else is sick.

• *Madeline's Rescue* by Ludwig Bemelmans (Viking, 1953).
Madeline falls in the Seine, then is rescued by a dog. Thus begins another adventure for the 12 little girls, Miss Clavel, the Board of Trustees, and Genevieve.

MADELINE ACTIVITIES

• MADELINE MAGIC: Do simple magic tricks like Madeline's friend the magician does. (*Madeline's Christmas*)

• MINE, MINE, MINE!: All the girls claim that Genevieve is "Mine." With a stuffed dog, act out the scene in mime. (*Madeline's Rescue*)

• MEANIE: Discuss what would make Pepito so mean. Make a list of things he could do to make positive changes. (*Madeline and the Bad Hat*)

Art Connection
MAKING MOSAICS

Using plaster of Paris instead of mortar, students can make mosaic pictures of Madeline or another "M" person or object.

Materials:

Plaster of Paris (mix according to directions), plastic lids from coffee or similar-sized cans (one per child), beads, pebbles, feathers

Directions:

1. For each child, fill a plastic coffee can lid with plaster of Paris. Have materials such as beads, feathers, and pebbles ready to set into these molds.
2. Let the students set some of the objects in the plaster. Have them work quickly as the plaster sets rapidly.
3. Display completed mosaics when dry on a low table in the classroom.

Note:

Mix only a manageable amount of plaster of Paris at a time. This material hardens very quickly!

Mm
Resources

More Madeline Books

- *Madeline and the Gypsies*
  by Ludwig Bemelmans
  (Viking, 1958).

Madeline and Pepito are whisked off with the circus and tour around France in this adventure.

- *Madeline in London*
  by Ludwig Bemelmans
  (Viking, 1961).

The next door neighbors move to London, the setting for this Madeline adventure.

French Books

- *L'alphabet: A Child's Introduction to the Letters and Sounds of French*
  (Passport Books, 1991).

The alphabet is humorously presented with illustrations of French phrases. This book also includes a pronunciation guide and some French definitions.

Audiotapes

- *Madeline*
  (Viking, 1975).

- *Madeline and the Bad Hat*
  (Viking, 1979).

- *Madeline and the Gypsies*
  (Viking, 1980).

- *Madeline in London*
  (Viking, 1977).

- *Madeline's Rescue*
  (Weston Woods, 1989).

- *Qu'il y ait toujours le solei*
  by Charlotte Diamond
  (Hug Bug Records, 1990).

A tape of French music.

Videotapes

- *Madeline*
  narrated by Christopher Plummer
  (Hi-Tops Video, 1988).

- *Madeline and the Bad Hat*
  (Golden Book, 1992).

- *Madeline's Christmas*
  (Golden Book, 1990).

- *Madeline and Cooking School*
  narrated by Christopher Plummer
  (Golden BookVideo, 1993).

- *Madeline and the Dog Show*
  narrated by Christopher Plummer
  (Golden BookVideo, 1993).

- *Madeline and the Easter Bonnet*
  narrated by Christopher Plummer
  (Golden BookVideo, 1993).

- *Madeline and the Gypsies*
  (Golden BookVideo, 1990).

- *Madeline and the Toy Factory*
  narrated by Christopher Plummer
  (Golden BookVideo, 1993).

- *Madeline in London*
  (Golden, 1991).

- *Madeline's Rescue*
  (Golden Book, 1991).

- *Madeline's Rescue and Other Stories About Madeline*
  (Wood, Knapp, 1992).

Other

- *Madeline* puzzle
  (Ravensburger, 1991).

A 25-piece puzzle of Madeline, Pepito, and Miss Clavel in front of the Eiffel Tower.

EXPLORE LETTER N

Discuss upper- and lower-case N's and read literature links featuring number books and books from the Nutshell Library.

 ## FIND THE "LETTER-OF-THE-WEEK"

• Use a permanent marker to write a letter "N" on the lid of a clear plastic deli tub. Place as many items for letter "N" in the tub as you can find, including a nut, a nickel, a noodle (uncooked), a plastic nose, a number, a noisemaker (the kind used at parties), and so on.

• Have children help you glue nuts onto a cardboard cutout of the letter "N."

• Purchase a bag of mixed nuts. Have students sort the nuts by size or color.

• Discuss the difference between being "naughty" and "nice."

• Discuss dreams and nightmares. (*There's a Nightmare in My Closet* by Mercer Mayer is an appropriate book link for this activity.)

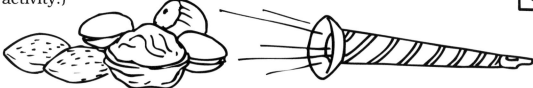

NICE "N" ACTIVITIES

• GO NUTS!: Chart your students' favorite nuts. Bring in a variety of nuts for children to sample. Then, on a large sheet of butcher paper, make a column for every type of nut that the students have tasted. Have children mark which nuts are their favorites in ranking order.

• NOSE FOR NEWS: Duplicate the nose pattern (see next page) to use to create a "Nose for News" bulletin board. Color and post on a bulletin board and surround with bits of information about your classroom. Each time your class does something "newsworthy" (takes a field trip, has a guest, plays a new game, learns a new song), post a "headline" on the bulletin board.

Reading Connections © 1996 Monday Morning Books, Inc.

Nn
Nose Pattern

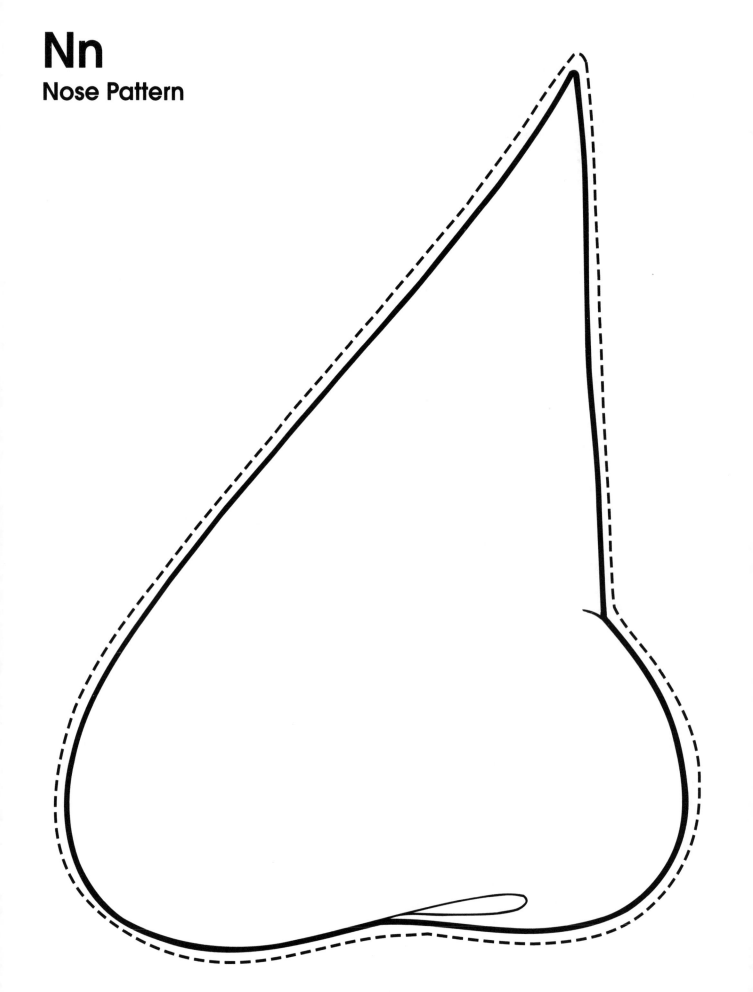

Nn

Needles and pins, **n**eedles and pins,
Needles starts with **N**.
So do words like **n**urse
And **n**est and **n**obody and **n**ine.
N starts words like **n**ewspaper
And **n**oodle, **n**et, and **n**o.
Can you think of more **N** words
Or shall we go to O?

Reading Connections © 1996 Monday Morning Books, Inc.

Nn
Upper- and Lower-case N

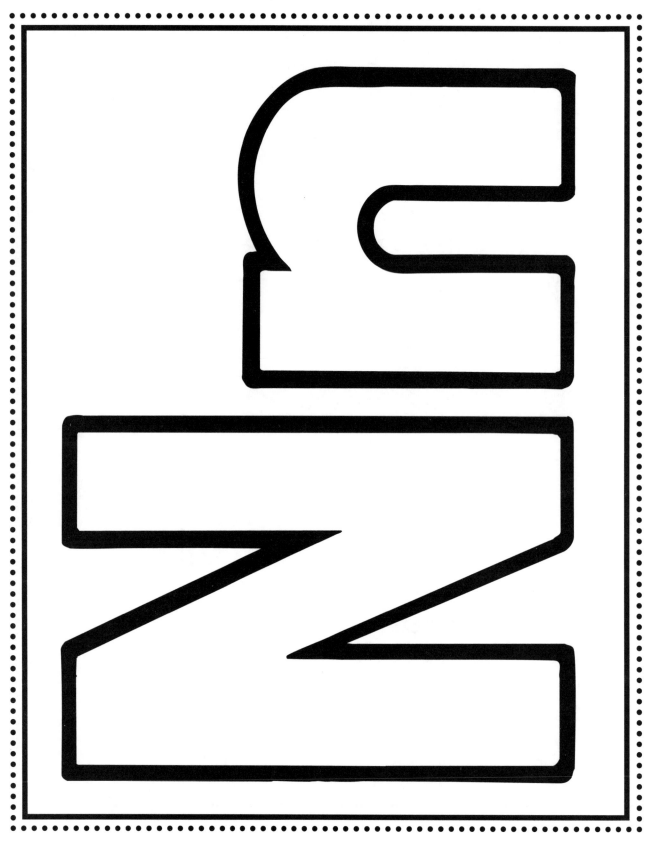

Nn
Alphabet Puzzle

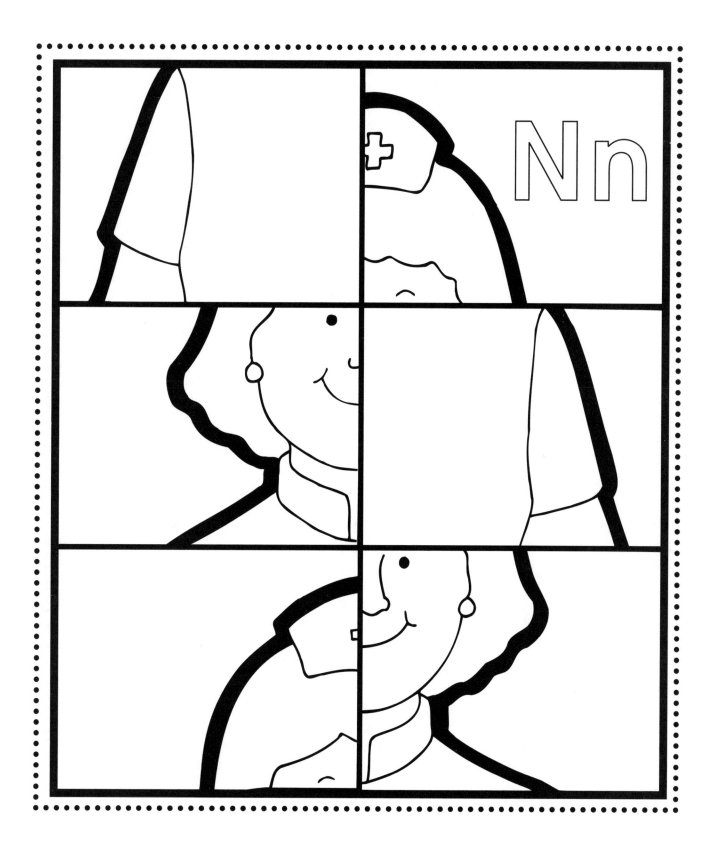

Reading Connections © 1996 Monday Morning Books, Inc.

Literature Connection
NUTSHELL LIBRARY

Maurice Sendak's classic books from the Nutshell Library are destined to be favorites with your students.

READ A BOOK

• *Alligators All Around: An Alphabet* by Maurice Sendak (Harper and Row, 1962).
This adorable book features the alphabet dramatized by alligators.

• *Chicken Soup with Rice: A Book of Months* by Maurice Sendak (Harper and Row, 1962).
This book follows the year with a monthly poem about chicken soup with rice.

• *One Was Johnny: A Counting Book* by Maurice Sendak (Harper and Row, 1962).
Numbers are featured in this simple counting book. Children will enjoy the odd procession of animals who parade into Johnny's house.

• *Pierre: A Cautionary Tale in Five Chapters and A Prologue* by Maurice Sendak (Harper and Row, 1962).
Pierre needs an attitude adjustment! But if you ask what he thinks, he'll tell you "I don't care!"

NUTSHELL ACTIVITIES

• NOSEY, NOSEY: Bring in a collection of plastic animal nose-masks from a novelty store. (These will be easiest to find during Halloween.) Students can wear the noses while acting out the comings and goings of the characters in this book. (*One Was Johnny*)

• POESY, POESY: Throughout the year, have students learn the poem for each month. For a special treat, serve chicken soup with rice after reading this story. (*Chicken Soup with Rice*)

• FROM A TO Z: Assign each student one (or more) letters of the alphabet to illustrate with pictures of alligators in action. (*Alligators All Around*)

Art Connection
NUTSHELL CREATURES

Materials:

Walnut shells (one half of a shell per child), tempera paint, paintbrushes, glue, yarn, marbles, felt, scissors, wiggly eyes (optional)

Directions:

1. Give each child a walnut shell to paint using tempera paint.
2. Once the shells have dried, provide felt for children to cut out and glue to their shell for decoration. They can use felt pieces to create animals from their shells. To make a mouse, they can glue two round ears to the front of the shell. For a cat, the ears should be pointed. For a bunny, the ears should be longer and thinner. Turtle shells can be made by gluing different pieces of felt to the shell for texture.
3. Provide wiggly eyes for children to glue to the front of the shells.
4. Give each child a marble to place under the shell. The children can roll their creatures on the floor.

Nn
Resources

More Sendak Books

- *In the Night Kitchen*
  by Maurice Sendak
  (Harper and Row, 1970).
This fantasy book is perfect for starting off discussions of dreams.

- *Maurice Sendak's Really Rosie*
  starring the Nutshell Kids
  lyrics and pictures by Maurice Sendak,
  music by Carole King
  (Harper Collins, 1975).
This book is based on the CBS network program.

- *Where the Wild Things Are*
  by Maurice Sendak
  (Harper and Row, 1963).
Max, a young boy, journeys to the land of the Wild Things, where he is made King.

Audiotapes

- *The Maurice Sendak Soundbook*
  performed by Tammy Grimes
  music by Wolfgang Amadeus Mozart and Carole King
  (Caedmon, 1976).
Four audiocassette tapes which include: *Higglety Piggelty Pop!*, *Really Rosie*, *Kenny's Window*, *Where the Wild Things Are*.

- *One Was Johnny: A Counting Book*
  (Weston Woods, 1976).

- *Pierre: A Cautionary Tale in Five Chapters and A Prologue*
  (Weston Woods, 1974).

- *Where the Wild Things Are and Other Stories*
  by Maurice Sendak
  performed by Tammy Grimes
  (Caedmon, 1988).
Includes *Where the Wild Things Are*, *In the Night Kitchen*, *Outside Over There*, the Nutshell Library, *The Sign on Rosie's Door*, and *Very Far Away*.

Videotapes

- *Really Rosie Starring the Nutshell Kids*
  by Maurice Sendak
  (Weston Woods Video, Weston, Ct 06883; [800] 243-5020).

Number Books

- *Animal Numbers*
  by Bert Kitchen
  (Dial, 1987).
This book features both exotic and familiar animals.

- *Annie's 1-100*
  by Annie Owens
  (Knopf, 1988).
Objects add up to ten in different combinations.

- *The Balancing Act: A Counting Song*
  by Merle Peek
  (Clarion, 1987).
Colorful elephants try to cross the high wire. Instructions for a game are included at the end of the book.

- *The Baron's Hunting Party*
  by Sally Kilroy
  (Viking, 1987).
Life in a castle is introduced with numbers from one to ten.

EXPLORE LETTER O

Discuss upper- and lower-case O's and read literature links featuring starts-with-O characters such as Otto.

FIND THE "LETTER-OF-THE-WEEK"

• Use a permanent marker to write a letter "O" on the lid of a clear plastic deli tub. Place as many items for letter "O" in the tub as you can find, including a picture of an octopus, a cut-out oval, anything orange, and so on.

• Paint a cardboard cutout of the letter "O" a bright orange. Or paste on oatmeal labels cut from boxes.

• Make a list of opposites. Start with "O" words such as over (under), off (on), odd (even), out (in), and so on.

• In math, focus on oblongs, octagons, and ovals.

• Serve oranges at snack time.

• Have students help you brainstorm animals that start with letter "O," including orangutans, ocelots, ostriches, octopuses, and so on.

• Set up an obstacle course for students to go over, on, off, and out of.

OUTSTANDING "O" ACTIVITIES

• OCEAN DISPLAY: Duplicate, color, and cut out pictures of octopuses and other ocean animals (see next page). Post these pictures on an ocean bulletin board. Display with factual photograph books nearby for students to observe.

• STRIKE OIL!: Provide oil pastels (Pentel) for children to use to draw ocean scenes.

Reading Connections © 1996 Monday Morning Books, Inc.

Oo
Ocean Patterns

O o

Over the river and through
    the woods,
And over starts with O.
So do words like ostrich
And onion, old, and "Oh!"
O starts words like octopus
And oranges and oak.
Can you think of other words
That start with letter O?

Oo

Upper- and Lower-case O

Oo
Alphabet Puzzle

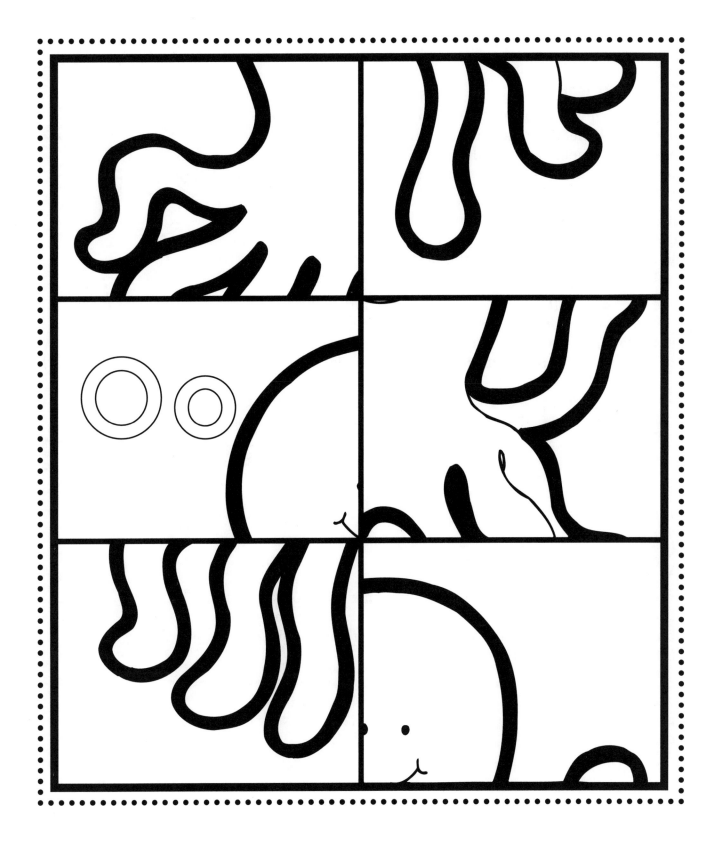

Reading Connections © 1996 Monday Morning Books, Inc.

Literature Connection
OTTO

Otto and Uncle Tooth do some fancy detective work using their powers of observation!

READ A BOOK

• *The Curse of the Cobweb Queen: An Otto and Uncle Tooth Adventure* by Geoffrey Hayes (Random House, 1994). Cousin Olivia helps famous detectives Otto and Uncle Tooth recover a stolen black pearl from their old enemy the Cobweb Queen.

• *The Mystery of the Pirate Ghost: An Otto and Uncle Tooth Adventure* by Geoffrey Hayes (Random House, 1985). Join Otto and Uncle Tooth in the first of their adventures as they set about finding the pirates disrupting life in Boogle Bay.

• *The Treasure of the Lost Lagoon: An Otto and Uncle Tooth Adventure* by Geoffrey Hayes (Random House, 1991). Ducky Doodle is forced to realize the value of true friends like Otto and Uncle Tooth when Sid Rat tries to cheat him.

OTTO ACTIVITIES

• PROPS USED PROPERLY: Hang up some fake cobwebs in the room before reading this book. Cover a rubber ball or a balloon with opalescent wrapping paper for the pearl. (*The Curse of the Cobweb Queen*)

• TERRIFIC TREASURE: Set out a cardboard treasure chest with "The Queen of the Sea" printed on it. Have children pretend to salvage it from a sunken ship. (*The Treasure of the Lost Lagoon*)

• PIRATE'S LIFE FOR ME: Make construction paper pirate eye patches like the one that One-eyed Eddy wore. (*The Curse of the Cobweb Queen/The Mystery of the Pirate Ghost*)

Art Connection
OCTOPUS BALLOONS

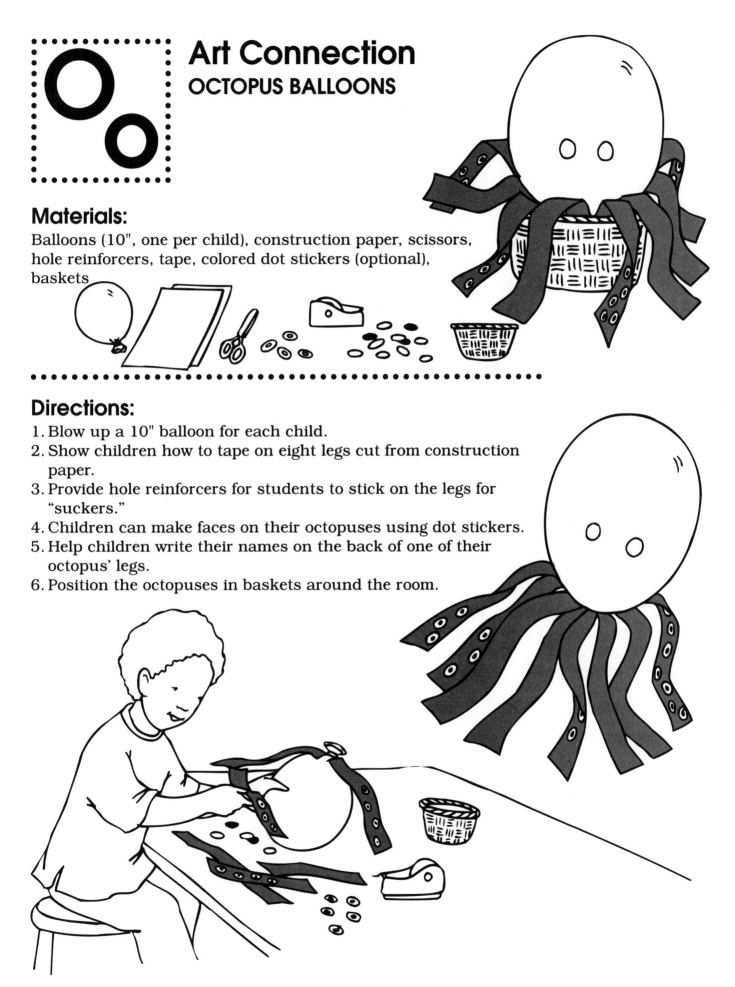

Materials:

Balloons (10", one per child), construction paper, scissors, hole reinforcers, tape, colored dot stickers (optional), baskets

Directions:

1. Blow up a 10" balloon for each child.
2. Show children how to tape on eight legs cut from construction paper.
3. Provide hole reinforcers for students to stick on the legs for "suckers."
4. Children can make faces on their octopuses using dot stickers.
5. Help children write their names on the back of one of their octopus' legs.
6. Position the octopuses in baskets around the room.

Oo Resources

Other Otto Books

• *Otto at Sea*
  by William Pene DuBois
  (Viking, 1936).
This Otto is a giant golden dog. He enjoys an ocean cruise until a storm comes up; then he saves the day and is awarded a parade in New York when the ship reaches port.

• *Otto in Africa*
  by William Pene DuBois
  (Viking, 1961).
Otto the otterhound earns his first medal.

• *Otto Is Different*
  by Franz Brandenberg
  (Greenwillow, 1985).
Otto the octopus discovers the advantages of having eight legs.

Ocean Books

• *Come Away from the Water, Shirley*
  by John Burningham
  (Thomas Y. Crowell, 1977).
Shirley has many imaginary adventures at the seaside, while her parents sit and relax in their beach chairs.

• *The Magic School Bus on the Ocean Floor*
  by Joanna Cole
  (Scholastic, 1992).
Ms. Frizzle's and her class learn about the ocean and its occupants.

• *My Cousin Has Eight Legs!*
  by Jasper Tomkins
  (Sasquatch, 1992).
An octopus poses as a young boy's cousin in this entertaining book.

• *Noah's Ark*
  by Peter Spier
  (Doubleday, 1977).
This nearly wordless book tells the story of Noah and his journey with two of every species.

• *The Ocean Alphabet Book*
  by Jerry Pallotta
  (Charlesbridge, 1986).
An alphabet book featuring O for octopus as well as an ocean creature for every letter of the alphabet.

• *An Octopus Is Amazing*
  by Patricia Lauber
  (Crowell, 1990).
This Let's Read and Find Out Science Book focuses on octopuses.

• *The Owl and the Pussy-cat*
  by Edward Lear
  (Atheneum, 1977).
"The Owl and the Pussy-cat went to sea in a beautiful pea-green boat." Lear's famous poem is whimsically illustrated by Gwen Fulton.

• *Sea Songs*
  by Myra Cohn Livingston
  (Scholastic, 1986).
Beautiful paintings enhance poetry about life below and above the sea.

• The *Underwater Alphabet* Book
  by Jerry Pallotta
  (Trumpet, 1991).
A beautifully illustrated alphabet book.

P p
EXPLORE LETTER P

Discuss upper- and lower-case P's and read literature links featuring starts-with-P characters such as Pooh and Piglet.

FIND THE "LETTER-OF-THE-WEEK"

• Use a permanent marker to write a letter "P" on the lid of a clear plastic deli tub. Place as many items for letter "P" in the tub as you can find, including a picture of a pumpkin, a pencil, a penny, a small bottle of perfume, a piece of unpopped popcorn, a pacifier, and so on.

• On a cardboard cutout of the letter "P," have children help you paste dried pasta or popcorn.

• Have children practice printing with colored pencils.

• Ask children to help you brainstorm names of foods that begin with "P," including peanuts, popcorn, popovers, peanut butter, popsicles, pork, pumpkins, pasta, plums, prunes, and so on. As a treat, bring popcorn in for children to eat while you read *Winnie-the-Pooh* stories.

• Do puzzles during this unit.

POSITIVE "P" ACTIVITIES

• PRESENTING...: Duplicate the present pattern (see next page) for children to use to draw their ideal gift. Enlarge one copy of the present pattern and post on a "Perfect Presents" bulletin board. Post the students' completed pictures around the present.

• PETER, PETER: Bring a pumpkin in for children to observe. Tell the Mother Goose rhyme until all students have it memorized.

Peter, Peter, pumpkin eater,
Had a wife and couldn't keep her;
He put her in a pumpkin shell
And there he kept her very well.

Peter, Peter, pumpkin eater,
Had another, and didn't love her;
Peter learned to read and spell,
And then he loved her very well.

Pp
Present Pattern

P p

Peter Peter Pumpkin Eater,
Pumpkin starts with P.
So do panda, pipe, and pig,
And penguin, pop, and peas.
P starts words like piggyback
And popcorn, pants, and please.
Can you think of other words
That start with letter P?

Pp
Upper- and Lower-case P

Pp
Alphabet Puzzle

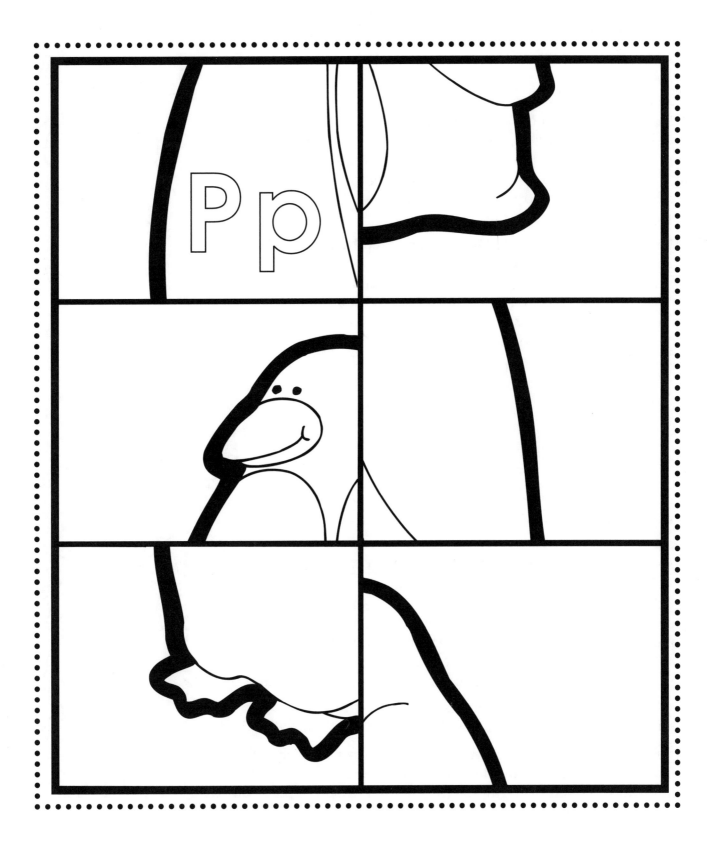

Reading Connections © 1996 Monday Morning Books, Inc.

Literature Connection
POOH

Winnie-the-Pooh has been a classic for many years. Have students share their favorite Pooh stories.

READ A BOOK

• *The House at Pooh Corner* by A. A. Milne, illustrated by Ernest H. Shepard (Dutton, 1928).
Contains 10 stories about Pooh, Eeyore (a donkey), Piglet (a little pig), Kanga and Roo (mama and baby kangaroo), Tigger (a tiger-like creature with a spring tail), wise old Owl, Rabbit, and Christopher Robin (a young boy).

• *Winnie-the-Pooh* by A. A. Milne, illustrated by Ernest H. Shepard (Dutton, 1926).
Contains 10 more stories about Pooh and his friends, including "In Which Piglet Meets a Heffalump," "In Which Piglet Is Entirely Surrounded by Water," and "In Which Eeyore Has a Birthday and Gets Two Presents."

POOH AND PIGLET ACTIVITIES

• A PLAN FOR PIGLET: Read the first several pages of the story. When you get to the part about needing help with a plan, stop reading. Transcribe the children's plan to help rescue Piglet. Then continue reading the story and compare endings. (*"In Which Piglet Is Entirely Surrounded by Water"*)

• POOH SAYS...: Play a game similar to Simon Says, substituting "Pooh says..." or "Piglet says..." (*Winnie-the-Pooh*)

• FRIENDS OF PIGLET: Invite students to write "help" notes from Piglet (who is stranded). Spread blue fabric on the floor. Let students send their notes (in plastic bottles) "upstream" by rolling them across the floor. (*"In Which Piglet Is Entirely Surrounded by Water"*)

Art Connection
POOH'S POT O' HONEY

Materials:

Empty plastic jars (one per child), gold-colored yarn, scissors, white glue (in pans)

Directions:

1. Have each student bring an empty plastic jar or container to school. (A peanut butter jar would be perfect.)
2. Have students dip pieces of yarn into pans of white glue.
3. Beginning at either the top or the bottom of their "Pooh pot," have students wrap the yarn around and around the pot, being careful to align each strand of yarn next to the previous one.
4. Children continue wrapping with a variety of colorful pieces of yarn.
5. Children can take their pots home to keep special prizes in.

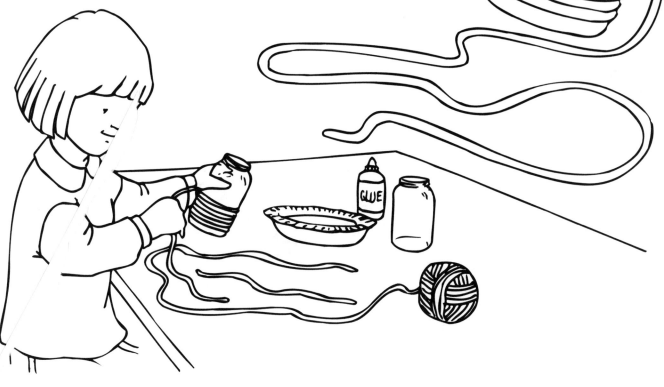

Reading Connections © 1996 Monday Morning Books, Inc.

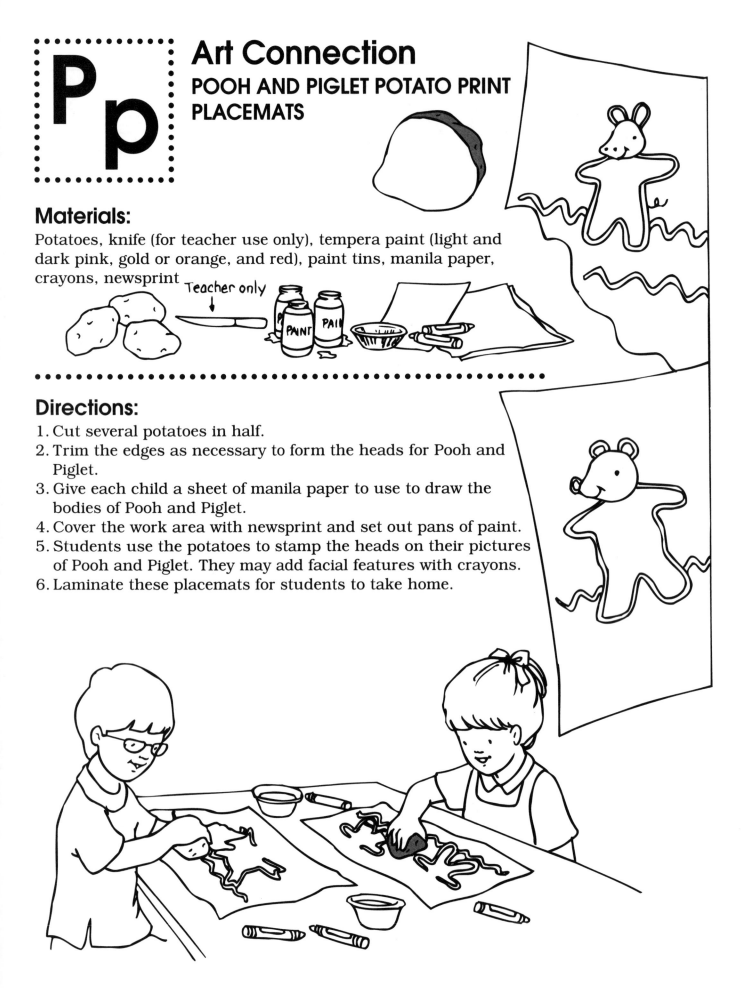

P p Art Connection
POOH AND PIGLET POTATO PRINT PLACEMATS

Materials:

Potatoes, knife (for teacher use only), tempera paint (light and dark pink, gold or orange, and red), paint tins, manila paper, crayons, newsprint

Teacher only

PAINT PAIN

Directions:

1. Cut several potatoes in half.
2. Trim the edges as necessary to form the heads for Pooh and Piglet.
3. Give each child a sheet of manila paper to use to draw the bodies of Pooh and Piglet.
4. Cover the work area with newsprint and set out pans of paint.
5. Students use the potatoes to stamp the heads on their pictures of Pooh and Piglet. They may add facial features with crayons.
6. Laminate these placemats for students to take home.

Pp
Resources

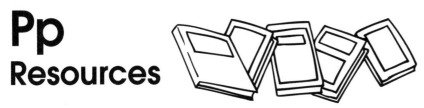

More Pooh Books

- *The Brilliant Career of Winnie-the-Pooh: The Definitive History of the Best Bear in All the World*
  by Ann Thwaite
  (Dutton, 1992).
This book focuses on Pooh with lots of photos and copies of Pooh memorabilia.

- *The Christopher Robin Book of Verse*
  by A. A. Milne
  (Dutton, 1967).
Twenty-four illustrated poems about Christopher Robin and his friends.

- *The Complete Tales of Winnie-the-Pooh*
  by A. A. Milne
  (Dutton, 1994).

- *Disney's Winnie the Pooh's A to Zzzz*
  by Don Ferguson
  (Disney Press, 1992).
Colorful illustrations set out the alphabet in the Hundred Acre Wood with Pooh and friends.

- *The Pooh Book of Quotations*
  by A. A. Milne
  compiled and edited by Brian Sibley
  (Dutton, 1986).
An excellent resource for any classroom. The book is divided into very short chapters.

- *The Pooh Cook Book*
  by Virginia H. Ellison
  (Dutton, 1969).
Inspired by the characters and stories in A. A. Milne's books.

- *The Pooh Craft Book*
  by Carol S. Friedrichsen
  (Dutton, 1976).
These craft ideas were inspired by *Winnie-the-Pooh* and *The House at Pooh Corner*.

- *The Pooh Get-Well Book: Recipes and Activities to Help You Recover from Wheezles and Sneezles*
  by Virginia Ellison
  (Dutton, 1973).
The first section of "Teazles" has puzzles, poems, and word games. This is followed by "Strengthening Things to Drink and Eat" and "Pleazles," things to make and do during recovery.

- *The Pooh Song Book* containing the "Hums of Pooh," "The King's Breakfast," and 14 songs from "When We Were Very Young" verses
  by A. A. Milne
  music by H. Fraser-Simson
  (Dutton, 1961).
A wonderful addition to any Pooh library collection!

- *The Pooh Story Book*
  by A. A. Milne
  (Dutton, renewed 1965).
This collection contains stories from *The House at Pooh Corner* and *Winnie-the-Pooh*.

- *Pooh's Bedtime Book*
  by A. A. Milne
  (Dutton, 1980).
Pooh and friends are featured in stories and poems which are perfect for bedtime.

- *Pooh's Counting Book*
  by A. A. Milne
  (Dutton, 1982).
The numbers from 1 to 10 are introduced in this small book.

Pp Resources

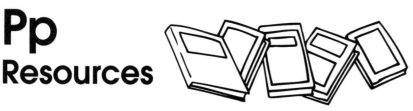

More Pooh Books

- *The Pooh Sketchbook*
  by Brian Sibley
  (Dutton, 1984).
A collection of sketches from the four favorite books.

- *The Pooh Party Book*
  by Virginia Ellison
  (Dutton, 1971).
Pooh has five special parties—one for each season and another for Eeyore's birthday.

- *Winnie-the-Pooh ABC*
  inspired by A. A. Milne
  (Dutton, 1995).
Pooh fans will be attracted to this simple alphabet book featuring illustrations from the original Pooh stories.

- *Winnie-the-Pooh's Trivia Quiz Book*
  inspired by A. A. Milne
  (Dutton, 1994).

More Milne Books

- *Now We Are Six*
  by A. A. Milne
  (Dutton, 1927).
A collection of verse about Pooh and Christopher Robin and many other characters.

- *When We Were Very Young*
  by A. A. Milne
  (Dutton, 1924).
A collection of verse about Pooh and Christopher Robin and many other characters.

Audiotapes

- *Carol Channing Sings the Pooh Song Book* words
  by A. A. Milne and music by H. Fraser-Simson
  (Caedmon, 1983).

Videotapes

- *Disney's Winnie-the-Pooh: Cowboy Pooh*
  (Disney Home Video, N.D.).
This 48-minute video features *Cowboy Pooh*.

- *Making Friends*
  (Disney Home Video, 1994).
Features Tigger from the *Winnie-the-Pooh* books.

- *Pooh to the Rescue*
  (Disney Home Video, N.D.).
This 44-minute videotape is in the "New Adventures of Winnie-the-Pooh" series.

- *Winnie-the-Pooh and the Blustery Day*
  (Disney Home Video, 1986).
This 24-minute videotape is based on A. A. Milne's characters.

- *Winnie-the-Pooh Fun 'n Games*
  (Disney Home Video, 1994).
This 33-minute videotape features new adventures of Winnie-the-Pooh.

EXPLORE LETTER Q

Discuss upper- and lower-case Q's and read literature links featuring starts-with-Q characters such as the Quimbys.

FIND THE "LETTER-OF-THE-WEEK"

• Use a permanent marker to write a letter "Q" on the lid of a clear plastic deli tub. Place as many items for letter "Q" in the tub as you can find, including a queen from a deck of cards, a quill (feather), a quarter, a picture of a quince, a quilt square, a plastic quail, and so on.

• On a cardboard cutout of the letter "Q," paste pieces of fabric in a quilt pattern.

• In math, use quarts to measure and quarters to count. Have students practice telling time to the quarter-hour.

• Challenge students to walk quickly and quietly.

QUIET "Q" ACTIVITIES

• QUESTIONS, ANYONE?: Duplicate the question mark pattern (see next page) to use to create a question and answer bulletin board. Transcribe questions that children may have and post on the board. Other children can help answer the questions, or you can invite students from upper grades to answer the questions.

• QUEUING UP: Have students queue for recess or snack. Explain that in England this word means "to form a line."

Qq
Question Mark Pattern

Q q

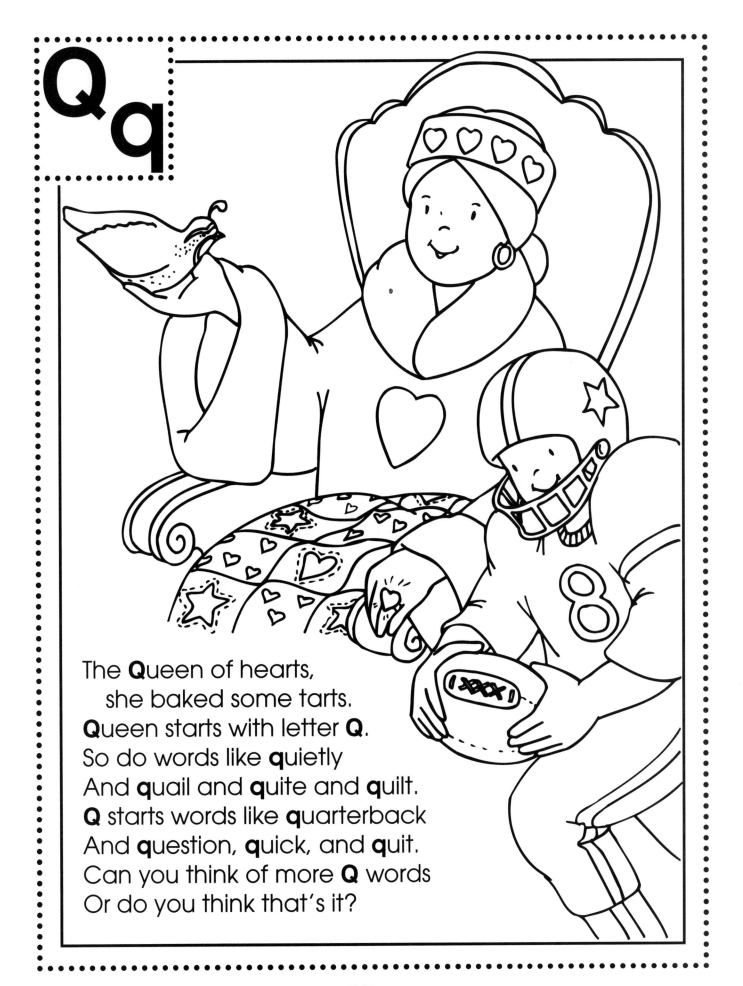

The **Q**ueen of hearts,
   she baked some tarts.
Queen starts with letter **Q**.
So do words like **q**uietly
And **q**uail and **q**uite and **q**uilt.
Q starts words like **q**uarterback
And **q**uestion, **q**uick, and **q**uit.
Can you think of more **Q** words
Or do you think that's it?

Qq

Upper- and Lower-case Q

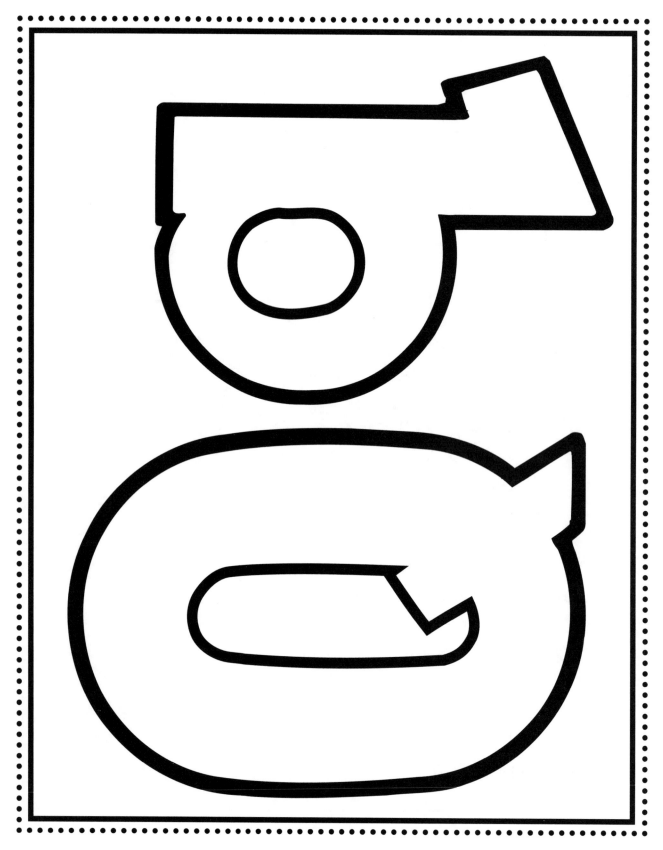

Qq
Alphabet Puzzle

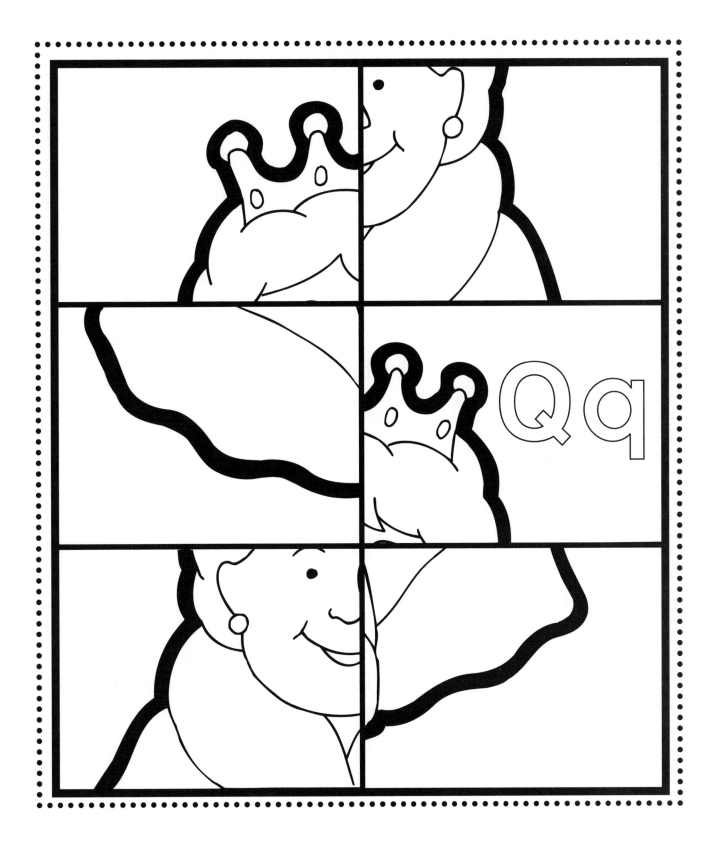

Literature Connection
QUIMBYS

The Quimbys are quite a family. Mother and Father, Beatrice (called "Beezus"), and Ramona have many adventures on Klickitat Street. Read aloud one of the Ramona books set when Ramona is the same age as your students.

Hi! I'm in the first grade at Madison Elementary school.

READ A BOOK

• *Ramona the Brave* by Beverly Cleary (Morrow, 1975).
In this book, Ramona is in the first grade. The Quimby adventures continue with Parents' Night, Ramona saying a bad word, Mrs. Quimby having a secret, and Mr. Quimby being proud of his spunky gal.

• *Ramona Forever* by Beverly Cleary (Morrow, 1984).
Ramona, now in third grade, has many changes in her life, including a new uncle, a new job for her dad, and a new sibling!

• *Ramona the Pest* by Beverly Cleary (Morrow, 1968).
In the first book devoted entirely to her, Ramona enters kindergarten; as her world expands, so do her antics.

• *Ramona Quimby, Age 8* by Beverly Cleary (Morrow, 1981).
Ramona is beginning third grade and has a quivery stomach. Does she even like her teacher this year? This is a Newbery Honor book.

QUIMBY ACTIVITIES

• A QUIMBY QUESTION QUIZ!: Have students take turns asking questions from the stories. Consider adding higher-level thinking questions for bonus rounds. (All Ramona books)

• FAMILIES FOREVER: Help each child make a family tree from construction paper and markers. (*Ramona Forever*)

• DOODLING AWAY: Ramona likes to read and draw. Provide drawing paper and crayons or colored pencils for children to use to make some sketches. (*Ramona Quimby, Age 8*)

Art Connection

QUIMBY QUILT

This project may be used as a literature "tie-in" after reading any book in the Quimby series.

Materials:

Paper, hole punch, yarn, crayons or markers

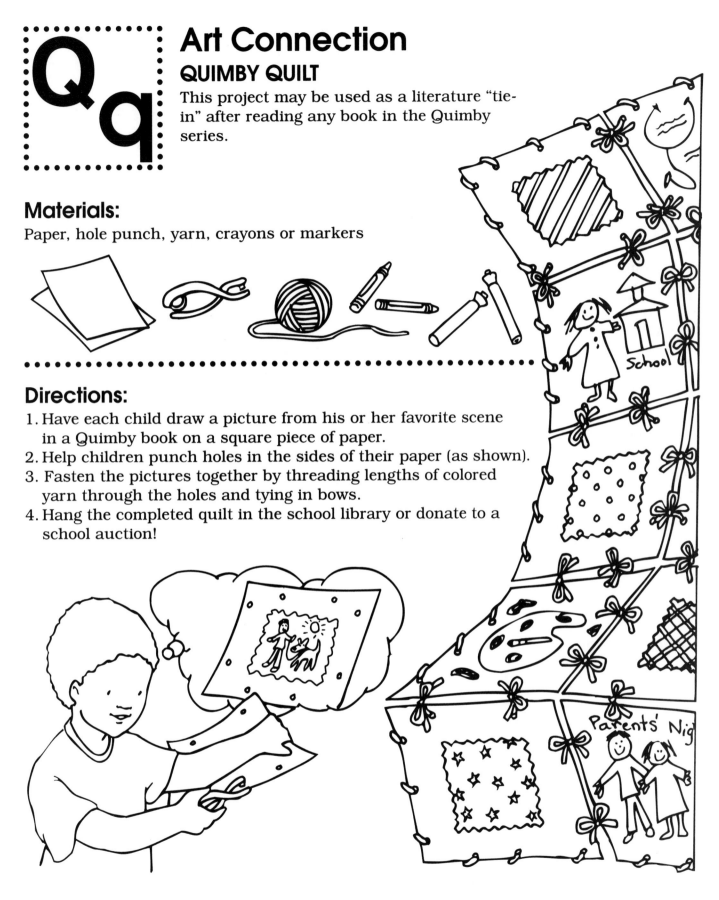

Directions:

1. Have each child draw a picture from his or her favorite scene in a Quimby book on a square piece of paper.
2. Help children punch holes in the sides of their paper (as shown).
3. Fasten the pictures together by threading lengths of colored yarn through the holes and tying in bows.
4. Hang the completed quilt in the school library or donate to a school auction!

Option:

Provide fabric scraps for children to use to glue to their quilt squares and mix with the art squares.

Reading Connections © 1996 Monday Morning Books, Inc.

Qq
Resources

More Beverly Cleary Books

- *Beezus and Ramona*
  by Beverly Cleary
  (Morrow, 1955).

Beezus' biggest problem in life is her pesky four-year-old sister Ramona. From a party of preschoolers to Ramona in the basement, life is interesting at the Quimby household.

- *Henry and Beezus*
  by Beverly Cleary
  (Morrow, 1952).

Meet these two special friends and the rest of the crowd on Klickitat Street.

- *Henry and the Clubhouse*
  by Beverly Cleary
  (Morrow, 1962).

Beezus and Ramona Quimby are excluded from Henry's clubhouse because they are girls.

- *Henry Huggins*
  by Beverly Cleary
  (Morrow, 1950).

Henry gets his dog Ribsy and suddenly his life is more interesting.

- *Henry and the Paper Route*
  by Beverly Cleary
  (Morrow, 1957).

Henry wants his own paper route. However, things seem to get in his way, including the neighbor girl, Ramona Quimby. Surely he can outsmart a four-year-old in order to get his route!

- *Ramona and Her Father*
  by Beverly Cleary
  (Morrow, 1977).

Ramona has many worries in second grade: her father loses his job and he won't quit smoking. A Newbery Honor book.

- *Ramona and Her Mother*
  by Beverly Cleary
  (Morrow, 1979).

Mrs. Quimby is the focus of this book as it details life in the Quimby household and the stresses on a working mother.

Videotapes

- *Beverly Cleary's Ramona "The Great Hair Argument*
  (Warner Home Video, 1987).

In this live-action video, the Quimby girls get their hair cut at Robert's School of Hair Design and Beezus' new haircut is terrible!

- *Beverly Cleary's Ramona "Mystery Meal; Rainy Sunday"*
  (Lorimar Home Video, 1988).

Two complete stories based on the popular series by Beverly Cleary.

- *Beverly Cleary's Ramona "New Pajamas"*
  (Warner Home Video, 1987).

In this live-action video, Ramona decides that she must run away after getting caught wearing her favorite pajamas to school.

EXPLORE LETTER R

Discuss upper- and lower-case R's and read literature links featuring starts-with-R characters such as Ralph.

FIND THE "LETTER-OF-THE-WEEK"

• Use a permanent marker to write a letter "R" on the lid of a clear plastic deli tub. Place as many items for letter "R" in the tub as you can find, including a rattle, a ribbon, a rose (real or silk), and something red.

• Use rhythm sticks.

• Sing "Row, Row, Row Your Boat" in a round.

• In math, use rulers.

• On a cardboard cutout of the letter "R," paste red ribbons or pictures of roses.

• Challenge students to brainstorm animals with names that start with "R," including rabbit, raccoon, ram, rat, rattlesnake, raven, reindeer, and rhinoceros.

• Help children brainstorm foods that start with "R," including radishes, raisins, raspberries, rhubarb, and rice.

RAVISHING "R" ACTIVITIES

• READ, READ, READ!: Make up "Remarkable Reader Recognition" awards. Duplicate the pattern (see next page), color, cut out, and distribute. Students can wear the awards as necklaces by punching two holes in the paper and threading through with a length of yarn.
• RAINBOW LESSONS: In science, study the spectrum of the rainbow by introducing Mr. Roy G. Biv (red, orange, yellow, green, blue, indigo, and violet). Let children make their own rainbows with tempera paint or watercolors on construction paper.

Rr

Remarkable Reader Awards

R r

Rain, rain, go away,
Rain starts with letter R.
So do ring and radio
And ribbon, run, and rare.
R starts words like reindeer
And rabbit, rip, and roar.
Can you think of other words
That start with letter R?

169

Rr
Upper- and Lower-case R

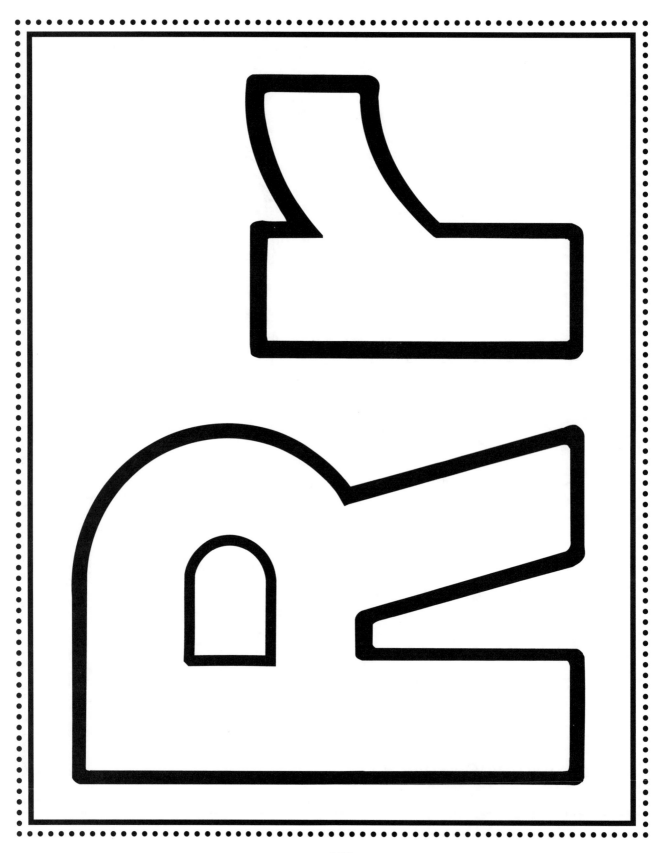

Rr

Alphabet Puzzle

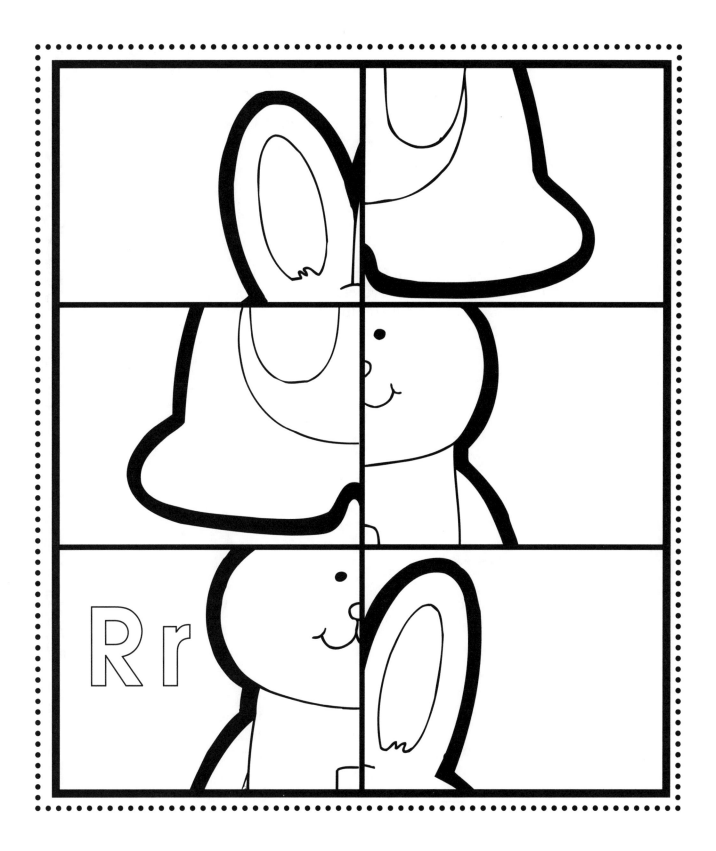

Reading Connections © 1996 Monday Morning Books, Inc.

Literature Connection

RALPH

Ralph, the soccer-loving rabbit, has difficulty focusing on his responsibilities. Follow him through his three adventures.

READ A BOOK

• *Bad, Bad Bunny Trouble* by Hans Wilhelm (Scholastic, 1994). The foxes are coming to collect the ingredients for rabbit stew. What will Ralph do?

• *Bunny Trouble* by Hans Wilhelm (Scholastic, 1985). Ralph has soccer on the brain, but the other bunnies are all busy the day before Easter. Oh, no! Will Ralph become Easter dinner?

• *More Bunny Trouble* by Hans Wilhelm (Scholastic, 1989). Ralph is supposed to be responsible for two chores: painting Easter eggs the day before Easter and watching his baby sister, Emily. When he doesn't do one of these jobs right, he has to call the other rabbits to the rescue.

Thursday—
Rabbit Stew

⚽ RALPH ACTIVITIES

• FUNNY BUNNY: Provide construction paper eggs for children to decorate in a soccer ball pattern. (*Bunny Trouble*)

• BUNNY GAMES: Play Musical Chairs and Pin the Tail on the Donkey. (*Bad, Bad Bunny Trouble*)

• OUTFOXING FOXES: Use masking tape to attach a long red scarf to the bottom of a plastic bucket. Stuff the scarf inside the bucket. Have some children pretend to be foxes, and one child pretend to be Ralph. When the foxes come with their ladder, Ralph can throw the red scarf "dye" on them. Let all children have a chance to play both roles. (*Bad, Bad Bunny Trouble*)

Art Connection
RED RUBBINGS

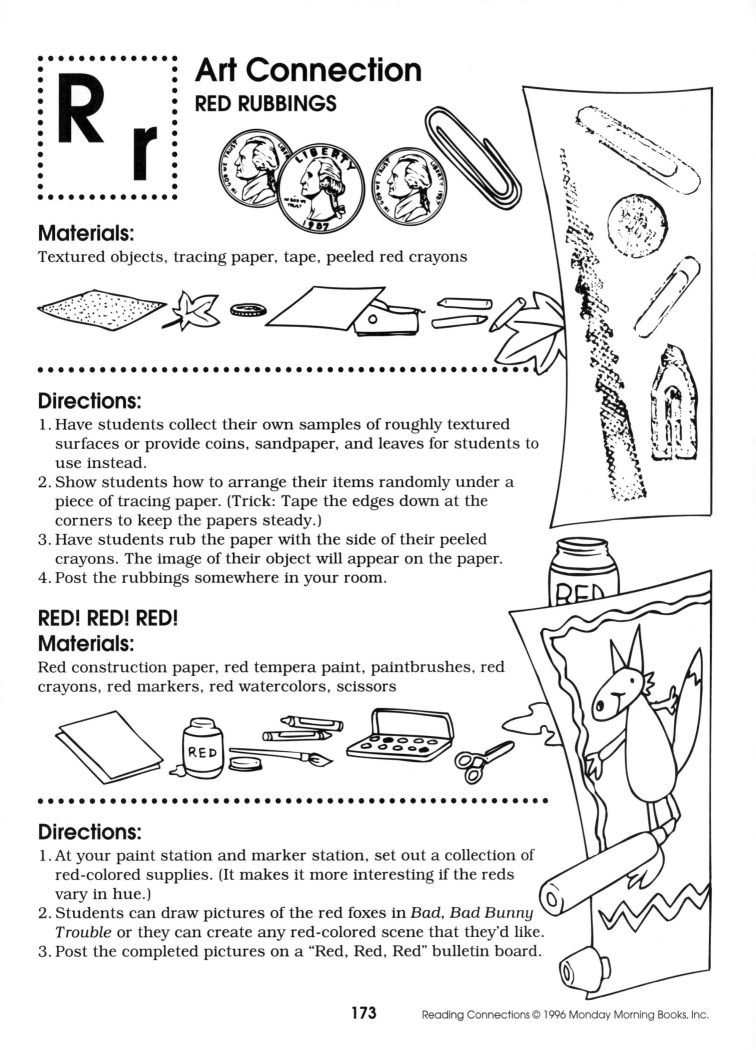

Materials:

Textured objects, tracing paper, tape, peeled red crayons

Directions:

1. Have students collect their own samples of roughly textured surfaces or provide coins, sandpaper, and leaves for students to use instead.
2. Show students how to arrange their items randomly under a piece of tracing paper. (Trick: Tape the edges down at the corners to keep the papers steady.)
3. Have students rub the paper with the side of their peeled crayons. The image of their object will appear on the paper.
4. Post the rubbings somewhere in your room.

RED! RED! RED!
Materials:

Red construction paper, red tempera paint, paintbrushes, red crayons, red markers, red watercolors, scissors

Directions:

1. At your paint station and marker station, set out a collection of red-colored supplies. (It makes it more interesting if the reds vary in hue.)
2. Students can draw pictures of the red foxes in *Bad, Bad Bunny Trouble* or they can create any red-colored scene that they'd like.
3. Post the completed pictures on a "Red, Red, Red" bulletin board.

Rr
Resources

More Rabbit Books

- *Big Trouble for Tricky Rabbit*
  by Gretchen Mayo
  (Walker, 1994).
  Contrast Tricky Rabbit's troubles with Ralph's troubles. Also by the author: *Here Comes Tricky Rabbit.*

- *Bunny Rabbit Rebus*
  by David Adler
  (Crowell, 1983).
  This small-format story about a hungry little bunny is told in words and rebus pictures.

- *Max and Ruby's First Greek Myth*
  by Rosemary Wells
  (Dial, 1993).
  In this retelling of Pandora's Box, Max's older sister Ruby tries to teach the young bunny about keeping out of things that don't belong to him.

- *Max's Dragon Shirt*
  by Rosemary Wells
  (Dial, 1991).
  Max and Ruby venture to the mall to buy Max some new pants. But Max would rather buy a dragon shirt.

- *Morris's Disappearing Bag:*
  A Christmas Story
  by Rosemary Wells
  (Dial, 1975).
  Morris's older brothers and sisters don't want to share their new Christmas toys with the little bunny. That is, until he discovers a final present under the tree!

- *Mr. Rabbit and the Lovely Present*
  by Charlotte Zolotow
  (Harper, 1962).
  Mr. Rabbit helps a little girl fill a basket with colorful fruit—the perfect present for her mother's birthday.

- *Rabbits on Roller Skates*
  by Jan Wahl
  (Crown, 1986).
  This book about busy rabbits is designed for the beginning reader.

- *Rabbit Wishes*
  by Linda Shute
  (Lothrop, 1995).
  This Afro-Cuban tale with strong, colorful illustrations explains why rabbits have long ears. Glossary of terms and pronunciations follows the story.

- *The Runaway Bunny*
  by Margaret Wise Brown
  (Harper, 1972).
  A young bunny with wanderlust discusses his future adventures with his mother.

- *The Tale of Rabbit and Coyote*
  by Tony Johnston and Tomie de Paola
  (Putnam, 1994).
  This story interweaves the tales of Br'er Rabbit, the "rabbit and the moon," and Coyote swallowing the moon.

- *Uncle Wiggly's Picture Book*
  by Howard R. Garis
  (Platt and Monk, 1989).
  Thirty stories of about 7-10 pages each, sparsely illustrated.

- *The Velveteen Rabbit*
  by Margery Williams
  (Avon, 1975).
  A toy rabbit turns real after a little boy loves him for a long, long time.

- *Zomo the Rabbit:*
  A Trickster Tale from West Africa
  by Gerald McDermott
  (Harcourt, 1992).
  In this vibrantly colored McDermott tale, Zomo must outwit the other animals in order to be granted wisdom. In the end, he becomes very fast, but isn't granted the wisdom.

EXPLORE LETTER S

Discuss upper- and lower-case S's and read literature links featuring starts-with-S characters such as Strega Nona.

FIND THE "LETTER-OF-THE-WEEK"

• Use a permanent marker to write a letter "S" on the lid of a clear plastic deli tub. Place as many items for letter "S" in the tub as you can find, including a seashell, a screw, a seed, a stamp, a silver crayon, and a picture of a sailboat.

• On a cardboard cutout of the letter "S," paste star stickers. Glue on sequins to make it sparkle!

• Have children brainstorm as many animals as they can think of that start with letter "S," including a seahorse, a seagull, a seal, a shark, a sheep, a skunk, a snake, a squirrel, and a swan.

• Have children brainstorm as many occupations that start with letter "S" as they can think of, including sailor, seamstress, songwriter, and singer.

• Ask children to name all of the foods they've eaten that start with "S," including spaghetti, salmon, a sandwich, scrambled eggs, spinach, spaghetti, seeds, squash, and strawberries.

SUPER "S" ACTIVITIES

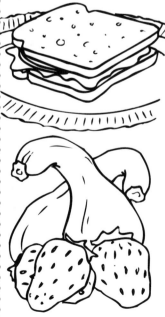

• SUPER STARS: Duplicate the star pattern (see next page) to create a "Super Star" bulletin board. Have children bring in photos from home and fasten a photo to each star pattern. Write children's names on the patterns.

• SPEAKING ITALIAN: Check out an Italian phrase book and look for words that start with "S," for example, "Si" means "Yes." *Spaghetti for Breakfast and Other Useful Phrases in Italian and English* by Sesyle Joslin, illustrated by Katharina Barry (Harcourt, 1965), is a good book to start with.

Ss
Super Star Pattern

S s

Sing a song of sixpence
Because sing starts with S.
So do seal and sun and snake
And silly, squirrel, and sis.
S starts words like scissors
And sometimes, shrimp, and sass.
Can you think of other words
That start with letter S?

Ss
Upper- and Lower-case S

Ss
Alphabet Puzzle

Reading Connections © 1996 Monday Morning Books, Inc.

Literature Connection

STREGA NONA

"Strega Nona" is an affectionate term in Italian which means "Grandma witch." Tomie de Paola's Strega Nona is a wonderful character who brews up some sensational spells.

READ A BOOK

• *Merry Christmas, Strega Nona* by Tomie de Paola (Harcourt, 1986).
Big Anthony gets tired of all the preparations for Christmas, but decides to surprise Strega Nona with a bit of his own Christmas magic.

• *Strega Nona* by Tomie de Paola (Prentice-Hall, 1975). This Caldecott Honor book introduces Strega Nona for the first time. Big Anthony, eager to try out some magic, learns part of a magic spell, but he doesn't learn all of it. This leads to a severe spaghetti problem in Calabria.

• *Strega Nona's Magic Lesson* by Tomie de Paola (Harcourt, 1982). Big Anthony wants to learn Strega Nona's magic, and in this silly attempt he tries to disguise himself as a girl.

STREGA NONA ACTIVITIES

• BUBBLE, BUBBLE: Place a pot at your props table and let children pretend that it's Strega Nona's pot. They can sing to the pasta pot, making up their own words. (*Strega Nona*)

• SHHH! IT'S A SECRET: Make up some special secrets. Write them in a book labeled "Strega's Special Secrets!" Have each child illustrate one page. (*Strega Nona's Magic Lesson*)

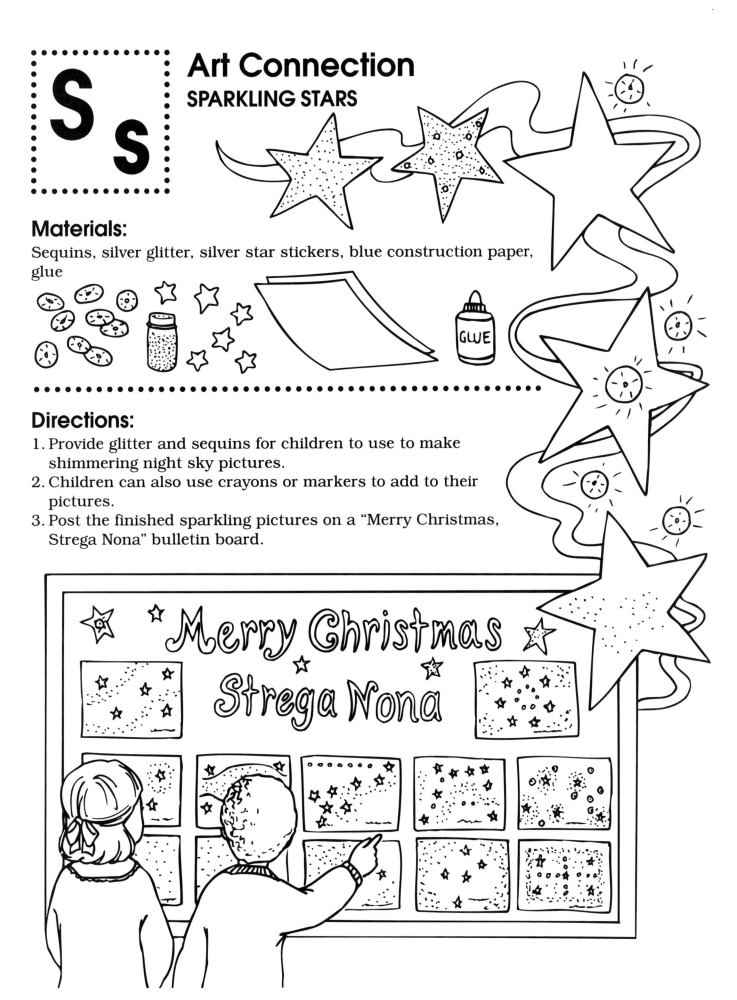

Art Connection
SPARKLING STARS

S s

Materials:

Sequins, silver glitter, silver star stickers, blue construction paper, glue

Directions:

1. Provide glitter and sequins for children to use to make shimmering night sky pictures.
2. Children can also use crayons or markers to add to their pictures.
3. Post the finished sparkling pictures on a "Merry Christmas, Strega Nona" bulletin board.

Merry Christmas Strega Nona

Ss
Resources

More Strega Nona Books

- *Big Anthony and the Magic Ring*
  by Tomie de Paola
  (Harcourt, 1979).
Tempted by the lure of Strega Nona's magic ring, Big Anthony gets himself into mischief.

- *Strega Nona Meets Her Match*
  by Tomie de Paola
  (Putnam, 1993).
Strega Nona's friend Strega Amelia sets up shop in town, bringing with her the new scientific secret ways. She proves no match for Strega Nona when Big Anthony is left to tend the new shop.

Spaghetti Books

- *Cloudy with A Chance of Meatballs*
  by Judi Barrett
  (Atheneum, 1978).
Strange weather descends on the town of Chewandswallow one Saturday. Great newspaper illustrations and headlines are shown as part of the story when "Spaghetti Ties Up Town."

- *Daddy Makes the Best Spaghetti*
  by Anna Grossnickle Hines
  (Clarion, 1986).
The family's evening ritual is detailed from the time that Dad picks Corey up from day care through a spaghetti dinner and bath/bedtime.

- *A Flying Saucer Full of Spaghetti*
  by Fernando Krahn
  (Dutton, 1970).
This book has humorous pictures, perfect for dictation and story starters for early readers.

- *Siggy's Spaghetti Works*
  by Peggy Thomson
  (Tambourine Books, 1993).
A tour through a factory where they make several kinds of pasta. Interesting book for background information.

- *Wednesday Is Spaghetti Day*
  by Maryann Cocoa-Leffler
  (Scholastic, 1990).
A cat and his friends party while the owners are away during the day.

Audiotapes

- *Merry Christmas, Strega Nona*
  (Listening Library, 1986).

- *Strega Nona*
  (Weston Woods, 1978).
Book by Tomie de Paola, music by Franticek Belfin.

- *Strega Nona and Other Stories*
  (Weston Woods, 1989).

Additional Resources

- *Big Anthony's Mixed-Up Magic*
  (Putnam New Media, 1993).
This package includes one computer laser optical disc, plus a book and a user's guide. A collection of games, activities, sing-along songs, music, and magic tricks feature Tomie de Paola's characters.

EXPLORE LETTER T

Discuss upper- and lower-case T's and read literature links featuring tales by Beatrix Potter.

🐢 FIND THE "LETTER-OF-THE-WEEK"

• Use a permanent marker to write a letter "T" on the lid of a clear plastic deli tub. Place as many items for letter "T" in the tub as you can find, including a thimble, a small toy, a picture of a tree, a ticket (from a movie or sports event), a tassel, and so on.

• On a cardboard cutout of the letter "T," paste drawings of different kinds of animal tails.

• Have children brainstorm as many animals as they can think of that start with letter "T," including tadpoles, tarantulas, tigers, tortoises, trout, and turtles.

• Ask children to list all of the foods that they've eaten that start with letter "T," including tacos, tortillas, tamales, tea, toast, turkey, and tuna.

⏰ TERRIFIC "T" ACTIVITIES

• TELLING TIME: Duplicate the clock pattern (see next page) to set up a time-telling station in your classroom. Bring in various kinds of clocks to keep around the classroom as well. Have children practice telling time during the day.

• TWISTING TONGUES: Tell tongue twisters (see "Resources" for books of tongue twisters).

183   Reading Connections © 1996 Monday Morning Books, Inc.

Tt

Clock Pattern

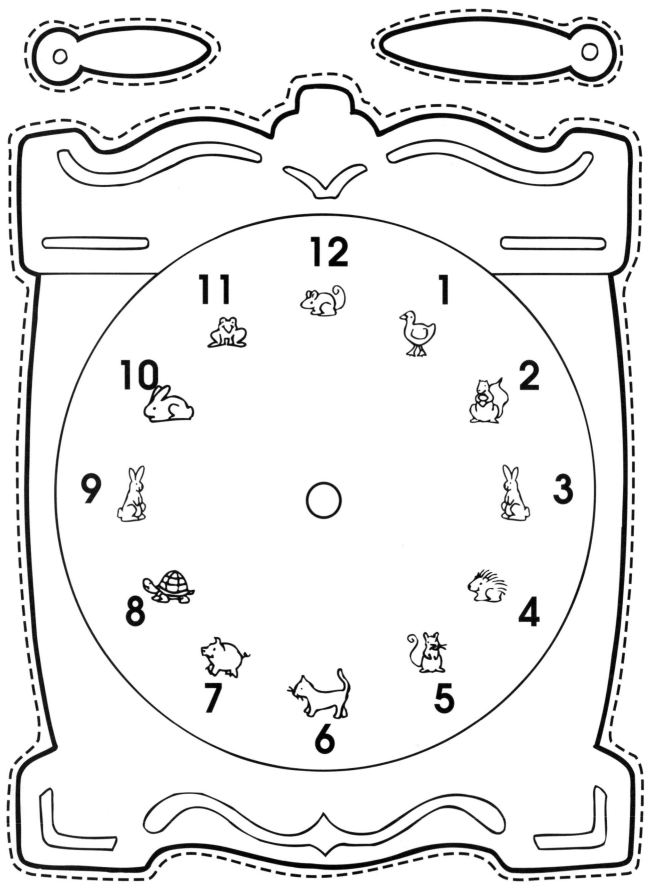

T t

Twinkle, twinkle, little star,
Twinkle starts with T.
So do top and telephone
And tiger and TV.
T starts words like turkey
And turtle, tongue, and tease.
Can you think of other words
That start with letter T?

185

Tt
Upper- and Lower-case T

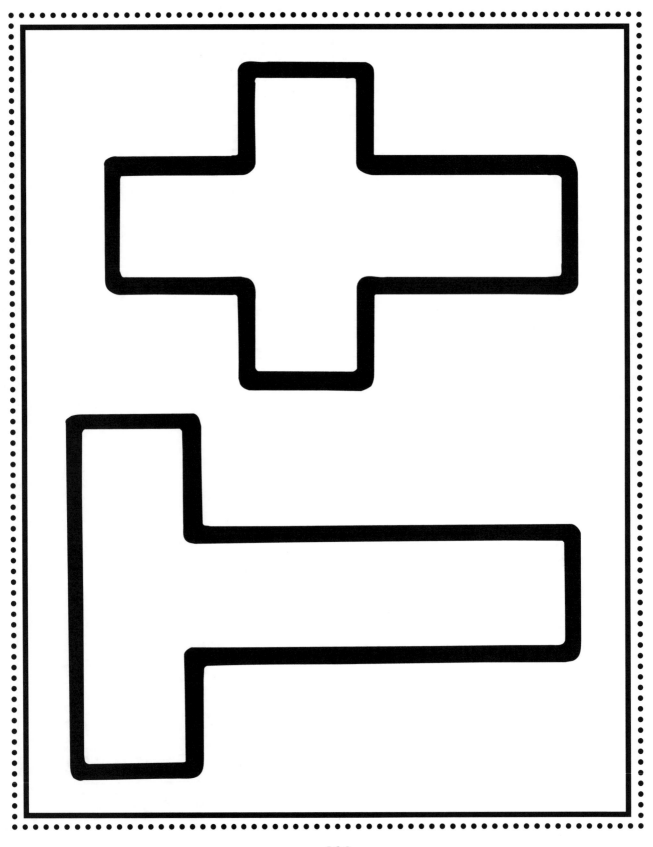

Tt
Alphabet Puzzle

Literature Connection

TALES

This treasury of tales features the work of Beatrix Potter.

READ A BOOK

• *The Tale of Peter Rabbit* by Beatrix Potter (Warne, 1902). This is the story of a naughty little rabbit who narrowly escapes from Farmer McGregor.

• *The Tailor of Gloucester* by Beatrix Potter (Warne, 1903). When the poor tailor becomes ill, some mice finish sewing the mayor's jacket.

• *The Tale of Benjamin Bunny* by Beatrix Potter (Warne, 1904). Benjamin and Peter venture into Mr. McGregor's garden to recover Peter's clothes.

• *The Tale of the Flopsy Bunnies* by Beatrix Potter (Warne, 1909). Benjamin Bunny married his cousin Flopsy, and their flopsy bunny children fortunately are rescued by Mrs. Tittlemouse in this adventure.

☕ "TALES" ACTIVITIES

• TEARFUL TALES: Cut tear shapes from colored paper. Each time you come upon a character in tears, write the character's name on a teardrop. (All)

• TEA PARTY: Have a tea party and serve chamomile tea in teacups. (*The Tale of Peter Rabbit*)

• TAILORS AND THREAD: Make up sewing cards for children to sew. (*The Tailor of Gloucester*)

• TREASURE HUNT: Hide a small blue jacket and a tiny pair of shoes somewhere in the classroom or playground. Then have a treasure hunt in which the students have to help Benjamin and Peter find Peter's clothes in Mr. McGregor's Garden. (*The Tale of Benjamin Bunny*)

Art Connection
TEA TRAYS

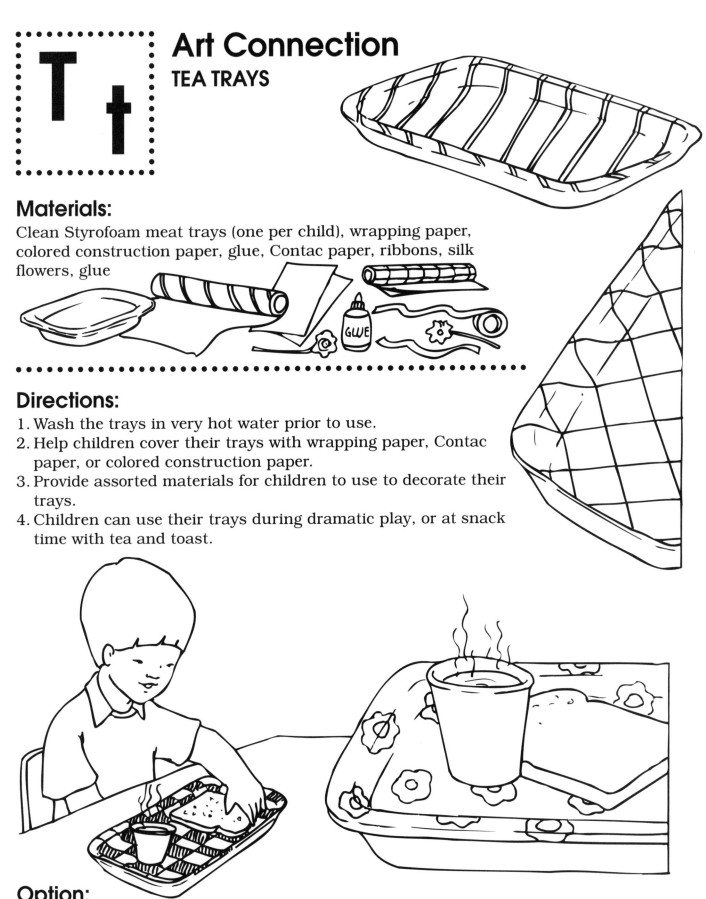

Materials:

Clean Styrofoam meat trays (one per child), wrapping paper, colored construction paper, glue, Contac paper, ribbons, silk flowers, glue

Directions:

1. Wash the trays in very hot water prior to use.
2. Help children cover their trays with wrapping paper, Contac paper, or colored construction paper.
3. Provide assorted materials for children to use to decorate their trays.
4. Children can use their trays during dramatic play, or at snack time with tea and toast.

Option:

Make a recipe from *Peter Rabbit's Cookery Book* compiled by Anne Emerson (Warne, 1987). This book contains 21 recipes inspired by various Beatrix Potter stories.

Tt
Resources

More Beatrix Potter Tales

- *The Tale of Ginger and Pickles*
  by Beatrix Potter
  (Warne, 1909).
  Ginger the cat and Pickles a terrier run a store which caters to dolls, mice, and rabbits.

- *The Tale of Jemima Puddle-Duck*
  by Beatrix Potter
  (Warne, 1908).
  Jemima meets a mysterious gentleman when she tries to find somewhere to build a nest to hatch her eggs.

- *The Tale of Mr. Jeremy Fisher*
  by Beatrix Potter
  (Warne, 1906).
  It's a good thing that Jeremy Fisher wears galoshes and a macintosh when he goes fishing...and that he has something else in the larder when his friends come to tea.

- *The Tale of Mrs. Tiggy-Winkle*
  by Beatrix Potter
  (Warne, 1905).
  While looking for her pocket-hankin', Lucie meets Mrs. Tiggy-Winkle.

- *The Tale of Mrs. Tittlemouse*
  by Beatrix Potter
  (Warne, 1910).
  Mrs. Thomasina Tittlemouse (a wood mouse with a long tail) has many unwelcome guests, including Mr. Jackson, a toothless toad.

- *The Tale of the Pie and the Patty Pan*
  by Beatrix Potter
  (Warne, 1905).
  The tale of a cat and dog planning to have supper together.

- *The Tale of Squirrel Nutkin*
  by Beatrix Potter
  (Warne, 1903).
  This book begins by stating that it is a tale about a tail!

- *The Tale of Timmy Tiptoes*
  by Beatrix Potter
  (Warne, 1911).
  This little grey squirrel lives in the tree-tops, until he is shoved down a woodpecker's hole by the other squirrels.

- *The Tale of Tom Kitten*
  by Beatrix Potter
  (Warne, 1908).
  Tom and his two sisters get into trouble while their mother prepares tea for her guests.

- *The Tale of Two Bad Mice*
  by Beatrix Potter
  (Warne, 1904).
  The mice are Tom Thumb and Hunca Munca and they like to get in trouble.

Tongue Twisters

- *Tongue Twisters*
  by Charles Keller
  (Simon and Schuster, 1989).
  A great collection with fun illustrations.

- *Faint Frogs Feeling Feverish and Other Terrifically Tantalizing Tongue Twisters*
  by Lilian Obligado
  (Puffin, 1983).
  This book has the added feature of having its twisters arranged alphabetically with funny animal illustrations.

- *Six Sick Sheep: 101 Tongue Twisters*
  by Joanna Cole and Stephanie Calmenson
  (Scholastic, 1993).

EXPLORE LETTER U

Discuss upper- and lower-case U's and read literature links featuring starts-with-U urban themes.

FIND THE "LETTER-OF-THE-WEEK"

• Use a permanent marker to write a letter "U" on the lid of a clear plastic deli tub. Place as many items for letter "U" in the tub as you can find, including a picture of a unicorn, the word "up," a drawing of an urn, a tiny paper umbrella, and so on.

• On a cardboard cutout of the letter "U," draw umbrellas.

• Look up "urban" in the dictionary. Explain the connection between the words "city" and "urban."

• Hide things *under* the sand in your sandbox or sand table. Students can dig for the hidden items and then rebury them for other students to find.

UNUSUAL "U" ACTIVITIES

• UNDERGROUND CONNECTION: Discuss different creatures and objects that can be found underground. (See "Resources" for books about "underground" areas.)

• UMBRELLA PAINTING: Duplicate and enlarge a copy of the umbrella pattern (see next page) for each child. Have students spatter blue paint onto the umbrella patterns by dipping a brush in blue paint, wiping the excess against the inside edge of the jar, holding the brush up, and shaking over the umbrella picture. (Note: This would be an appropriate outdoor activity done over newsprint.) Post the finished pictures.

Uu
Umbrella Pattern

U u

Upon my word and honor,
Upon begins with U.
So do words like unicorn,
Umbrella, up, and use.
U starts words like unicycle
And uncle, us, and urn.
Can you think of more U words
Or shall V have a turn?

Uu

Upper- and Lower-case U

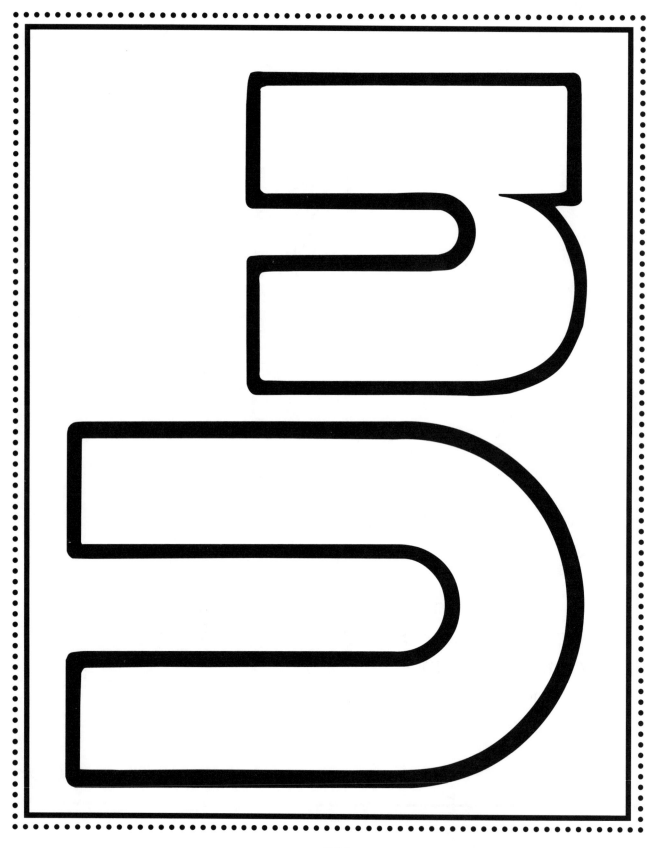

Uu

Alphabet Puzzle

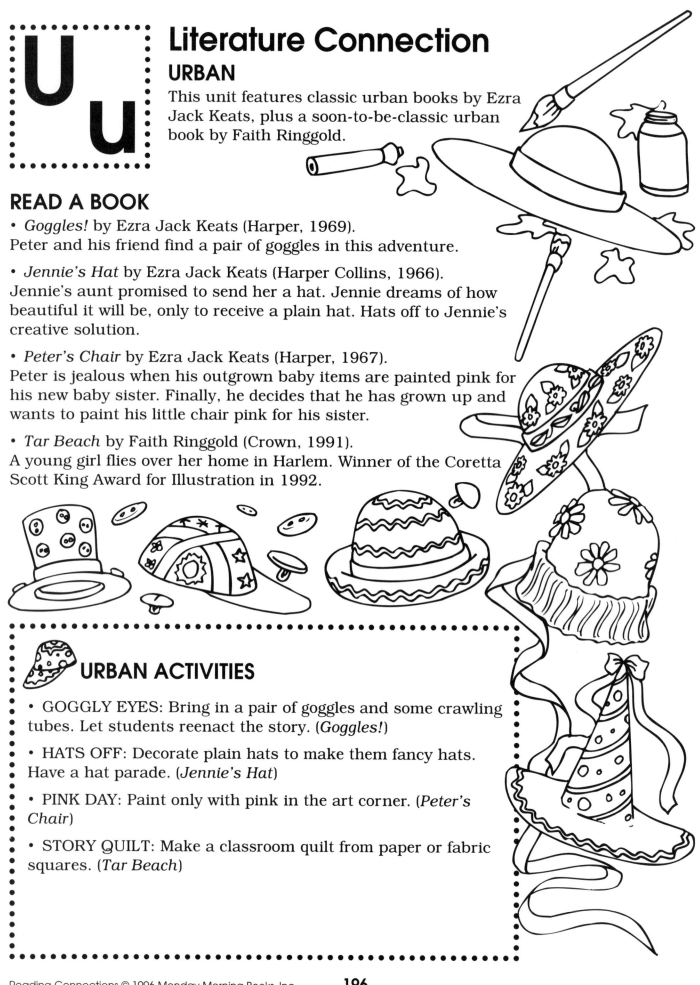

U u Literature Connection

URBAN

This unit features classic urban books by Ezra Jack Keats, plus a soon-to-be-classic urban book by Faith Ringgold.

READ A BOOK

• *Goggles!* by Ezra Jack Keats (Harper, 1969).
Peter and his friend find a pair of goggles in this adventure.

• *Jennie's Hat* by Ezra Jack Keats (Harper Collins, 1966).
Jennie's aunt promised to send her a hat. Jennie dreams of how beautiful it will be, only to receive a plain hat. Hats off to Jennie's creative solution.

• *Peter's Chair* by Ezra Jack Keats (Harper, 1967).
Peter is jealous when his outgrown baby items are painted pink for his new baby sister. Finally, he decides that he has grown up and wants to paint his little chair pink for his sister.

• *Tar Beach* by Faith Ringgold (Crown, 1991).
A young girl flies over her home in Harlem. Winner of the Coretta Scott King Award for Illustration in 1992.

URBAN ACTIVITIES

• GOGGLY EYES: Bring in a pair of goggles and some crawling tubes. Let students reenact the story. (*Goggles!*)

• HATS OFF: Decorate plain hats to make them fancy hats. Have a hat parade. (*Jennie's Hat*)

• PINK DAY: Paint only with pink in the art corner. (*Peter's Chair*)

• STORY QUILT: Make a classroom quilt from paper or fabric squares. (*Tar Beach*)

Art Connection
URBAN UTOPIA

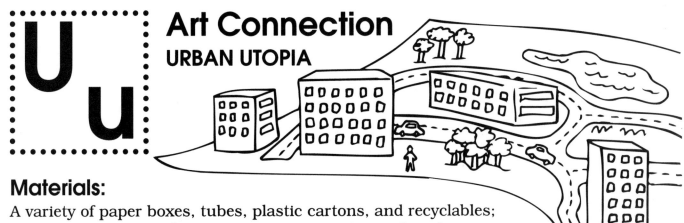

Materials:

A variety of paper boxes, tubes, plastic cartons, and recyclables; construction paper; glue; tape; tempera paint; paintbrushes; butcher paper; crayons or markers; plastic toy vehicles and people

Directions:

1. Dedicate a table top to this project for the week.
2. Spread out a large sheet of butcher paper on the table top.
3. Students can draw or paint roads, parks, rivers, lakes, etc., on the butcher paper.
4. Have students cover the containers with construction paper or paint them.
5. Students can arrange the buildings upon the urban utopia!
6. Set out small plastic vehicles and people for children to use to create city life.

197

Uu
Resources

More Urban Books

- *Dreams*
  by Ezra Jack Keats
  (Macmillan, 1974).
  Roberto has trouble falling asleep one night and then getting up the next morning. *Note*: This story would be best enjoyed when students are familiar with the other characters in these books; references are made to the other neighborhood children.

- *A Letter to Amy*
  by Ezra Jack Keats
  (Harper, 1968).
  Peter has mixed feelings as he goes off to mail a birthday party invitation to a *girl*!

- *Louie*
  by Ezra Jack Keats
  (Greenwillow, 1975).
  Louie is entranced by the puppets in the neighborhood puppet show.

- *Maggie and the Pirate*
  by Ezra Jack Keats
  (Four Winds Press, 1979).
  The new pirate on the block takes Maggie's pet cricket. Before the hostage can be freed, it dies. However, this sad event brings the neighborhood children together.

- *Pet Show*
  by Ezra Jack Keats
  (Macmillan, 1972).
  Archie can't find the cat for the pet show, so he brings a pet germ!

- *The Snowy Day*
  by Ezra Jack Keats
  (Puffin, 1962).
  In this Caldecott winner, Peter wakes up to discover that it snowed during the night. He puts on his snowsuit, goes outside, and explores.

- *The Trek*
  by Ann Jonas
  (Greenwillow, 1985).
  An imaginative girl sees all types of jungle animals on her walk to school.

- *The Trip*
  by Ezra Jack Keats
  (Greenwillow, 1978).
  When Louie's family moves to a new neighborhood, he dreams of being with his friends on Halloween.

- *Underground*
  by David Macaulay
  (Houghton Mifflin, 1976).
  Includes detailed drawings of the underside of urban areas.

- *Whistle for Willie*
  by Ezra Jack Keats
  (Viking, 1964).
  Willie practices whistling all day so that he can whistle for his dog.

Audiotapes
- *Goggles!*
  (Weston Woods, 1974).

- *A Letter to Amy*
  (Weston Woods, 1991).

- *Peter's Chair*
  (Weston Woods, 1991).

Additional Resources
- *Tar Beach* puzzle
  (JTG of Nashville): 1-800-327-5113.

EXPLORE LETTER V

Discuss upper- and lower-case V's, practice assorted "V" sounds, and read literature links featuring starts-with-V books, such as Eric Carle's *Very. . .* series.

FIND THE "LETTER-OF-THE-WEEK"

• Use a permanent marker to write a letter "V" on the lid of a clear plastic deli tub. Place as many items for letter "V" in the tub as you can find, including a valentine, a picture of a violin, a violet (or a violet-hued crayon), a picture of a volcano, a picture of a vacuum (could be cut from an advertisement), and so on.

• On a cardboard cutout of the letter "V," draw vegetables and color them using crayons or markers.

• Have children make valentines for each other.

• Let children take turns vacuuming. Or they can pretend to vacuum in your "home" play area.

• Play recorded violin music. Or have a violin player put on a performance for your classroom.

• Play volleyball, or use a volleyball to roll back and forth in a circle so that children get used to the size, shape, and weight of it.

VIVACIOUS "V" ACTIVITIES

• VERY, VERY VIOLET: Provide purple tissue paper for children to use to make little paper violets. Children can glue the violets to green pipe cleaners and then place their paper violets in vases.

• VALENTINES: Duplicate the valentine pattern (see next page) to use to create a "Very, Very Valentine" bulletin board. Color and decorate as you'd like, then post on a bulletin board. Have children make valentines for each other, and add them to the board. Use the valentine format when you give children awards or certificates.

Vv
Valentine Pattern

V v

When she was good, she was **v**ery,
 very good,
And **v**ery starts with **V**.
So do words like **v**alentine
And **v**ase and **v**an and **v**ine.
V starts words like **v**iolin
And **v**acuum, **v**est, and **v**ent.
Can you think of more **V** words
Or is it time we went?

Reading Connections © 1996 Monday Morning Books, Inc.

Vv

Upper- and Lower-case V

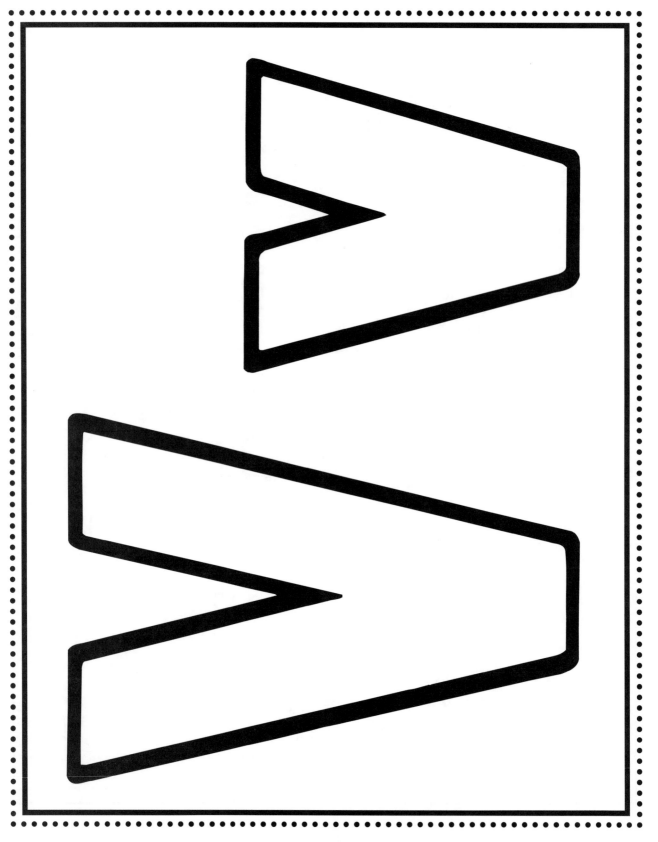

Vv
Alphabet Puzzle

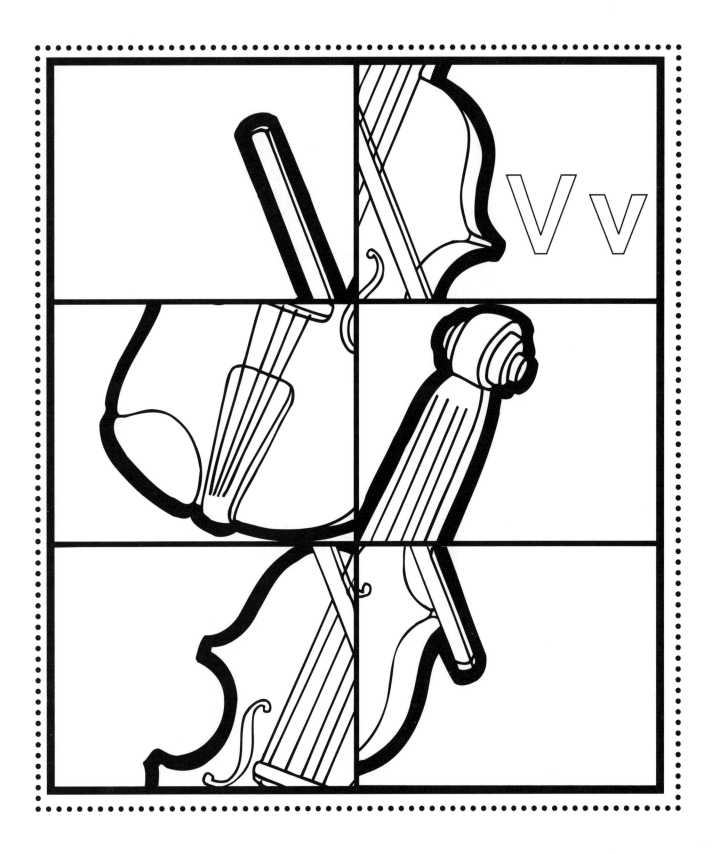

Reading Connections © 1996 Monday Morning Books, Inc.

Literature Connection
VERY, VERY, VERY

This unit focuses on Eric Carle's *Very. . .* books. Visit with a caterpillar, spider, cricket, and firefly.

READ A BOOK

• *The Very Busy Spider* by Eric Carle (Philomel, 1984). This book will hold special appeal, as the spider and web are raised up off the page.

• *The Very Hungry Caterpillar* by Eric Carle (Philomel, 1969). Students learn the stages of metamorphosis as they follow a hungry caterpillar through his journey to become a butterfly.

• *The Very Lonely Firefly* by Eric Carle (Philomel, 1995). The firefly looks for other fireflies, but finds only other sources of light. . . until the final page. The book has fireflies that actually light up.

• *The Very Quiet Cricket* by Eric Carle (Philomel, 1990). As a cricket proceeds through the day, he is unable to make noises like the other insects, until he finally meets a female cricket. (This book has a "chirping" device.)

VERY ACTIVITIES

• CHIRPING CRICKETS: Play a version of sound tag. One student (the "cricket") is blindfolded. All of the other students make an insect noise and the cricket has to locate them by sound alone. (*The Very Quiet Cricket*)

• SILVER WEBS: Provide small squeeze bottles filled with white glue for children to use to make "glue webs" on black or gray paper. Students can make "webby" designs on the paper with the glue, then sprinkle on a little silver glitter to make their webs shimmer. (*The Very Busy Spider*)

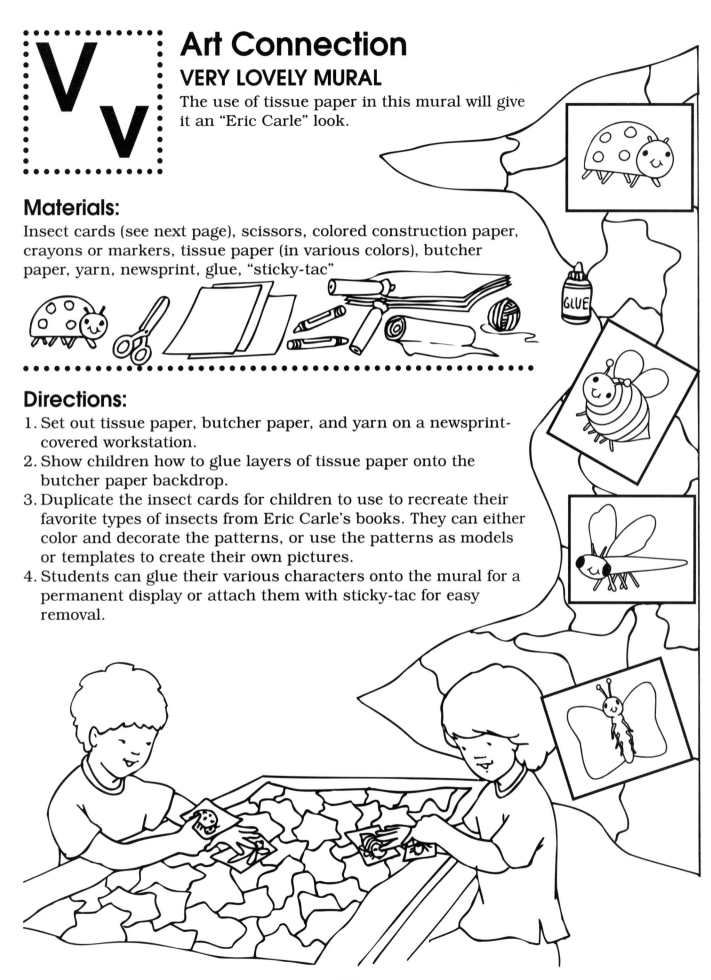

Vv

Art Connection

VERY LOVELY MURAL

The use of tissue paper in this mural will give it an "Eric Carle" look.

Materials:

Insect cards (see next page), scissors, colored construction paper, crayons or markers, tissue paper (in various colors), butcher paper, yarn, newsprint, glue, "sticky-tac"

Directions:

1. Set out tissue paper, butcher paper, and yarn on a newsprint-covered workstation.
2. Show children how to glue layers of tissue paper onto the butcher paper backdrop.
3. Duplicate the insect cards for children to use to recreate their favorite types of insects from Eric Carle's books. They can either color and decorate the patterns, or use the patterns as models or templates to create their own pictures.
4. Students can glue their various characters onto the mural for a permanent display or attach them with sticky-tac for easy removal.

Vv
Insect Cards

Vv
Resources

More Eric Carle Books

- *All About Arthur: An Absolutely Absurd Alphabet*
  by Eric Carle
  (Watts, 1974).
  An animal alphabet book in which Arthur the ape travels to meet other animals.

- *Do You Want to Be My Friend?*
  by Eric Carle
  (Harper Collins, 1976).
  A mouse searches for a friend.

- *Draw Me A Star*
  by Eric Carle
  (Philomel, 1992).
  The artist starts the story with a request to draw a star, and continues until an entire universe is drawn. The book ends with a letter to the reader about how this book came to be.

- *Eric Carle's Animals, Animals*
  (Philomel, 1989).
  This book is a compilation of poems about pets and animals by a variety of authors.

- *Eric Carle's Dragons, Dragons and Other Creatures*
  (Philomel, 1991).
  This poetry book is similar to *Animals, Animals*, but focuses on mythical creatures.

- *Eric Carle's Storybook: Seven Tales by Grimm*
  (Watts, 1976).
  Carle illustrations accompany classic tales.

- *Eric Carle's Treasury of Classic Stories*
  (Orchard, 1988).
  Twenty-two folk and fairy tales are retold with Carle's illustrations.

- *The Grouchy Ladybug*
  by Eric Carle
  (Crowell, 1977).
  This ladybug is looking for a fight! The book also introduces telling time.

- *Have You Seen My Cat?*
  by Eric Carle
  (Picture Book Studio, 1987).
  Various wild cats are encountered as a young boy looks for the cat he lost.

- *The Honeybee and the Robber*
  by Eric Carle
  (Philomel, 1981).
  One bee saves the hive when a bear attacks it. This book also includes factual info about bees.

- *A House for Hermit Crab*
  by Eric Carle
  (Picture Book Studios, 1987).
  A crab has outgrown his shell and decorates his new one.

- *The Mixed-Up Chameleon*
  by Eric Carle
  (Crowell, 1975).
  A chameleon colorfully mixes up various animal parts.

- *1, 2, 3 to the Zoo*
  by Eric Carle
  (Philomel, 1968).
  A counting book with animals on a zoo train.

- *Pancakes, Pancakes*
  by Eric Carle
  (Picture Book Studios, 1990).
  Jack makes his morning breakfast from scratch.

Vv
Resources

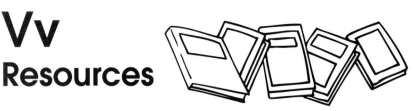

More Eric Carle Books

• *Papa, Please Get the Moon for Me*
  by Eric Carle
  (Picture Book Studio, 1986).
Monica's father tries to fulfill her wish for the moon.

• *Rooster's Off to See the World*
  by Eric Carle
  (Picture Book Studio, 1972).
Rooster meets sets of animals from 1 to 14 on his adventure in this counting book.

• *The Secret Birthday Message*
  by Eric Carle
  (Crowell, 1972).
Coded instructions help a boy find his birthday present.

• *The Tiny Seed*
  by Eric Carle
  (Picture Book Studio, 1987).
The life cycle of a flowering plant is followed in this simple book.

• *Today Is Monday*
  by Eric Carle
  (Philomel, 1993).
Animals introduce new foods for every day of the week until the children eat on Sunday.

• *Very First Book of Colors*
  by Eric Carle
  (Harper Collins, 1974).
This book presents puzzles about colors.

• *Very First Book of Heads and Tails*
  by Eric Carle
  (Crowell, 1976).
With this flip-format book, students can create a variety of very odd creatures.

• *Very First Book of Numbers*
  by Eric Carle
  (Harper Collins, 1974).

• *Very First Book of Shapes*
  by Eric Carle
  (Crowell, 1974).
This puzzle format asks children to find a particular shape in each picture.

• *Very First Book of Tools*
  by Eric Carle
  (Crowell, 1986).
A split-page format is used for mix and match playing.

• *The Very First Book of Words*
  by Eric Carle
  (Crowell, 1974).

• *Watch Out! A Giant!*
  by Eric Carle
  (Collins-World, 1978).
Two children are caught by a hungry giant.

• *What's for Lunch?*
  by Eric Carle
  (Philomel, 1982).
A monkey looks for lunch in this "fruity" counting book.

Videotapes

• *The Very Hungry Caterpillar and Other Stories*
  (Disney Home Video, 1993).
Five of Eric Carle's most popular stories are presented in this 25-minute video tape.

This way to a counting adventure.

EXPLORE LETTER W

Discuss upper- and lower-case W's and read literature links featuring starts-with-W books such as *World Famous Muriel*.

 **FIND THE "LETTER-OF-THE-WEEK"**

• Use a permanent marker to write a letter "W" on the lid of a clear plastic deli tub. Place as many items for letter "W" in the tub as you can find, including a whistle, a picture of a whale, a walnut, a plastic worm, a picture of a window, and so on.

• On a cardboard cutout of the letter "W," paste wagon wheel pasta.

• Make a welcome mat from pieces of burlap.

• Study whales. Listen to audiotapes of whale songs, such as "Songs and Sounds of Orcinus Orca" (Total Records, 1987).

• In math, work with weights and weighing.

• Set up daily activities at your water table.

• Have your students wiggle, giggle, then wiggle some more! (Do you have a class of wiggle worms?)

• Have children brainstorm as many foods that start with "W" as they can think of, including watermelon, waffles, watercress, and walnuts.

WILD "W" ACTIVITIES

• THE WHOLE WORLD: Create a "Whole Wide World" bulletin board. Post a world map on your bulletin board. Then paste stickers on the countries that your students' ancestors originally came from.

• IF WISHES WERE HORSES: Create a wishing well by covering a clean waste paper basket with fancy wrapping paper. Give each child a penny to toss into the "wishing well." Children can dictate their wishes or keep them secrets.

• WONDERFUL WANDS: Provide paper towel tubes for children to decorate with wrapping paper and streamers. Let children wave their wands to waltz music.

 Reading Connections © 1996 Monday Morning Books, Inc.

W **W**

Wee is **W**illie **W**inkie,
Wee starts with **W**.
So do **w**ords like **w**heelbarrow
And **w**ater, **w**atch, and **w**oo.
W starts **w**indmill
And **w**ishbone, **w**and, and **w**in.
Can you think of other words
That **W** begins?

Ww
Upper- and Lower-case W

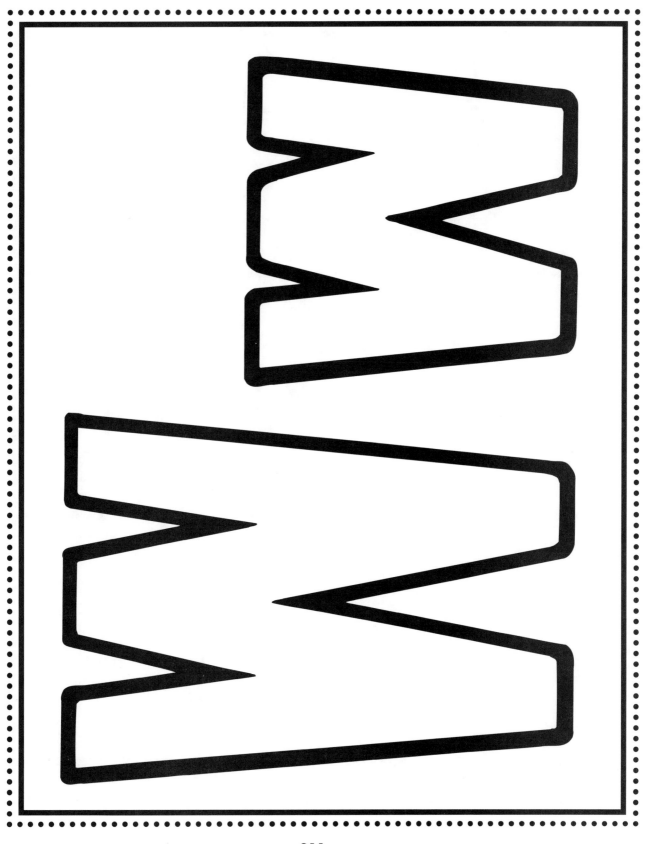

Reading Connections © 1996 Monday Morning Books, Inc.

Ww

Alphabet Puzzle

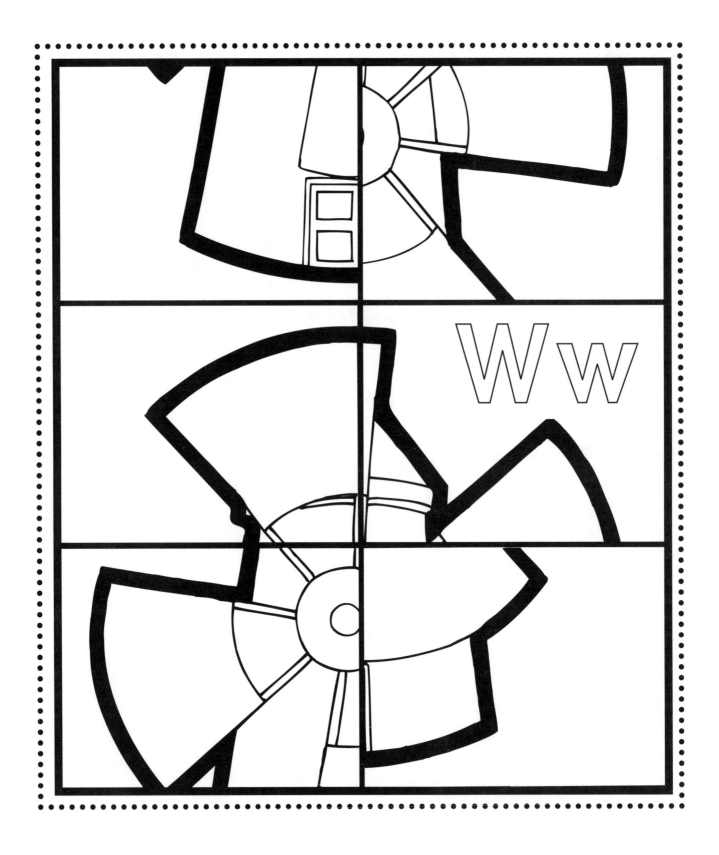

Literature Connection
WORLD FAMOUS MURIEL

Sue Alexander has written three books about her world famous character Muriel.

READ A BOOK

• *World Famous Muriel* by Sue Alexander, illustrated by Chris Demarest (Little, Brown, 1984).
Muriel is asked to tightrope walk at the queen's party, but her detective skills are called into service when all the paper lanterns end up missing.

• *World Famous Muriel and the Magic Mystery* by Sue Alexander, illustrated by Marla Frazee (Crowell, 1990).
Muriel sets about being a smart detective as she searches for her friend Hocus Pocus, who disappears while rehearsing his act. Muriel is kept energized by peanut butter cookies!

• *World Famous Muriel and the Scary Dragon* by Sue Alexander, illustrated by Chris Demarest (Little, Brown, 1985).
The king asks Muriel to rid the kingdom of a terrible dragon!

🌎 WORLD FAMOUS ACTIVITIES

• IT'S A WONDERFUL WORLD: Use an inflatable "world" ball to toss around a circle of students. Students can take turns trying to balance the beach ball on one finger while they stand on one foot. (*World Famous Muriel*)

• WORLD FAMOUS COOKIES: Make peanut butter cookies to enjoy as an afternoon snack. (*World Famous Muriel and the Magic Mystery*)

• WORLD FAMOUS PUPPET SHOW: Reenact this World Famous Muriel story using hand puppets. (*World Famous Muriel and the Scary Dragon*)

Reading Connections © 1996 Monday Morning Books, Inc.

Art Connection
WATERCOLOR-WORLD WALL MURAL

Children can use watercolors to create their own "World Famous" mural.

Materials:

Masking tape, butcher paper, watercolors, paintbrushes, pencils, newspaper or plastic tarps

Directions:

1. Use masking tape to attach a sheet of butcher paper to a wall in your classroom or hallway.
2. Spread newspaper or plastic tarps on the floor.
3. Set out several watercolor stations.
4. Have students consider their ideal world. They should think about topics such as pollution and the environment before they paint.
5. Provide pencils for children to use to sketch in their paintings ahead of time.
6. Let students paint their ideal world.

EXPLORE LETTER X

Discuss upper- and lower-case X's and read literature links featuring ends-with-X characters such as the Lorax.

FIND THE "LETTER-OF-THE-WEEK"

• Use a permanent marker to write a letter "X" on the lid of a clear plastic deli tub. Place as many items for letter "X" in the tub as you can find, including a picture of a xylophone, a small x-ray, and *ends*-with-X items, such as a picture of a fox, a small box, a picture of an ox, and so on.

• On a cardboard cutout of the letter "X" draw X's and O's to represent hugs and kisses!

• Ask a doctor or dentist to lend your classroom old x-rays to examine.

• Invite an x-ray technician to talk to your class about the job and equipment.

X-TRA-SPECIAL "X" ACTIVITIES

• "X" MARKS THE SPOT: Hide a treasure in your classroom and draw a treasure map, marking the treasure with an "X." Have children hunt for the "X" on the map and then in the classroom.

• XOX: Teach children how to play Tic-Tac-Toe.

• MARVELOUS MOTHER GOOSE: Teach the Mother Goose rhyme "X shall stand for playmates ten, V for five stout stalwart men, I for one, as I'm alive, C for hundred and D for five, M for a thousand soldiers true, and L for fifty, I'll tell you." (This is a mnemonic to help remember Roman numerals.)

 Reading Connections © 1996 Monday Morning Books, Inc.

X x

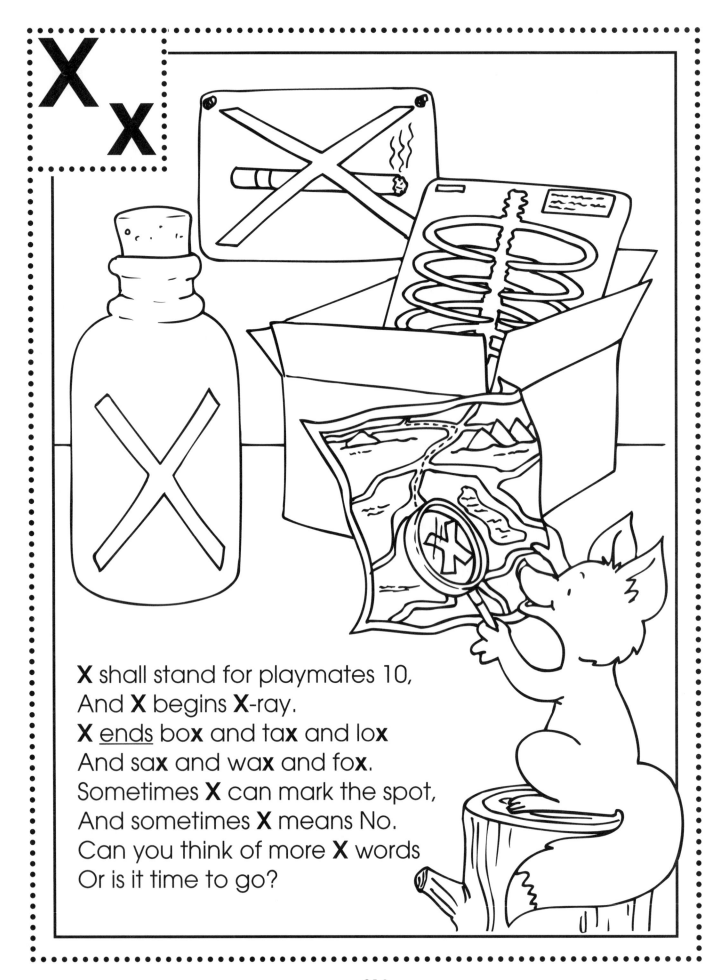

X shall stand for playmates 10,
And **X** begins **X**-ray.
X <u>ends</u> bo**x** and ta**x** and lo**x**
And sa**x** and wa**x** and fo**x**.
Sometimes **X** can mark the spot,
And sometimes **X** means No.
Can you think of more **X** words
Or is it time to go?

Xx
Upper- and Lower-case X

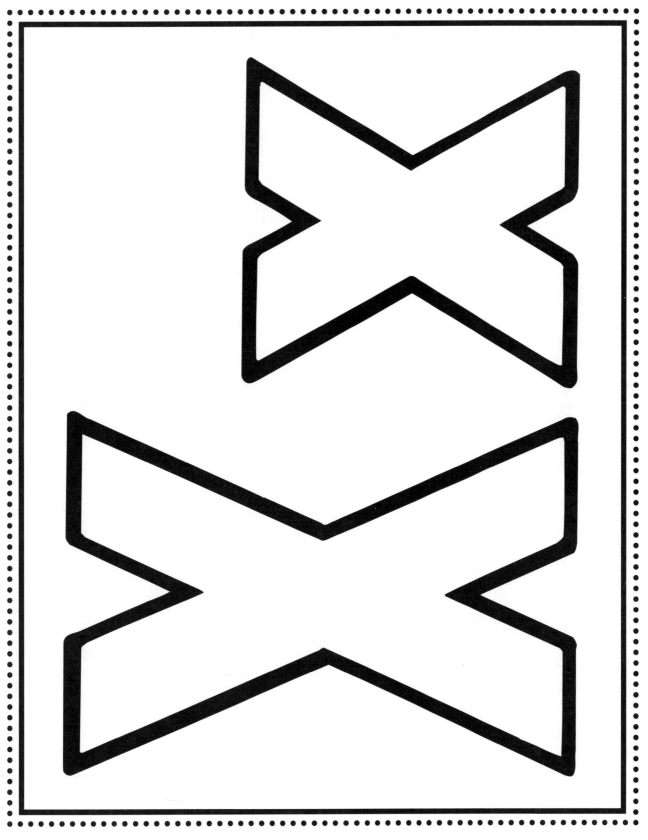

Xx
Alphabet Rhyme

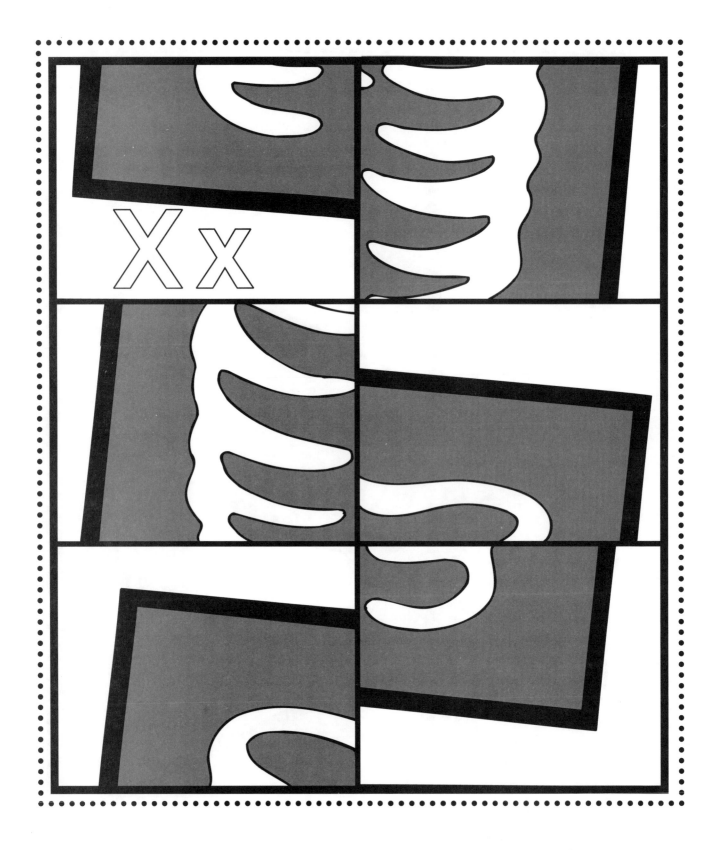

Literature Connection

THE LORAX

This unit focuses on the Lorax, a character whose name ends in X. The Lorax is a small environmentally concerned creature who stars in Dr. Seuss' classic tale. The Fox in Socks is another Seuss character that ends in X.

READ A BOOK

• *Fox in Socks: A Tongue Twister for Super Children* (Beginner Books, 1965).
The reader's tongue is supposed to get tangled in this Dr. Seuss delight!

• *The Lorax* by Dr. Seuss (Random House, 1971).
The Lorax speaks out on behalf of the trees and the animals to the developer who is polluting the area.

ENDS-IN-X ACTIVITIES

• UNLESS: Create a small stage area with building bricks from your manipulatives center. If you have room, build the Once-ler's home, as well. Dangle a small pail from a string. Label a nearby spot with the word "Unless." Set out 15 cents, a nail, and a shell. Students can pretend to be the Lorax and stand on the spot labeled "UNLESS." (*The Lorax*)

• MUSTACHIOED: Make Lorax mustaches from cotton or felt. Attach two pieces of yarn to the sides of each mustache. Children can take turns wearing the mustaches. (*The Lorax*)

• SEEDLINGS: Plant seeds in pots or in your yard. Pretend that they will grow to be Truffula trees. (*The Lorax*)

• SOCK HOP: Have children take off their shoes while you read *Fox in Socks*.

Art Connection
TRUFFULA TREES

Materials:

Butcher paper, sponges, scissors, tempera paint (in assorted colors), paintbrushes, pie tins, newsprint

Directions:

1. Cover a flat working area with newsprint.
2. Place the butcher paper over the newsprint.
3. Pour different colors of tempera paint into pie tins.
4. Cut sponges into small circles that fit easily in the children's hands.
5. Have children use the sponges to paint fluffy Truffula treetops on the butcher paper.
6. Provide brushes for children to use to paint the Truffula trunks.
7. Post the completed colorful mural on a wall in the classroom.

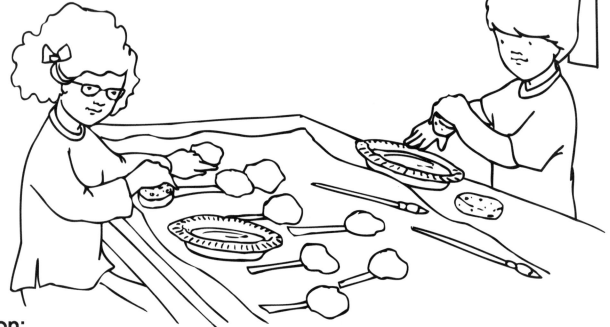

Option:

• Make Truffula tree axes by fastening triangles of construction paper to paper towel tubes.

Xx Resources

More Dr. Seuss Books

- *The Foot Book*
  by Dr. Seuss
  (Bright and Early, 1968).
  The world of Dr. Seuss isn't limited to simply left and right feet. Step into this fun book!

- *Great Day for Up*
  by Dr. Seuss
  (Bright and Early Books, 1974).
  Many things and people get up in the morning, but not the sleepy little boy on the final page.

- *Mr. Brown Can MOO, Can You?*
  by Dr. Seuss
  (Bright and Early Books, 1970).
  This book must be read aloud to appreciate it fully.

- *There's A Wocket in My Pocket*
  by Dr. Seuss
  (Bright and Early Books, 1974).
  A young boy imagines an assortment of rhyming creatures that inhabit locations of the house.

Beginner Books

- *The Cat in the Hat*
  by Dr. Seuss
  (Random House, 1957).
  Two children sitting at home are visited by the very zany Cat in the Hat. This cat knows all sorts of games that can be played indoors on a rainy day.

- *The Cat in the Hat Comes Back*
  by Dr. Seuss
  (Beginner Books, 1958).
  Joining the Cat in the striped hat are little cats from A to Z.

- *Dr. Seuss' ABC*
  (Beginner Books, 1963).
  An extra-special alphabet book as only Dr. Seuss can do!

- *Green Eggs and Ham*
  by Dr. Seuss
  (Beginner Books, 1960).
  In this classic, the main character does not even want to try Sam's green eggs and ham—regardless of time, location, or circumstance.

- *Hop on Pop*
  by Dr. Seuss
  (Beginner Books, 1963).
  Rhymes introduce the simplest vocabulary words in Seuss' inimitable style.

- *I Am Not Going to Get Up Today!*
  by Dr. Seuss
  (Beginner Books, 1987).
  No matter what the family, neighbors, and city folks do, this boy refuses to get up.

- *I Can Read with My Eyes Shut*
  by Dr. Seuss
  (Beginner Books, 1978).
  The Cat in the Hat finds that it is easier to read if he leaves his eyes open!

- *Oh Say Can You Say? Oh My Brothers! Oh My Sisters! These Are Terrible Tongue Twisters*
  by Dr. Seuss
  (Beginner Books, 1979).
  These tongue twisters are a paragraph or more long and will tie up the tongue for sure!

Xx
Resources

Beginner Books

- *Oh, The Thinks You Can Think*
  by Dr. Seuss
  (Beginner Books, 1975).
A little imagination goes a long way! A *lot* of imagination makes this a Dr. Seuss delight!

- *One Fish Two Fish Red Fish Blue Fish*
  by Dr. Seuss
  (Beginner Books, 1960).
An odd assortment of creatures do unusual "funny" things everywhere.

Environmental Books

- *50 Simple Things Kids Can Do to Save the Earth*
  by The EarthWorks Group
  (Andrews and McMeel, 1990).
The EarthWorks encourages kids to write to them at:
  The Kids' EarthWorks Group
  1400 Shattuck Avenue, #25
  Berkeley, CA 94709

- *The Great Kapok Tree*
  by Lynne Cherry
  (Harcourt, 1990).
A man begins to chop down a great kapok tree in the middle of the rain forest. But animals who live in the tree come to tell him why he should not chop it down.

- *A River Ran Wild*
  by Lynne Cherry
  (Harcourt, 1992).
This book follows the Nash-a-way River through six centuries, beginning when its waters were clear enough to merit the Native American name that means "River with the Pebbled Bottom."

Audiotapes

- *The Cat in the Hat*
  (Random House, 1987).

- *The Lorax*
  (Random House, 1992).
Narrated by Ted Danson, music by Bruce H. Zimmerman.

Videotapes

- *The Cat in the Hat*
  (Playhouse Video, 1989).

- *The Cat in the Hat Comes Back*
  (Random House, 1989).
Includes "The Cat in the Hat Comes Back," "There's A Wocket in My Pocket," and "Fox in Socks."

- *Dr. Seuss's ABC and Other Stories*
  (Random House, 1989).
Includes "Dr. Seuss's ABC," "I Can Read with My Eyes Shut," and "Mr. Brown Can MOO! Can You?"

- *Dr. Seuss on the Loose*
  (PlayHouse Video, 1989).
Includes "Sneetches on the Beaches," "The Zax," and "Green Eggs and Ham."

- *Hop on Pop and Other Stories*
  (Random House, 1989).
Includes "Hop on Pop," "Oh Say Can You Say?", and "Marvin K. Mooney, Will You Please Go Now!"

- *One Fish Two Fish Red Fish Blue Fish and Other Stories*
  (Random House, 1989).
"One Fish Two Fish Red Fish Blue Fish," "Oh, the Thinks You Can Think!", and "The Foot Book" are included.

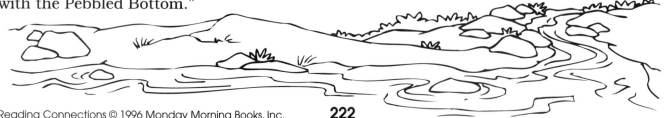

EXPLORE LETTER Y

Discuss upper- and lower-case Y's and read *You're the Scaredy Cat* and other Mercer Mayer books.

FIND THE "LETTER-OF-THE-WEEK"

• Use a permanent marker to write a letter "Y" on the lid of a clear plastic deli tub. Place as many items for letter "Y" in the tub as you can find, including a yo-yo, a piece of yarn, a yellow crayon, and a picture of a yak.

• On a cardboard cutout of the letter "Y," paste yellow yarn.

• Have the children practice reciting all of the months of the year.

• Have a Yellow Day. Encourage students to wear something yellow to school. Provide yellow ribbon for children who forget.

• Go outside to yodel and yell in the school yard.

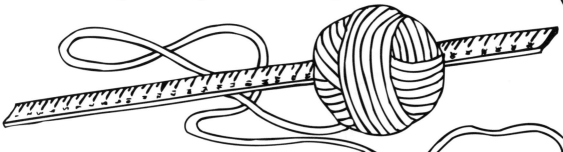

YOWZA! "Y" ACTIVITIES

• YOU AND ME: Play "Free to Be You and Me" by Marlo Thomas (Arista, 1972) for the children. Teach your students the words to this song and then sing it as a class.

• "YOU" MOTHER GOOSE RHYMES: Learn the following rhymes to recite with your class:

Do you love me, or do you not? You told me once, but I forgot.

If you love me as I love you, no knife shall cut our love in two!

A dillar, a dollar, a ten o'clock scholar! What makes you come so soon? You used to come at ten o'clock, but now you come at noon.

Tickly, tickly, on your knee; if you laugh you don't love me.

Y y

Yankee Doodle came to town,
And Yankee starts with Y.
So do words like yak and yam
And yo-yo, yes, and yea!
Y starts words like yarn and yawn
And yellow and yahoo!
Can you think of more Y words
Or will that do for you?

Yy
Upper- and Lower-case Y

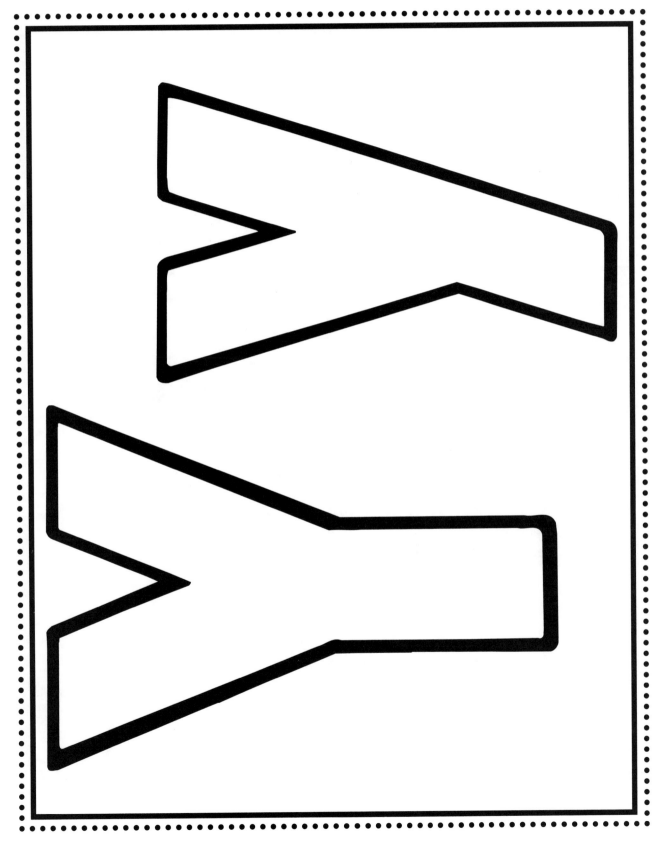

Reading Connections © 1996 Monday Morning Books, Inc.

Yy
Alphabet Rhyme

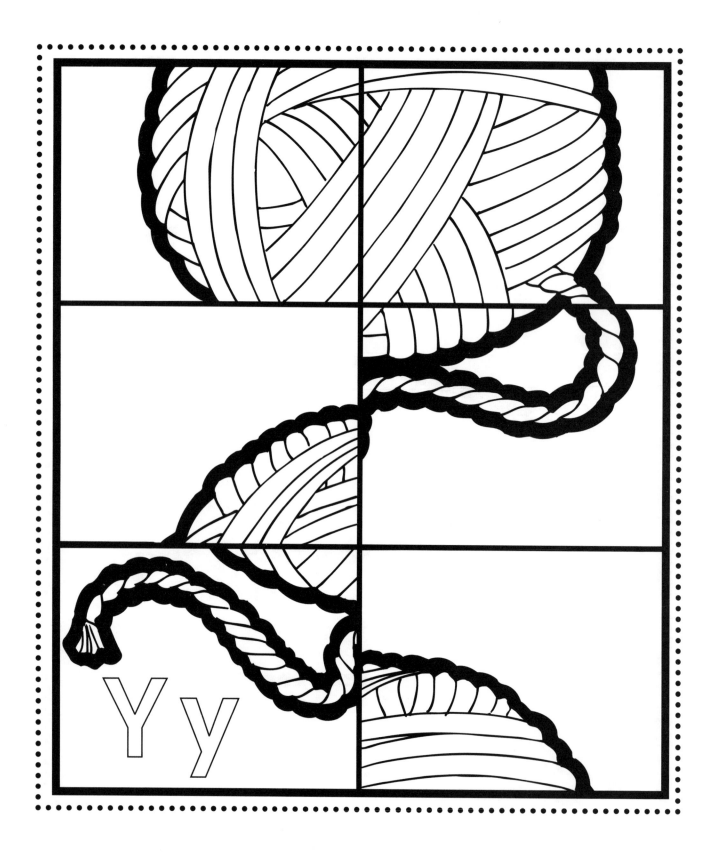

 **Yy**

Literature Connection
YOU'RE THE SCAREDY CAT

Mercer Mayer's *You're the Scaredy Cat* is a classic tale of bravery winning out over fear. The other books in this unit follow the same theme.

READ A BOOK

• *There's An Alligator Under My Bed* by Mercer Mayer (Dial, 1987). A young boy decides to solve his alligator problem by tempting it out from under his bed with a path of food to the garage. But will Dad need help getting into his car?

• *There's A Nightmare in My Closet* by Mercer Mayer (Dial, 1968).
The nightmare that inhabits a little boy's closet turns out to be less frightening than frightened.

• *There's Something in My Attic* by Mercer Mayer (Dial, 1988).
A brave young girl goes up into the attic, prepared to catch a toy-snatching nightmare with her lasso.

• *You're the Scaredy Cat* by Mercer Mayer (Four Winds Press, 1974).
Two brothers, camping in their back yard, frighten each other with scary stories. When they hear a scary noise nearby, they retreat to the safety of their bedroom.

MERCER MAYER ACTIVITIES

• NIGHTMARES: Fold sheets of drawing paper in half. Have children draw nightmares on the inside of the paper and a closet door on the outside. Post on a "Nightmarish Bulletin Board." (*There's A Nightmare in My Closet*)

• YOU'RE THE SCAREDY CAT: Gather children in a circle and give each child a chance to share a time that he or she was frightened of something. Ask how the child overcame his or her fear. (*You're the Scaredy Cat*)

Yy Art Connection
"YOU'RE THE SCAREDY CAT" SELF-PORTRAITS

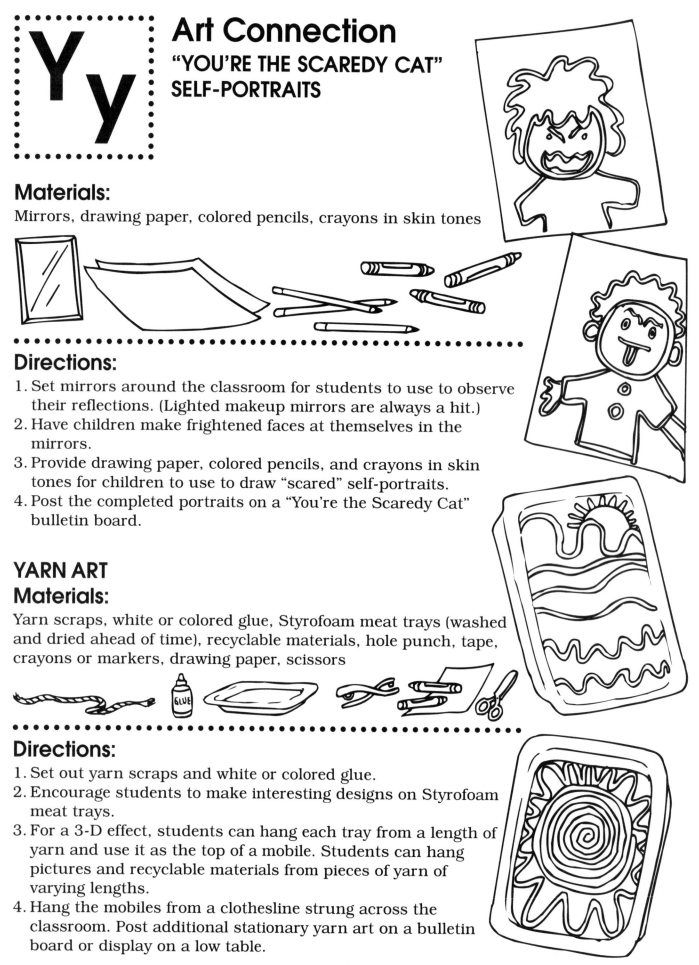

Materials:

Mirrors, drawing paper, colored pencils, crayons in skin tones

Directions:

1. Set mirrors around the classroom for students to use to observe their reflections. (Lighted makeup mirrors are always a hit.)
2. Have children make frightened faces at themselves in the mirrors.
3. Provide drawing paper, colored pencils, and crayons in skin tones for children to use to draw "scared" self-portraits.
4. Post the completed portraits on a "You're the Scaredy Cat" bulletin board.

YARN ART
Materials:

Yarn scraps, white or colored glue, Styrofoam meat trays (washed and dried ahead of time), recyclable materials, hole punch, tape, crayons or markers, drawing paper, scissors

Directions:

1. Set out yarn scraps and white or colored glue.
2. Encourage students to make interesting designs on Styrofoam meat trays.
3. For a 3-D effect, students can hang each tray from a length of yarn and use it as the top of a mobile. Students can hang pictures and recyclable materials from pieces of yarn of varying lengths.
4. Hang the mobiles from a clothesline strung across the classroom. Post additional stationary yarn art on a bulletin board or display on a low table.

Yy Game Connection

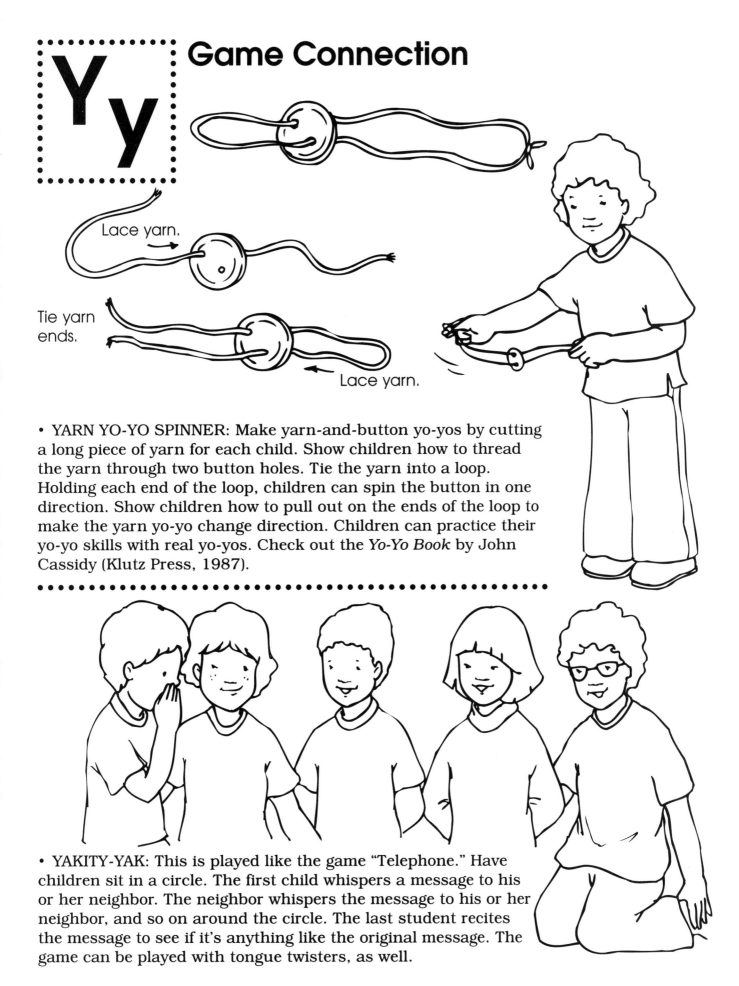

Lace yarn.

Tie yarn ends.

Lace yarn.

• YARN YO-YO SPINNER: Make yarn-and-button yo-yos by cutting a long piece of yarn for each child. Show children how to thread the yarn through two button holes. Tie the yarn into a loop. Holding each end of the loop, children can spin the button in one direction. Show children how to pull out on the ends of the loop to make the yarn yo-yo change direction. Children can practice their yo-yo skills with real yo-yos. Check out the *Yo-Yo Book* by John Cassidy (Klutz Press, 1987).

• YAKITY-YAK: This is played like the game "Telephone." Have children sit in a circle. The first child whispers a message to his or her neighbor. The neighbor whispers the message to his or her neighbor, and so on around the circle. The last student recites the message to see if it's anything like the original message. The game can be played with tongue twisters, as well.

229   Reading Connections © 1996 Monday Morning Books, Inc.

Yy
Resources

More "You" Books

- *Are You My Mother?*
  by P. D. Eastman
  (Beginner Books, 1960).
  This classic beginning reading book is
  about a little bird looking for his mother.

- *Guess How Much I Love You*
  by Sam McBratney
  (Candlewick Press, 1995).
  Big Nutbrown Hare and Little Nutbrown
  Hare star in this new classic about a father
  and his child. This book reinforces the idea
  that parent-child love will always exist.

- *If You Listen*
  by Charlotte Zolotow
  (Harper and Row, 1980).
  A young girl longs for her father. She is
  reassured by her mother that her father
  loves her even though he is far away.

- *I Love You, Good Night*
  by Jon Buller and Susan Schade
  (Simon and Schuster, 1988).
  At bedtime, a mother and daughter
  exclaim their love for each other.

- *Mama, Do You Love Me?*
  by Barbara M. Joose
  (Chronicle, 1991).
  An Inuit girl asks how much her mama
  loves her. "More than the raven loves his
  treasure," answers her mother. This
  reassuring tale is set in the Arctic, and is
  accompanied by a detailed glossary that
  explains Inuit words.

- *Mama, If You Had a Wish*
  by Jeanne Modesitt
  (Green Tiger Press, 1993).
  A young rabbit is reassured that his
  mother wishes for him to only be himself.

- *Why Do You Love Me?*
  by Martin Baynton
  (Greenwillow, 1988).
  A boy and father share a beautiful
  afternoon as the boy questions Dad about
  his paternal love.

EXPLORE LETTER Z

Discuss upper- and lower-case Z's and read literature links featuring A to Z alphabet books.

FIND THE "LETTER-OF-THE-WEEK"

• Use a permanent marker to write a letter "Z" on the lid of a clear plastic deli tub. Place as many items for letter "Z" in the tub as you can find, including a zipper, a picture of a zebra, your Zip code, a sign of the zodiac, and a drawing of a zucchini.

• On a cardboard cutout of the letter "Z" draw zigzag lightning bolts.

• Read books about zoos, such as *I Spy at the Zoo* by Maureen Roffey (Four Winds Press, 1988), *If I Ran the Zoo* by Dr. Seuss (Random House, 1950), *Zachary Goes to the Zoo* by Jill Krementz (Random House, 1986), or *Zoo* by Anthony Browne (Random House, 1992).

• In math, work on the number zero.

• Have children practice self-help skills using zippers.

ZEALOUS "Z" ACTIVITIES

• CLASSROOM ZOO: Duplicate and color the zoo patterns (see next page) to use to create a zoo-themed bulletin board. Use the patterns to play animal charades. Duplicate the patterns and give one to each child to act out in front of the class. Add verbal clues, if necessary.

• WHAT A WONDERFUL DAY: Sing "Zippity-do-dah" with your students.

• ZOOM!: Have students zip and zoom around the playground.

Zz

Zoo Patterns

Z z

Zippity-doo-dah, zippity-ay,
Zippity starts with Z.
So do words like zigzag
And zero, zip, and zing.
Z starts words like zebra
And zipper, zoo, and zounds.
Can you think of more Z words
Or is that all you found?

Zz

Upper- and Lower-case Z

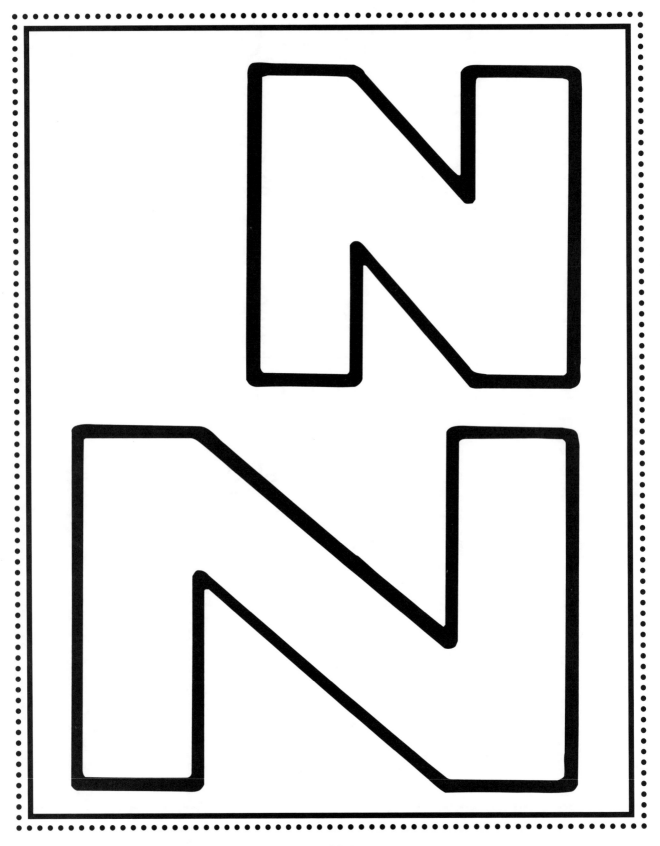

Zz

Alphabet Puzzle

Literature Connection

A TO Z

This unit focuses on alphabet books including *The Z Was Zapped* by Chris Van Allsburg.

READ A BOOK

• *An Edible Alphabet* by Bonnie Christenson (Dial, 1994).
Wood engravings are used to depict edible plants from apples to zucchini. The book concludes in a short description of each plant.

• *Elfabet: An ABC of Elves* by Jane Yolen, illustrated by Lauren Mills (Little, Brown, 1990).
On each page, an elf is busy doing some activity that begins with the same letter as his or her name. The borders include other objects that begin with the same letter of the alphabet.

• *The Z Was Zapped* by Chris Van Allsburg (Houghton Mifflin, 1987).
The letters of the alphabet are struck by mishap in this illustrated play in 26 one-page acts.

A TO Z ACTIVITIES

• CLASSROOM ABC: Make a classroom ABC book. (If you have more than 26 children in your class, have children work cooperatively. If you have fewer than 26 children, let those who finish first illustrate a second letter.)

• ELVES 'R US: Have children draw their own "Elfabets." Children can draw elves doing other activities than the ones in Yolen's book. (*Elfabet: An ABC of Elves*)

• ALPHABET MURAL: Have children use the alphabet to illustrate a mural. They can draw mishaps on their mural in homage to Van Allsburg. (*The Z Was Zapped*)

• ALPHABET ART: Children can make their own "edible alphabet art" by gluing alphabet pasta or alphabet cereal to drawing paper. (*An Edible Alphabet*)

Art Connection
ZEBRA ART

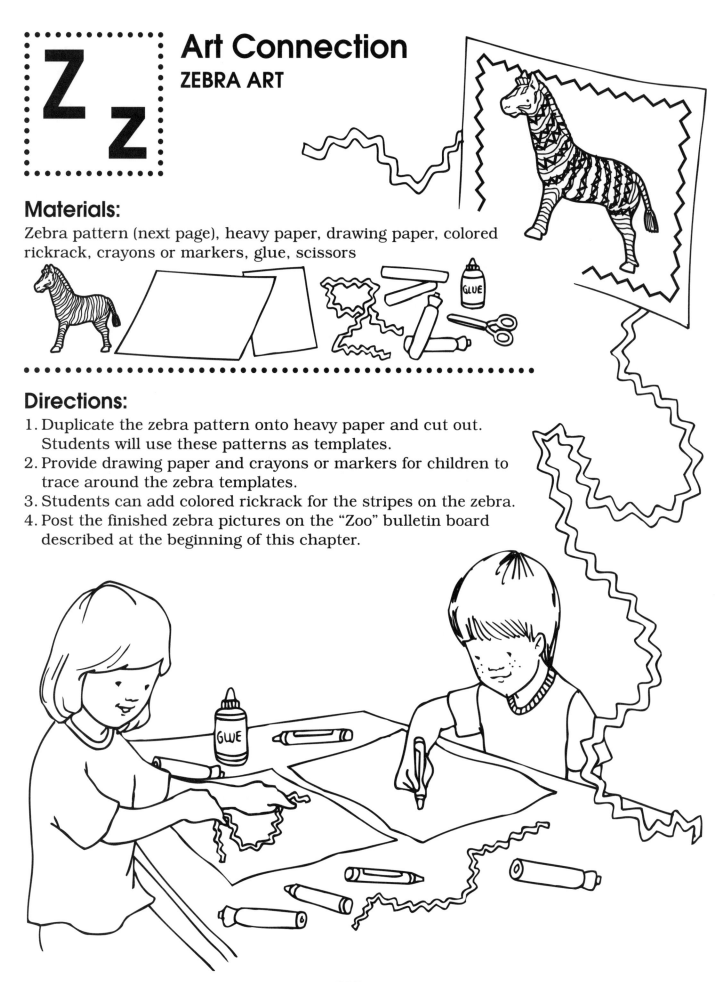

Materials:

Zebra pattern (next page), heavy paper, drawing paper, colored rickrack, crayons or markers, glue, scissors

Directions:

1. Duplicate the zebra pattern onto heavy paper and cut out. Students will use these patterns as templates.
2. Provide drawing paper and crayons or markers for children to trace around the zebra templates.
3. Students can add colored rickrack for the stripes on the zebra.
4. Post the finished zebra pictures on the "Zoo" bulletin board described at the beginning of this chapter.

Zz
Zebra Pattern

Zz
Resources

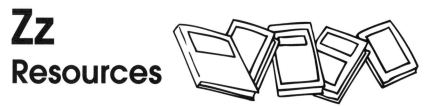

More ABC Books

- *A Apple Pie*
  by Kate Greenway
  (Warne, 1886).
This book alphabetically lists all the things to do with an apple pie, with a notable exception of "I"—for historical reasons.

- *ABC de Babar*
  by Jean de Brunhoff
  (Random, 1939).
This book, in English and French, features detailed illustrations. There are translations at the back of the book.

- *A B Cedar: An Alphabet of Trees*
  by George Ella Lyon
  (Orchard, 1989).
This book introduces the leaves of trees A-Z.

- *All About Arthur: An Absolutely Absurd Alphabet*
  by Eric Carle
  (Watts, 1974).
An animal alphabet book in which Arthur the ape travels to meet other animals.

- *Alphabears: An ABC Book*
  by Kathleen and Michael Hague
  (Holt, 1984).
There is a bear for every letter of the alphabet.

- *Alphabet Soup*
  by Kate Banks
  (Knopf, 1988).
A boy and an imaginary bear go on an adventure in a bowl of alphabet soup.

- *A My Name is ALICE*
  by Jane Bayer
  (Puffin Pied Piper, 1984).
Each letter of the alphabet is represented by an animal whose name and spouse's name begin with the letter. The book is based on a playground ball game. Directions for how to play the game are given at the end of the book.

- *An Alphabet of Dinosaurs*
  by Peter Dodson
  (Scholastic, 1995).
Full-page colorful, beautiful paintings accompany pages depicting dinosaur skeletons.

- *Animal Alphabet*
  by Bert Kitchen
  (Dial, 1984).
"In this book there lies a game: spot the creatures, give each its name." Large realistic illustrations of each animal accompany the letters of the alphabet. A list of the animals is on the final page.

- *Animalia*
  by Graeme Base
  (Abrams, 1986).
Enormous, detailed pictures are given for each letter of the alphabet.

- *Anno's Alphabet: An Adventure in Imagination*
  (Crowell, 1974).
Each letter of the alphabet is pictured in a woodcut.

- *Antler, Bear, Canoe: A Northwoods Alphabet Year*
  by Betsy Bowens
  (Little, Brown, 1991).
Woodcuts alphabetically depict the changing seasons in the Minnesota woods.

Zz
Resources

More ABC Books

- *April Bubbles Chocolate: An ABC of Poetry*
  selected by Lee Bennett Hopkins
  (Simon, 1994).
This book includes 26 wonderfully diverse poems by favorite children's poets.

- *The Bird Alphabet Book*
  by Jerry Pallotta
  (Children's Press, 1986).
Birds are depicted and detailed in alphabetical order. Bird lovers will delight in this book.

- *The Christmas Alphabet*
  by Robert Sabuda
  (Orchard, 1994).
This elegant Christmas alphabet book displays the many symbols of Christmas using paper sculpture.

- *Day Care ABC*
  by Tamara Phillips
  (Albert Whitman, 1989).
Twenty-six children in a day care center perform activities that begin with the same letter of the alphabet as their name, such as "Vincent volunteers to vacuum." The concluding pages list items to look for in the pictures that start with various letters of the alphabet.

- *The Dinosaur Alphabet Book*
  by Jerry Pallotta
  (Children's Press, 1991).
Lesser-known dinosaurs are presented in this dinosaur ABC.

- *Disney's Winnie-the-Pooh's A to Zzzz*
  by Don Ferguson
  (Disney Press, 1992).
Colorful illustrations set out the alphabet in the Hundred Acre Wood with Pooh and friends.

- *The Extinct Alphabet Book*
  by Jerry Pallotta
  (Charlesbridge, 1993).
For each letter of the alphabet, this book tells about a creature that no longer exists. Vibrant colors and a paragraph of text per page.

- *Gretchen's ABC*
  by Gretchen Dow Simpson
  (HarperCollins, 1991).
Gretchen has painted a familiar object for each letter of the alphabet.

- *The Guinea Pig A, B, C*
  by Kate Duke
  (Dutton, 1983).
A guinea pig acts out a word for each letter of the alphabet.

- *It Begins with an A*
  by Stephanie Calmenson
  (Hyperion, 1993).
Rhyming riddles are presented with picture clues.

- *The Ocean Alphabet Book*
  by Jerry Pallotta
  (Charlesbridge, 1986).
An alphabet book featuring an ocean creature for every letter of the alphabet.

- *A Prairie Alphabet*
  by Yvette Moore
  (Tundra, 1992).
Both artist and author are prairie residents of Canada, and bring their love of and experience in the prairie environment to this alphabet book.

- *Sandra Boynton A to Z*
  (Little Simon, 1984).
A simple board book with each letter of the alphabet humorously illustrated by an animal doing an activity.

Learning to Read with Mini-Books

The four sets of mini-books introduce pre-kindergarten and kindergarten children to beginning reading experiences.

In **Set I**, children are introduced to letters and pictures that start with the letter sound. In **Set II**, children work on sound-symbol associations of the letters. The letters are placed in a simple format and children name, sound, and match them to the key picture. In **Set III**, children read and work with short vowel word patterns. The vowel pattern is boldly placed on the title page of each book with a supporting picture. Words on subsequent pages follow that pattern. Supporting pictures help guide children in giving the correct pattern word. A few beginning sight words are introduced. In **Set IV**, children read and work on short vowel words in context using the vowel patterns in Set III. Picture clues help children work out special vowel patterns and sight words.

A chart listing letters, word patterns, and sight words begins on page 243. Check the listing and work on the letters, patterns, and sight words covered in the particular mini-book set before introducing the book.

mini-books can be used with individual children or with a small group of two or three. When working with a group, each child should have a book to work with.

How to Make

Duplicate the pages for each book in each set. Cut the pages apart and assemble by page number. Staple pages together on the left side. If desired, make a construction paper cover for the book. Write the title on the cover with a felt pen.

How to Use

For **Set I**, have the child name the letters on the title page. Ask the child to give the sounds for the letters. If he or she is unable to, give words, names of objects in the classroom, or names of classmates that begin with the letter sounds. Elicit from the child the letter sounds for the symbols and pictures on the next page.

For **Set II**, again have the child name the letters. Then turn to the next page. Have the child point to or trace the first letter on the page. Have the child name it, give the sound, and then name the key picture across from the letter to check. If the child has difficulty giving the sound, say that it starts the same way as the key picture on the right side of the page. Continue through the book. The child may want to "read" the book again alone or with a friend.

For **Set III**, have the child look at the key picture on the title page and name it. Tell the child that the last part of the word/name rhymes with the vowel pattern on the page. Have the child trace the vowel pattern with a finger, naming the letters aloud. Then have the child give the sound of the vowel pattern.

Tell the child that the next words in the book will have that same vowel pattern. If the child forgets, remind him or her of the key picture on the title page. Guide the child to read the words on the next pages using the vowel pattern sound. Supporting pictures guide the child. Help the child read the sight words and the vowel pattern words, blending them smoothly into a phrase.

To study the sight words introduced in each book, make sight word cards from 3 x 5 index cards. Write one word with a black felt pen on each card. Tell the sight word. Have the child trace the letters of the word and say the word a few times. Do the same for the other sight words.

For **Set IV**, discuss the picture on the title page. Have a child read the title. Say that the title tells what the story will be about. Children may want to guess what will happen in the story. Have them say the title again. Turn to the next page. Discuss what is on the page or what is happening. Remind the child of the title again if necessary. Have the child read the sentence below the picture. If the child has difficulty, point out any vowel patterns previously studied or the sounds of the letters learned. Blend and read. Slowly running a finger under or over the words as the child reads helps the child visually track from left to right. Reread any page that needs more practice. Have the child read the book again, alone or with a friend.

As in Set III above, make sight word cards for the sight words introduced in this set. Have children practice them until mastery is achieved.

1

Set III	Set IV		
	Title	**Phonetic Word Patterns**	**Sight Words****
[at] hat mat cat rat bat fat flat (sight word: a)	The Hat	hat mat bat man	a this the on is in look no
[an] fan can man tan pan van plan (sight word: the)	Dan	Dan can ran man bat	the at is look has can and on not get
[am] ham ram jam yam dam clam (sight words: a the and)	Sam	Sam cat cab in jam	a on is in has can go up stop not
[ig] wig pig dig jig fig big (sight words: a the to in)	The Fig	fig pig big jig at can rat	look at the said big it is up we are down I go has
[in] fin pin spin twin tin bin in win (sight words: a the to)	Spin, Spin!	spin in	the in up said down come to see me go and out *bee *spider

*A few words not covered in the **Set III** Word Pattern books are included. Children work these out using picture clues and phonetics.

**Some phonetic words are repeated as sight words due to frequency in early reading material.

The suffix s, meaning more than one, is introduced. Guide children to add the /s/ after the base word with picture support for plurals and the s present tense verb ending, i.e. I jump. She jumps.

Overview

Set III	Set IV — Title	Phonetic Word Patterns	Sight Words**
[ip] lips rip flip zip drip tip ship (sight words: a to the)	Skip and Kip	Skip Kip trips *pals *swim	go and are good to like play ball they take *hide-and-seek *good-night
[op] stop pop mop top hop hops (sight words: a the and one two)	Flip, Flop!	hop flop dig pig *sad *had *glad am flip	the is look said I so up stop down funny one oh me my *ear *ears *bunny am will give you this two are to
[ot] hot tot cot dot spot pots (sight words: a the big two three)	The Pot	dot spot hot got pot lot stop at cat rat *had *nap *map dig	this is the said to saw he here stop we are at it was and a got up they
[og] jog log hog dog, frog, frogs (sight words: a the one two three)	The Log	log bog hog dog frogs in hop *jump *bump	a the on in three little saw jump and splash went into
[ub] sub rub club tub tubs cub cubs (sight words: a the to one four)	The Tub	rub dub tub cub cubs	a the one two three four are in now there jumps out is

*A few words not covered in the **Set III** Word Pattern books are included. Children work these out using picture clues and phonetics.

**Some phonetic words are repeated as sight words due to frequency in early reading material.

The suffix s, meaning more than one, is introduced. Guide children to add the /s/ after the base word with picture support for plurals and the s present tense verb ending, i.e. I jump. She jumps.

Set IV	Title	Phonetic Word Patterns	Sight Words**	Set III
	The Jug	jug rug bugs snug get stop	a the one two three four five little go up stop do not into are in help said get us out down	[ug] jug jug rug mug hug bug bugs plug (sight words: a the big one five)
	Rum-Tum-Tum	rum tum drum gum plum hum chum can tin pop get lot got	a I can play my get do with	[um] gum drum chum plums (sight words: a big my two three four)
	The Pet	pet get gets met got man hen then	me eggs said here is a the to give I girl with yellow for *Mama *bird *goat will you got then now she my gets from	[et] wet pet pets net vet jet (sight words: a the big my)
	My Red Hen	hen pen den red	come here my little to me is not here she no in the oh look baby one two *chicks three four five	[en] hen hens pen pens ten men den (sight words: a the in three four five)
	Ned and His Sled	Ned sled can *fast	the to got out his green here I go said up and is on down can in	[ed] Ned red fed sled wed bed beds (sight words: a the to five)

*A few words not covered in the **Set III** Word Pattern books are included. Children work these out using picture clues and phonetics.
**Some phonetic words are repeated as sight words due to frequency in early reading material.

The suffix s, meaning more than one, is introduced. Guide children to add the /s/ or /s/ after the base word with picture support for plurals and the s present tense verb ending, i.e. I jump. She jumps.

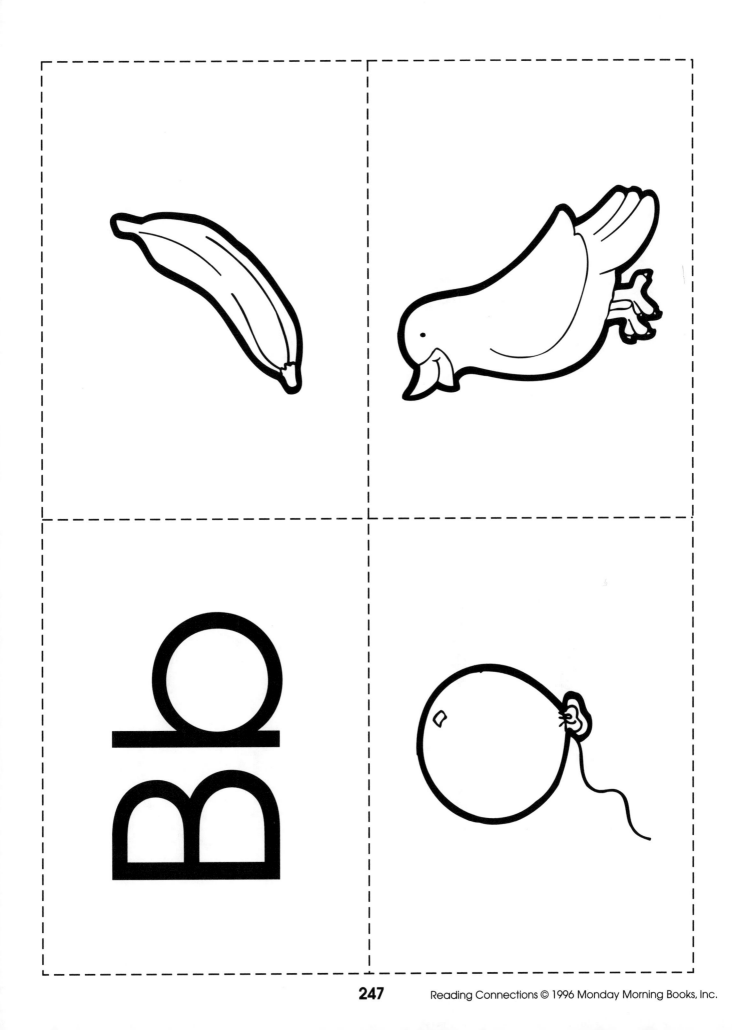

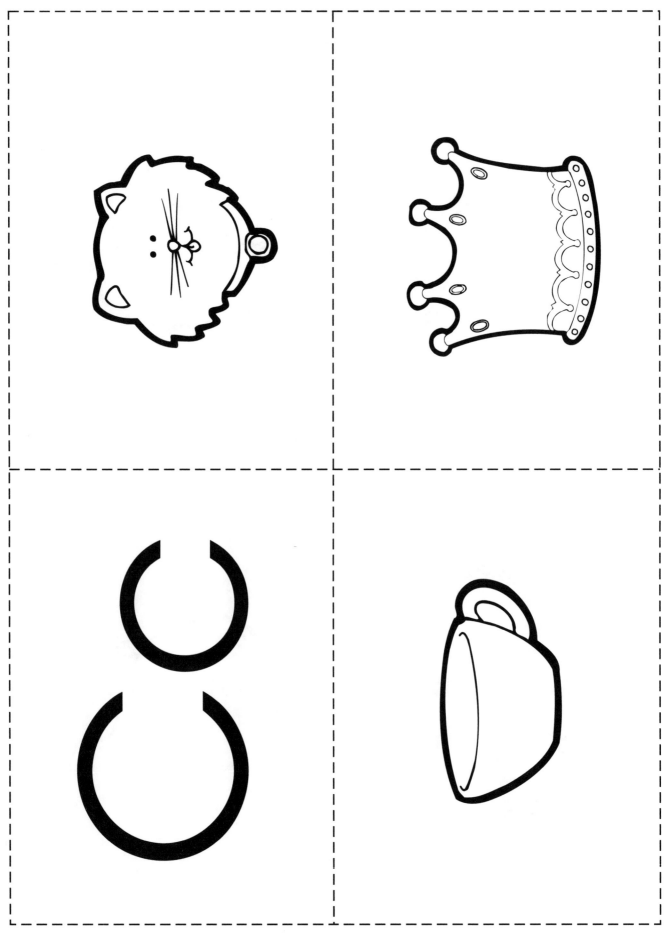

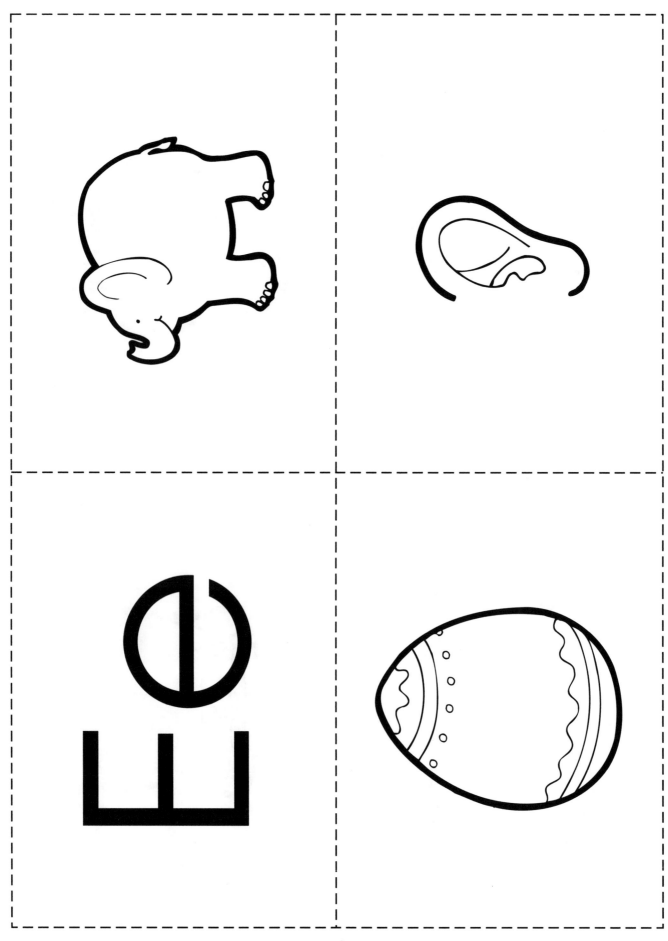

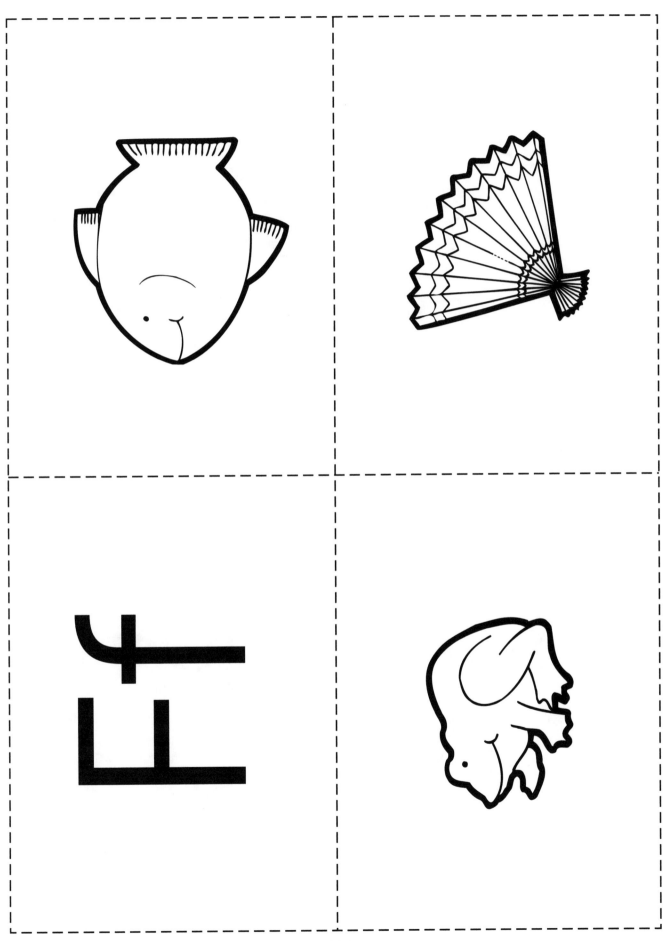

F f

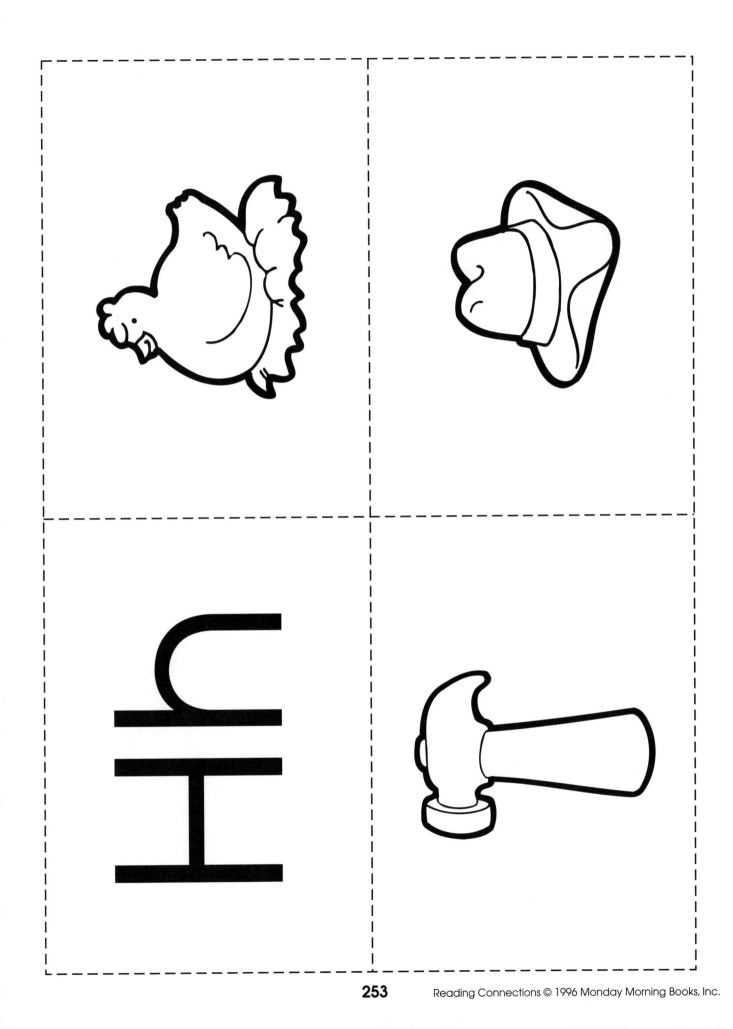

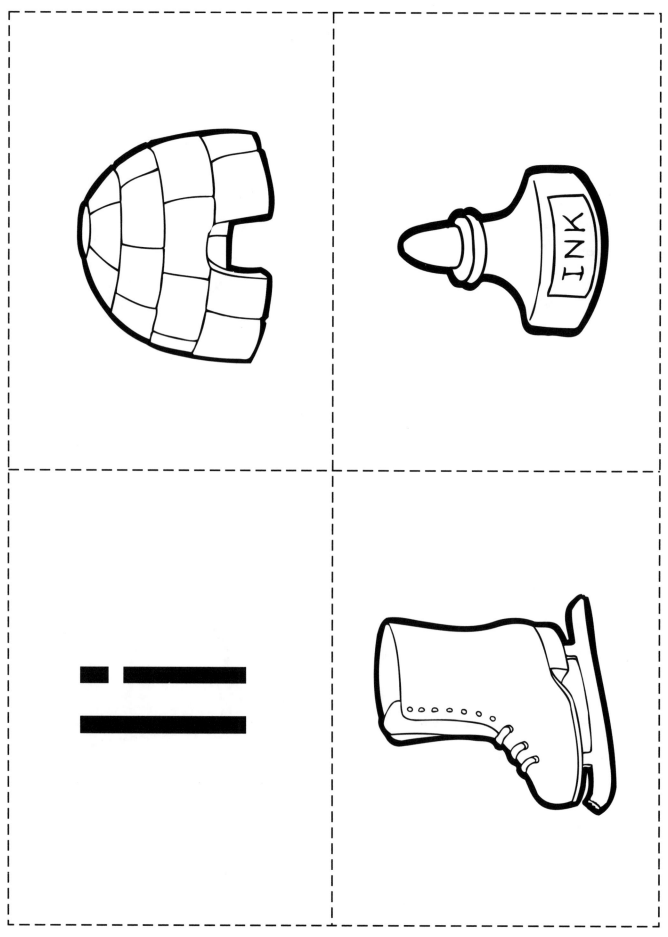

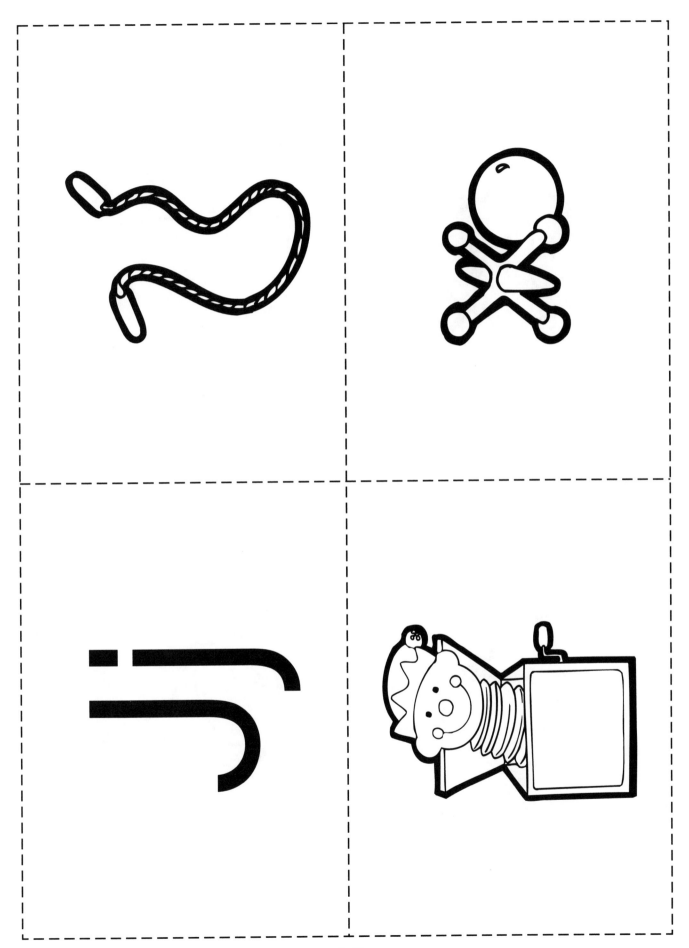

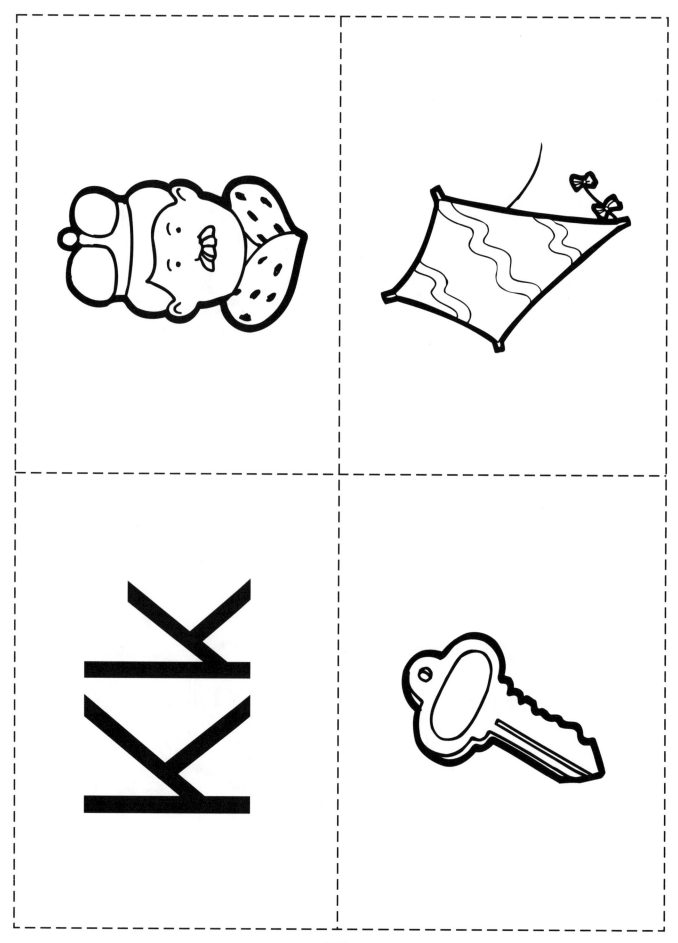

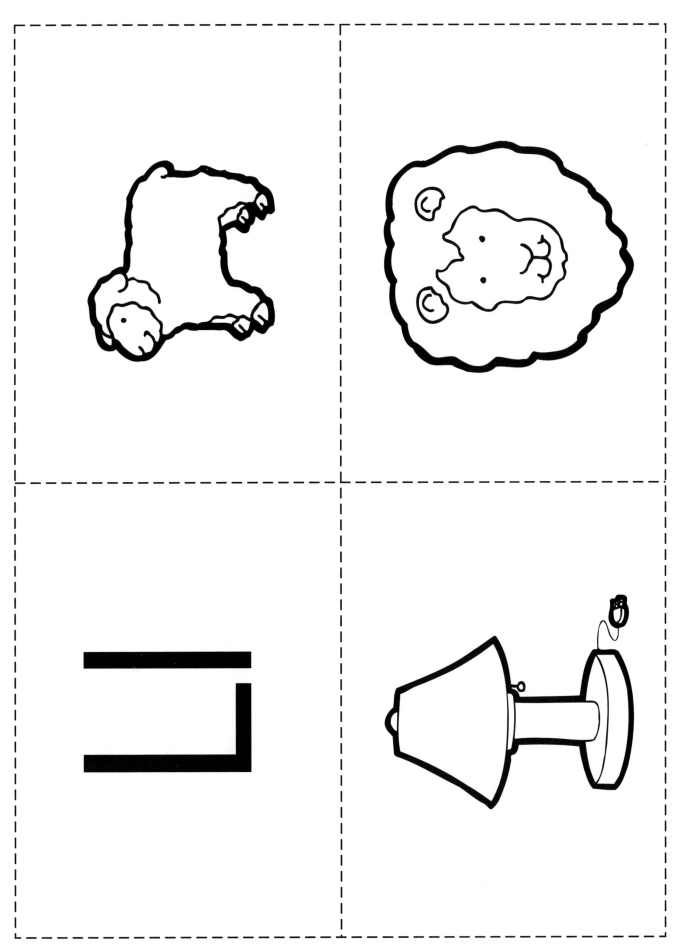

Reading Connections © 1996 Monday Morning Books, Inc.

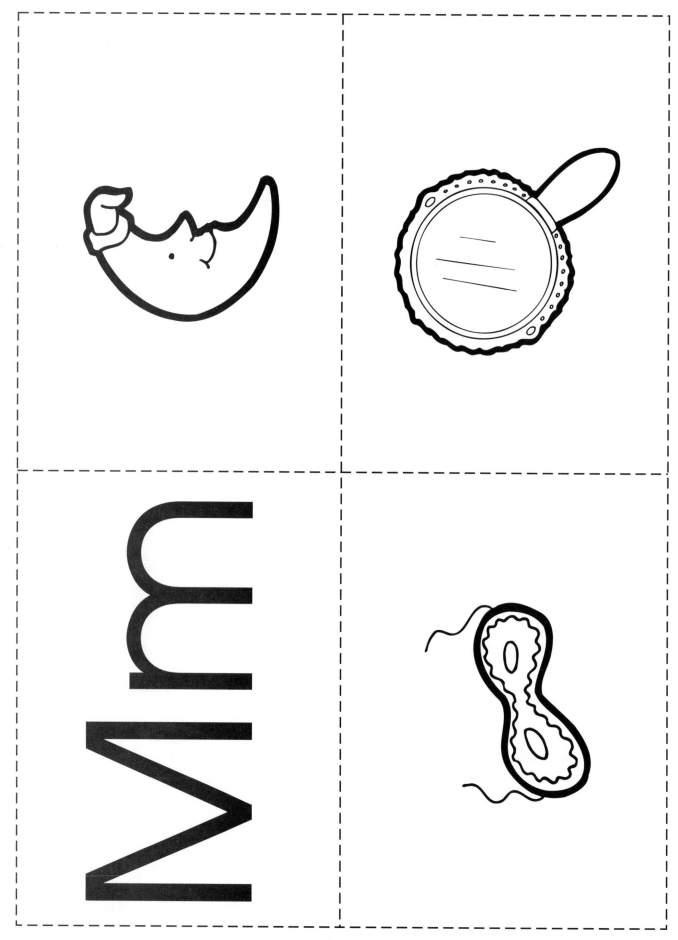

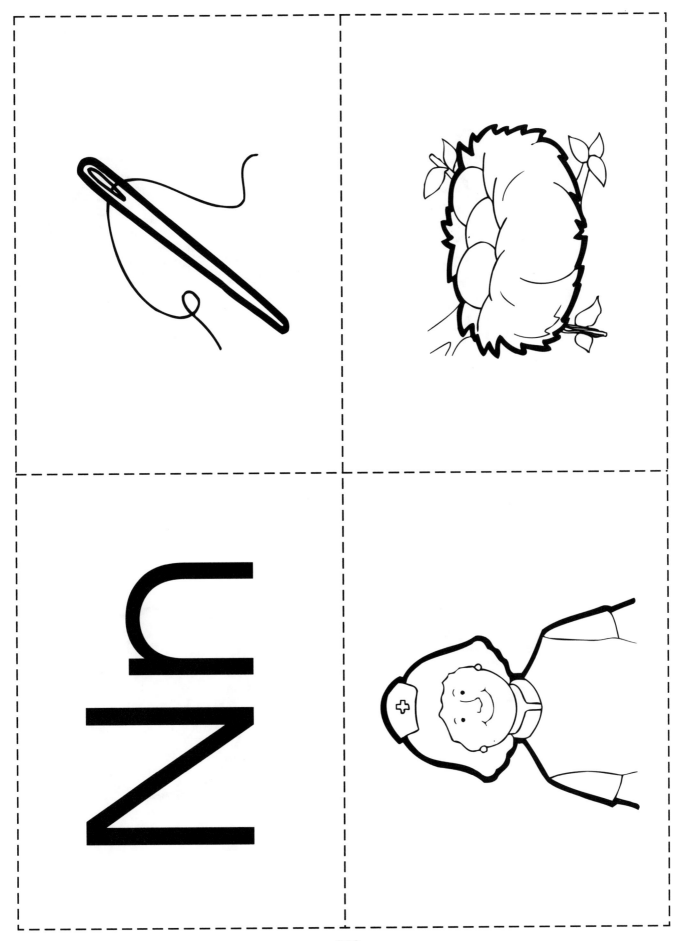

Reading Connections © 1996 Monday Morning Books, Inc.

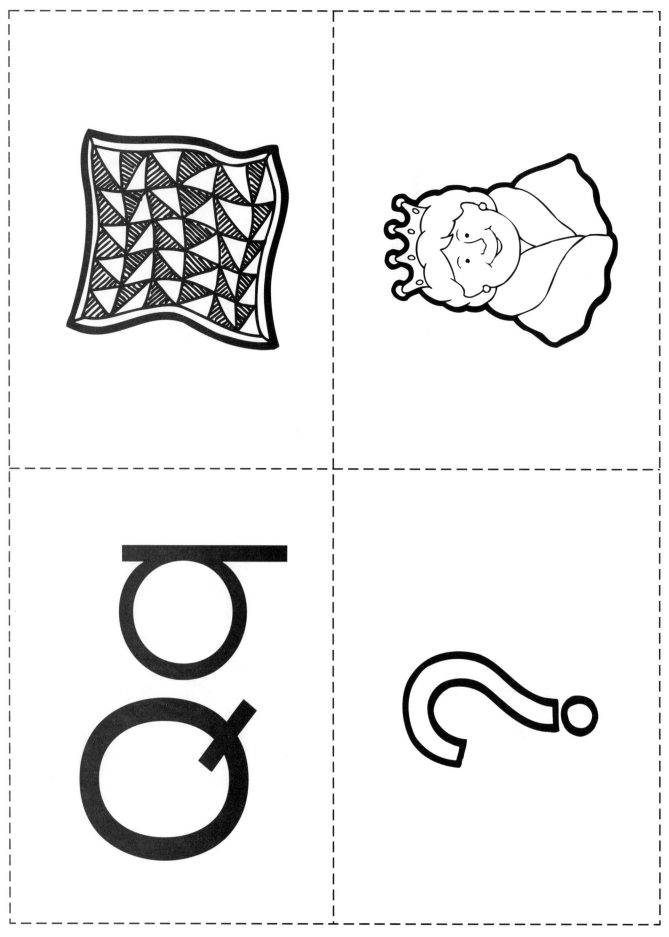

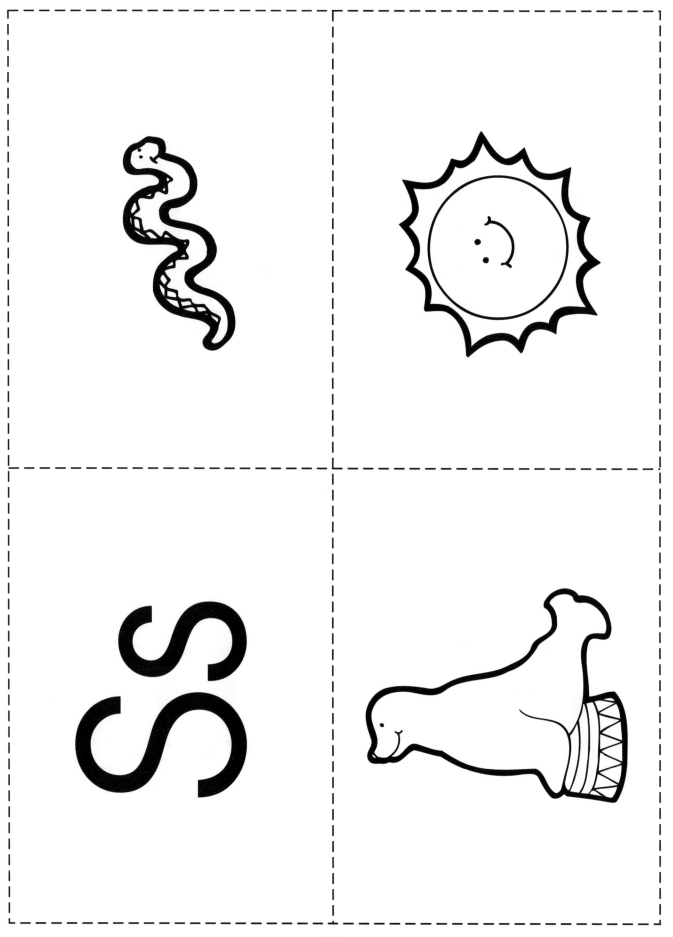

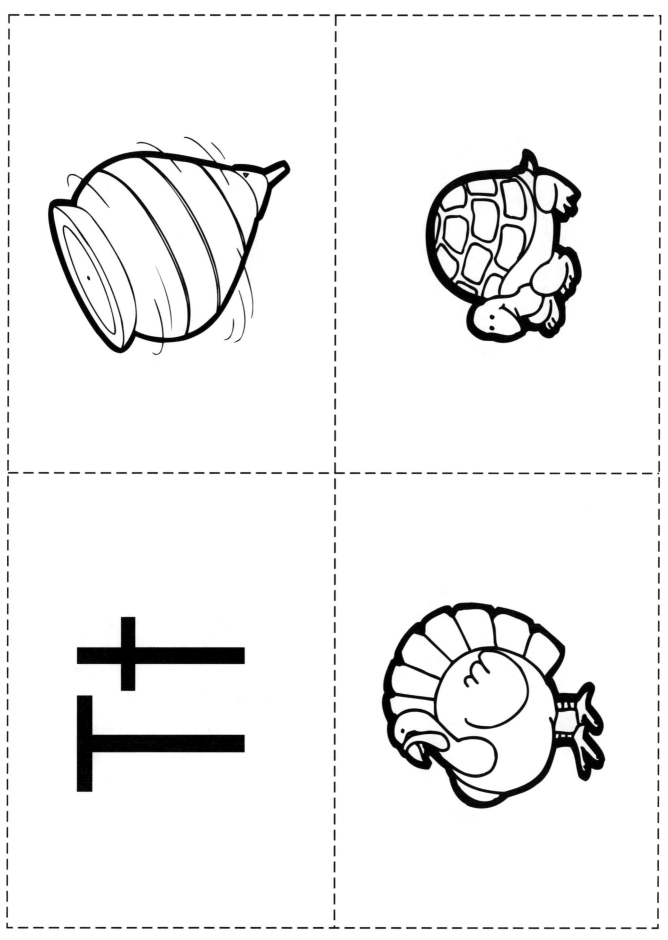

Reading Connections © 1996 Monday Morning Books, Inc.

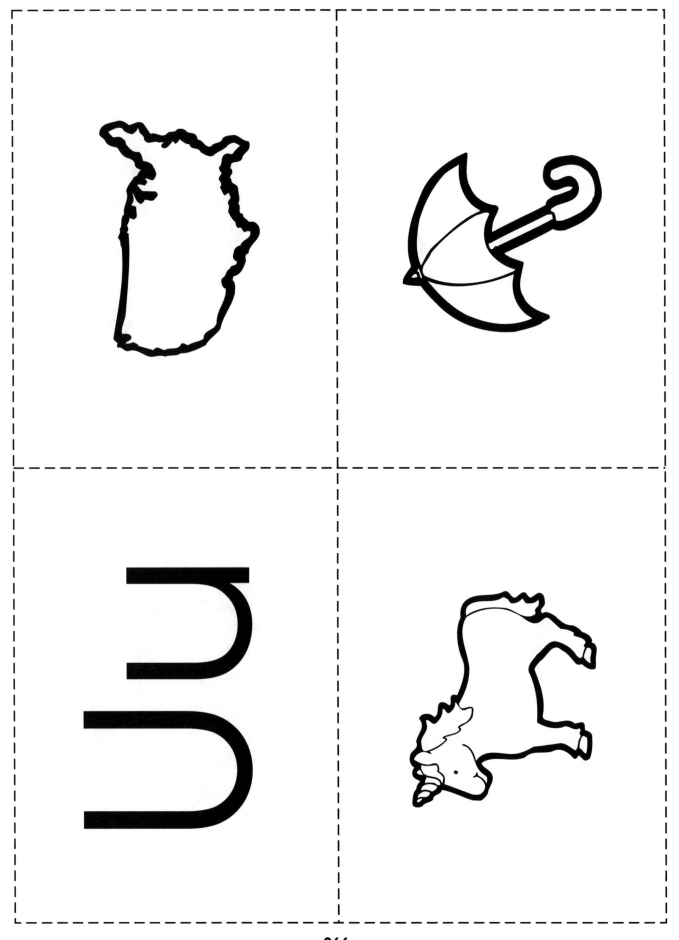

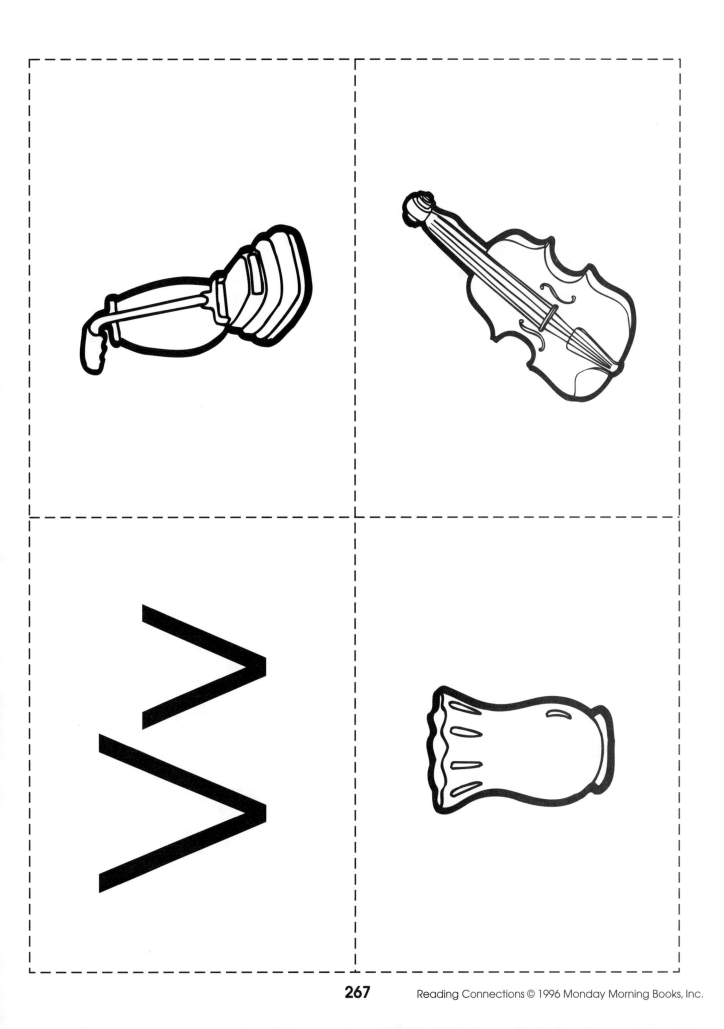

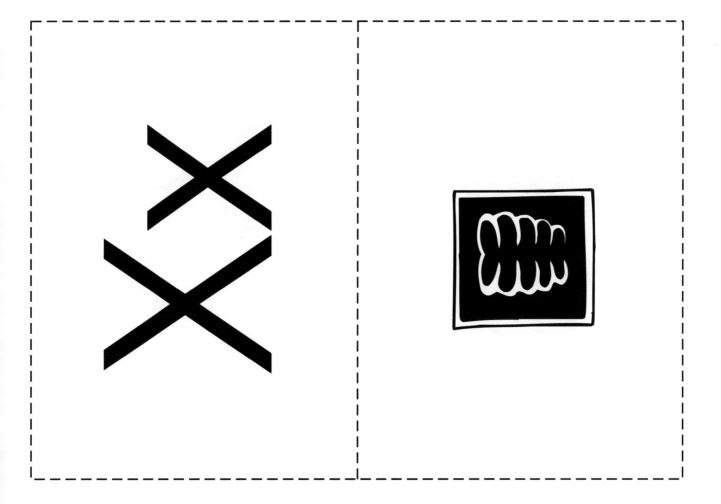

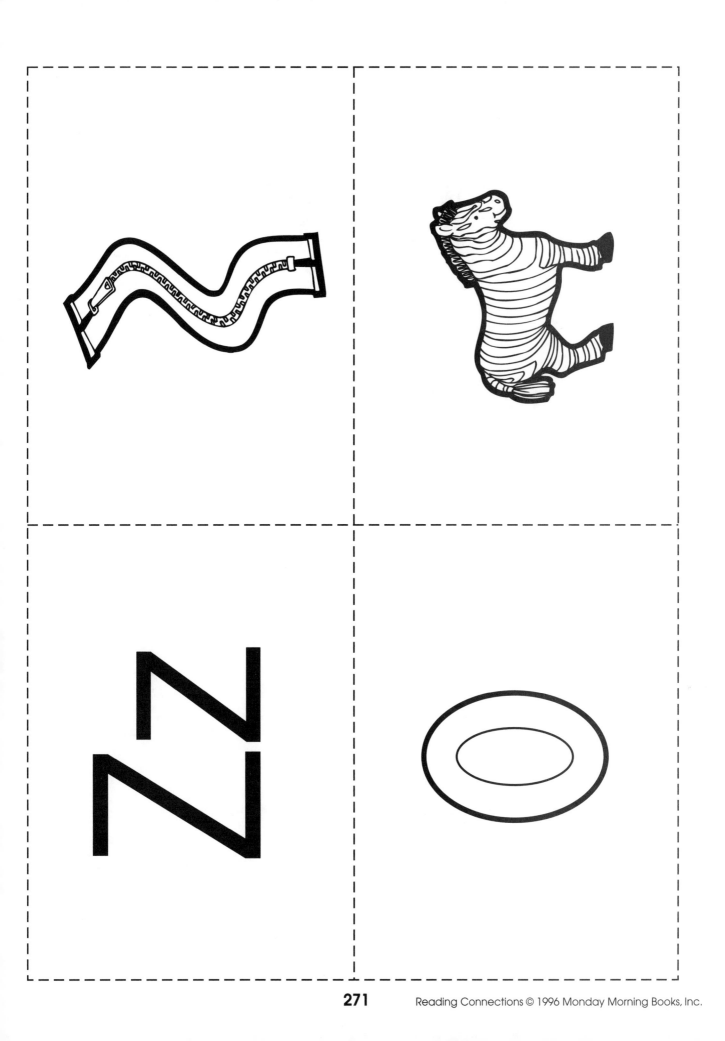

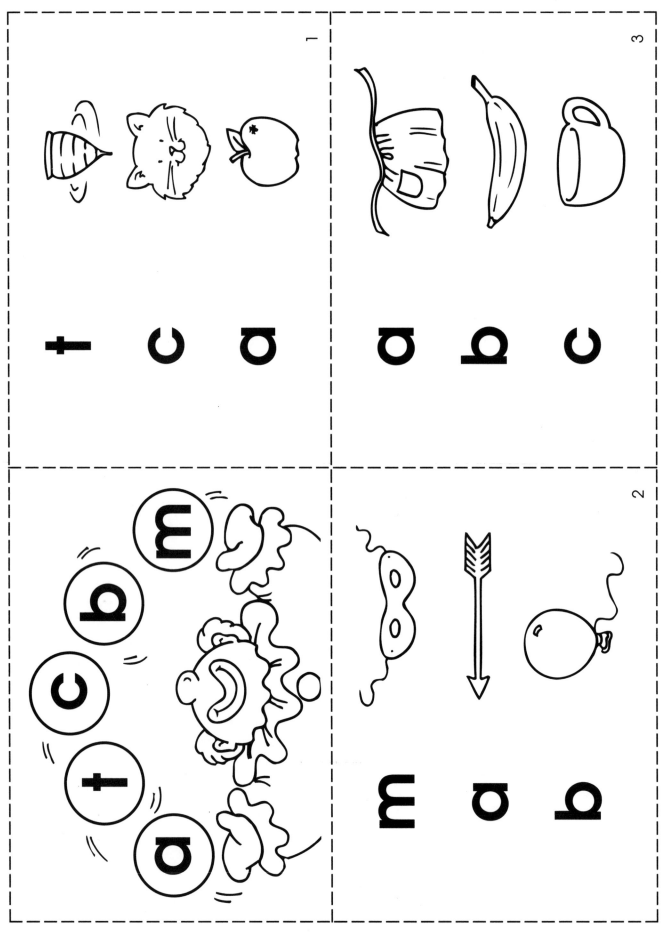

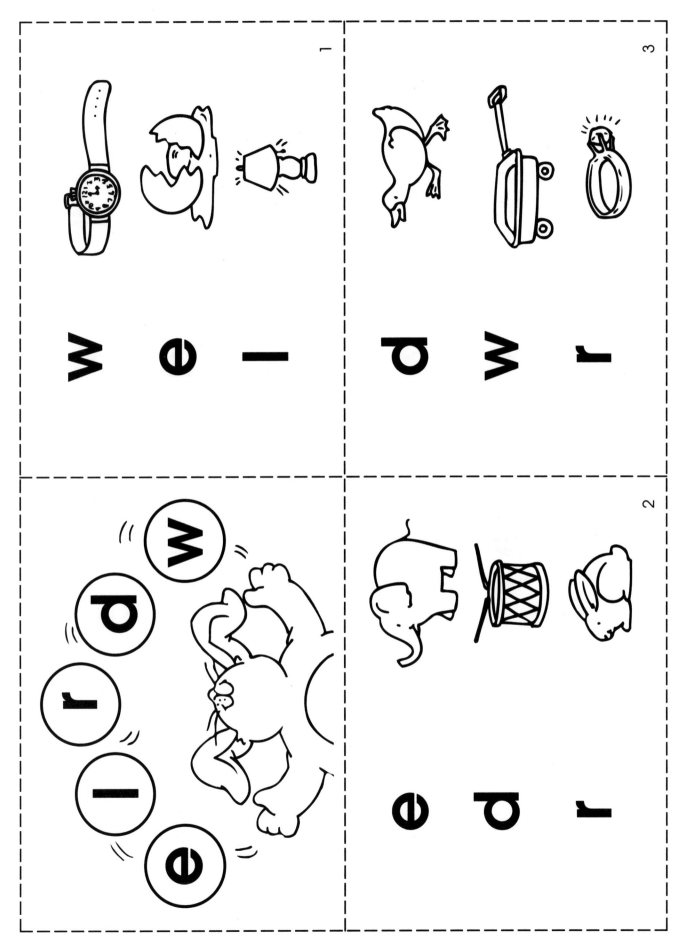

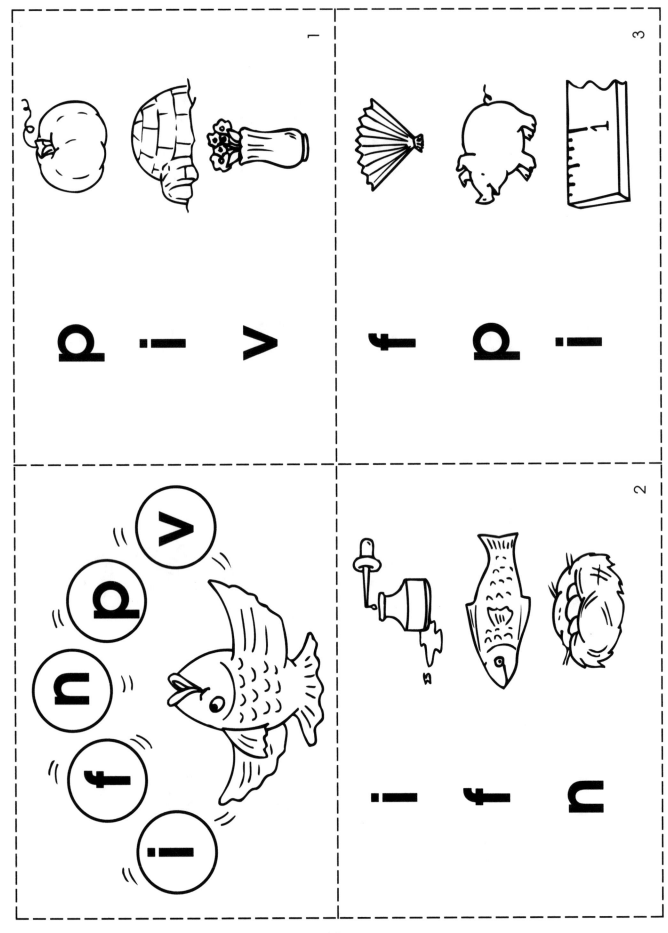

1

p i v

3

f p i

2

i f n

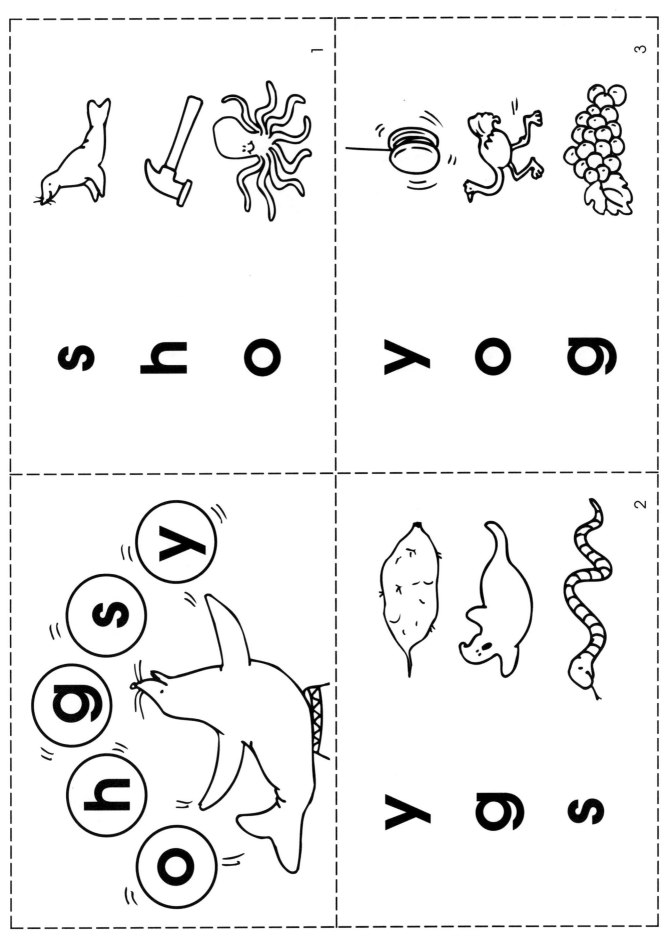

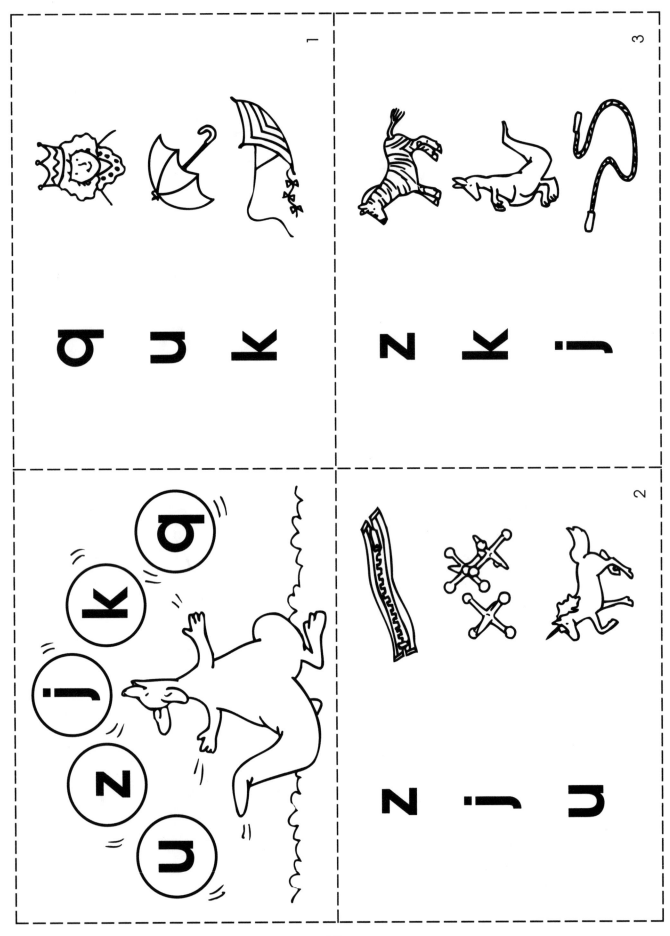

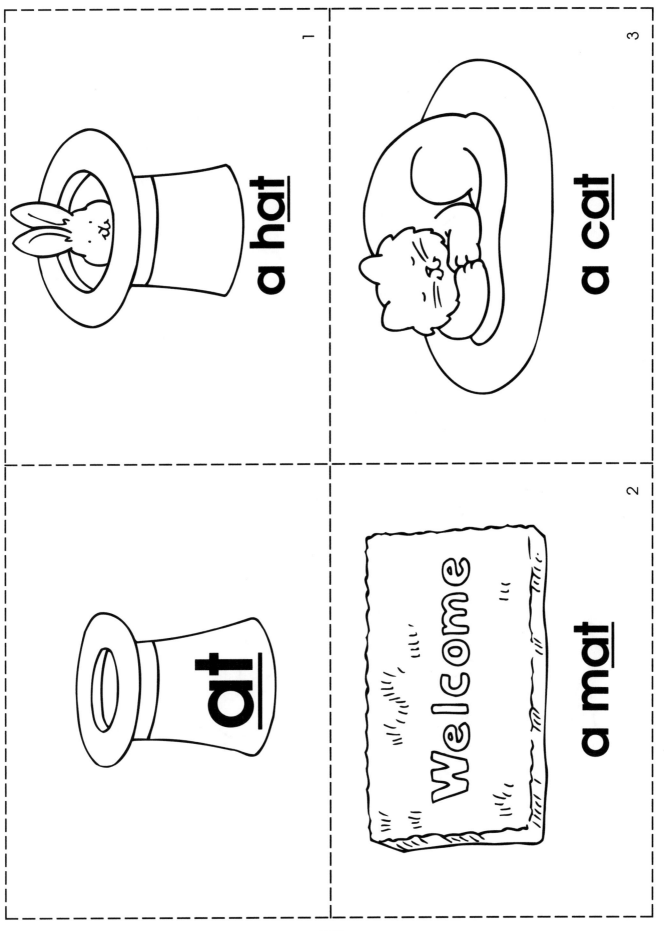

1

a hat

3

a cat

at

2

Welcome

a mat

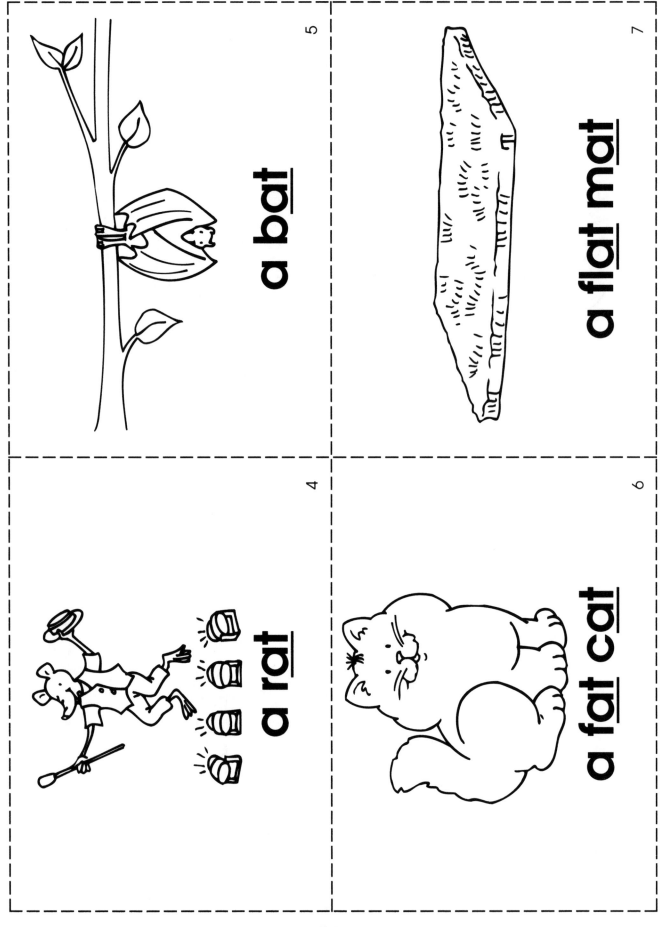

a bat

a flat mat

a rat

a fat cat

5

7

4

6

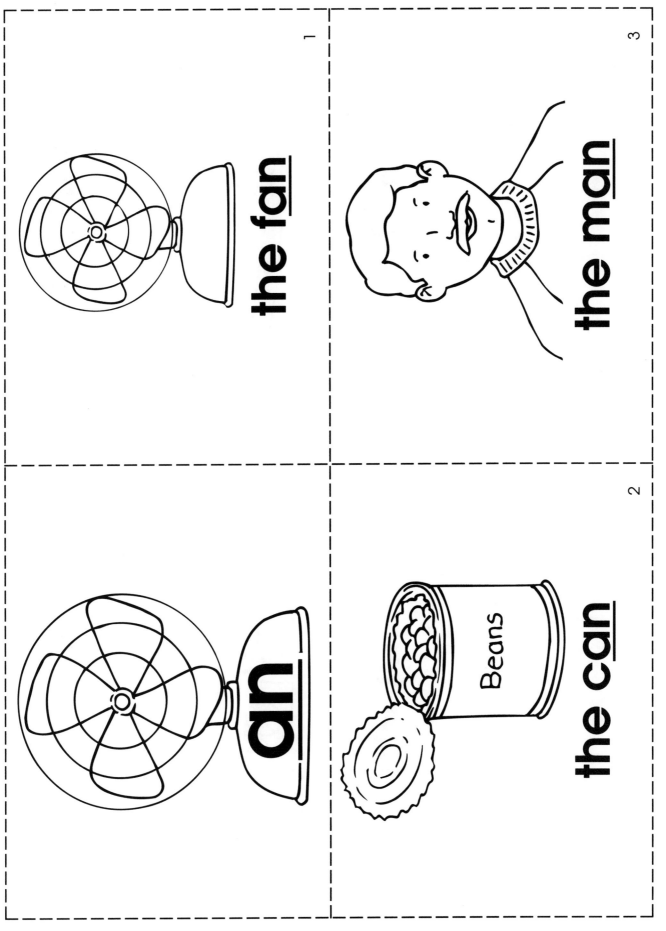

the fan

1

the man

3

an

the can

2

279

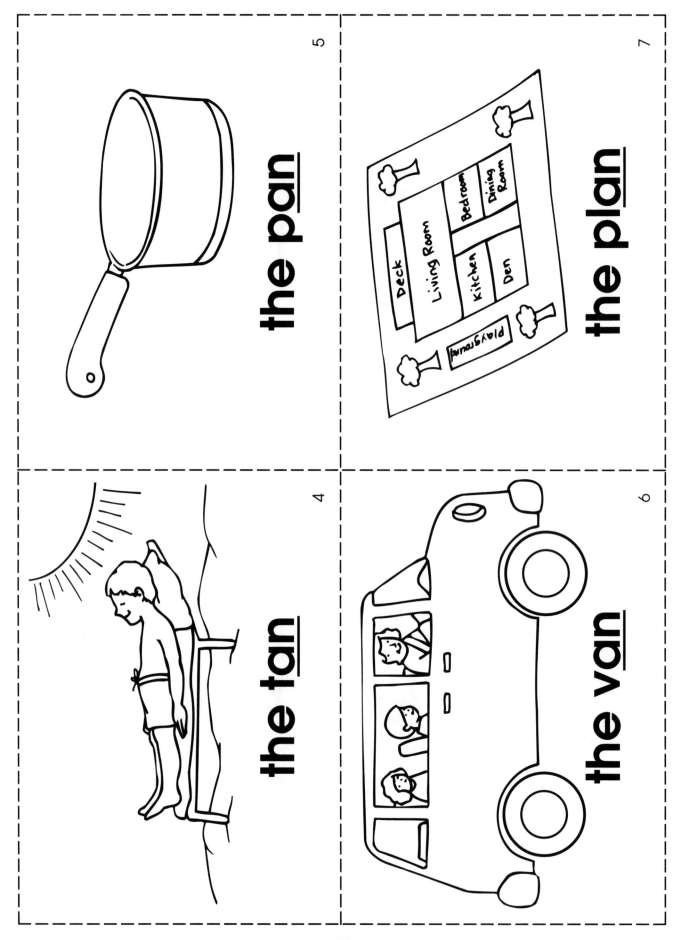

the pan

5

the plan

7

the tan

4

the van

6

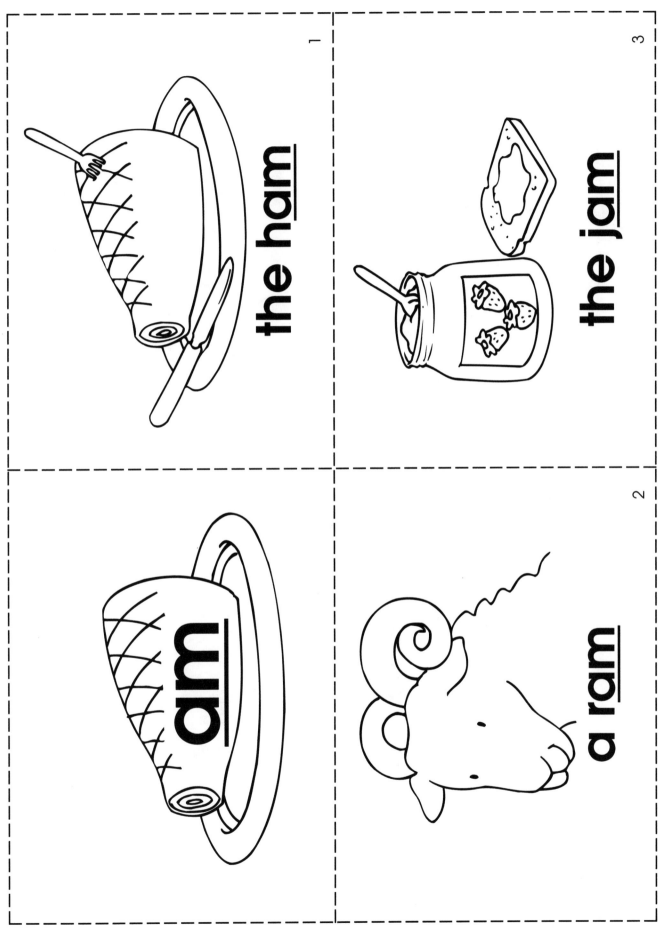

1

the ham

3

the jam

ham

2

a ram

Reading Connections © 1996 Monday Morning Books, Inc.

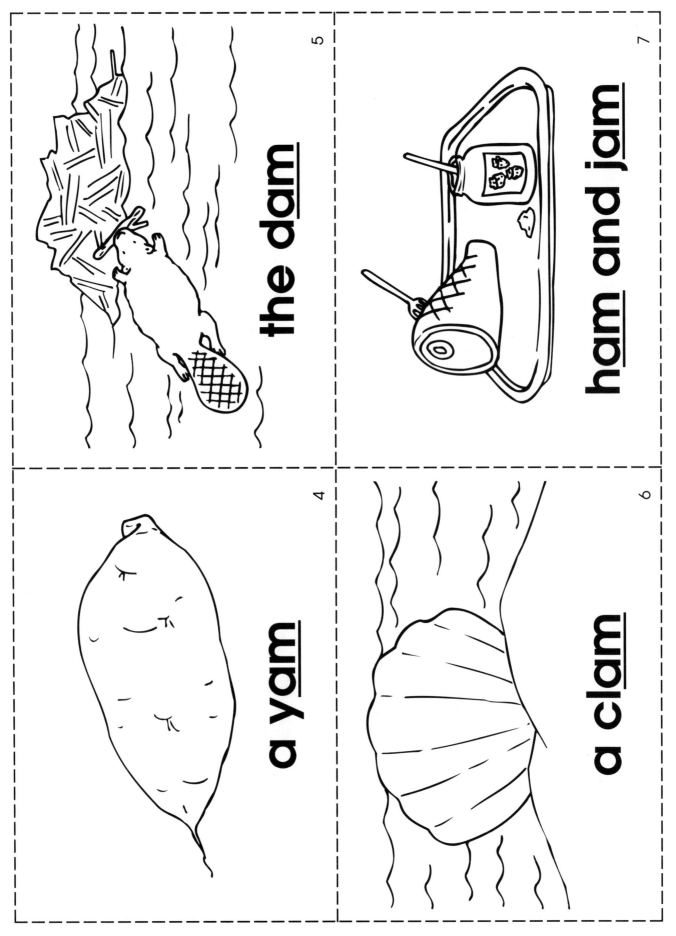

the dam

5

ham and jam

7

a yam

4

a clam

6

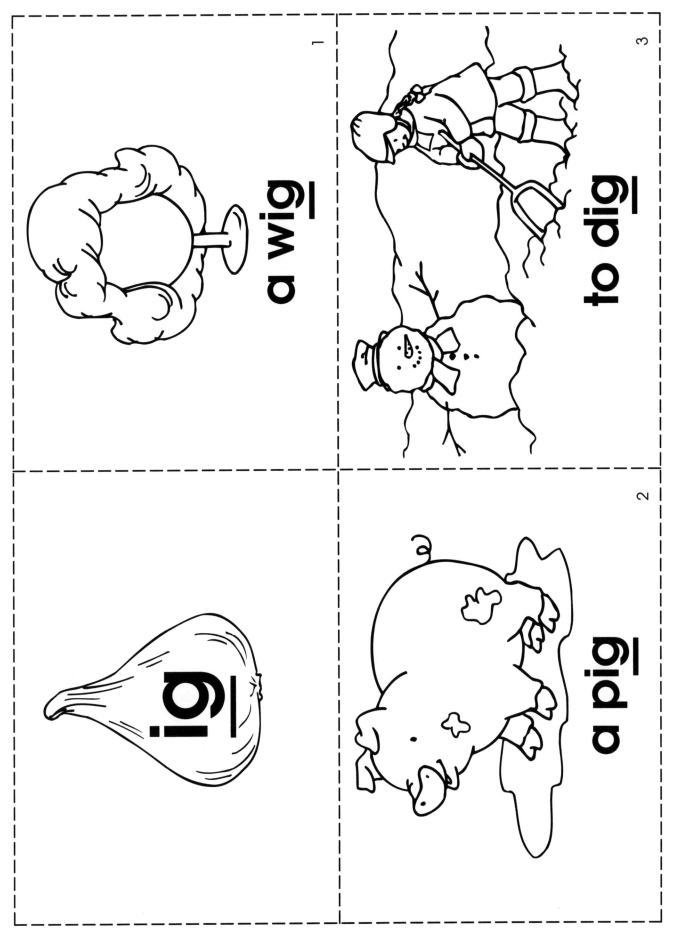

a wig

to dig

a pig

ig

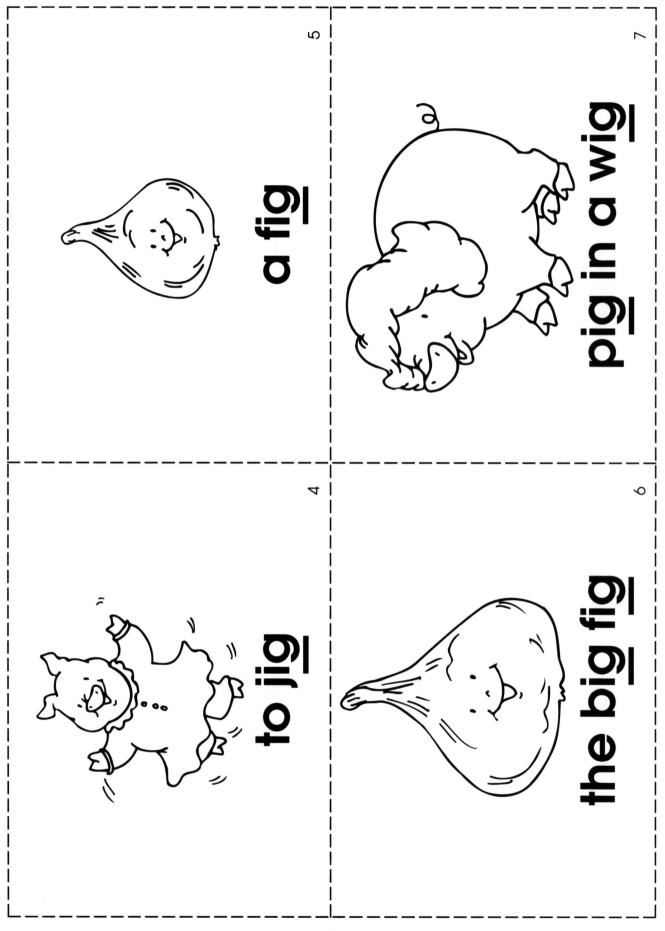

a fig

5

pig in a wig

7

to jig

4

the big fig

6

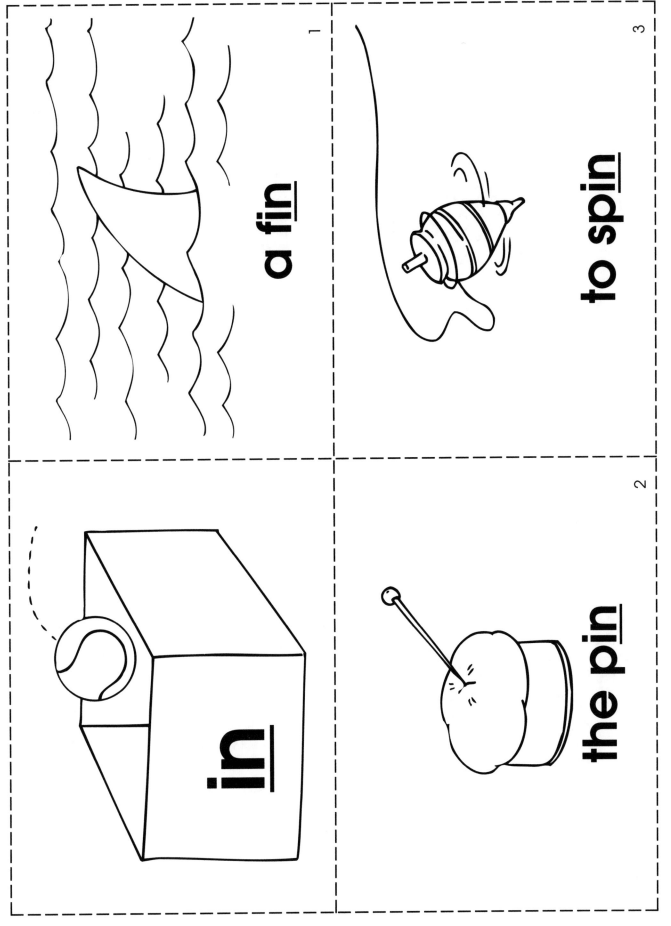

a fi<u>n</u>

1

to spi<u>n</u>

3

in

the pi<u>n</u>

2

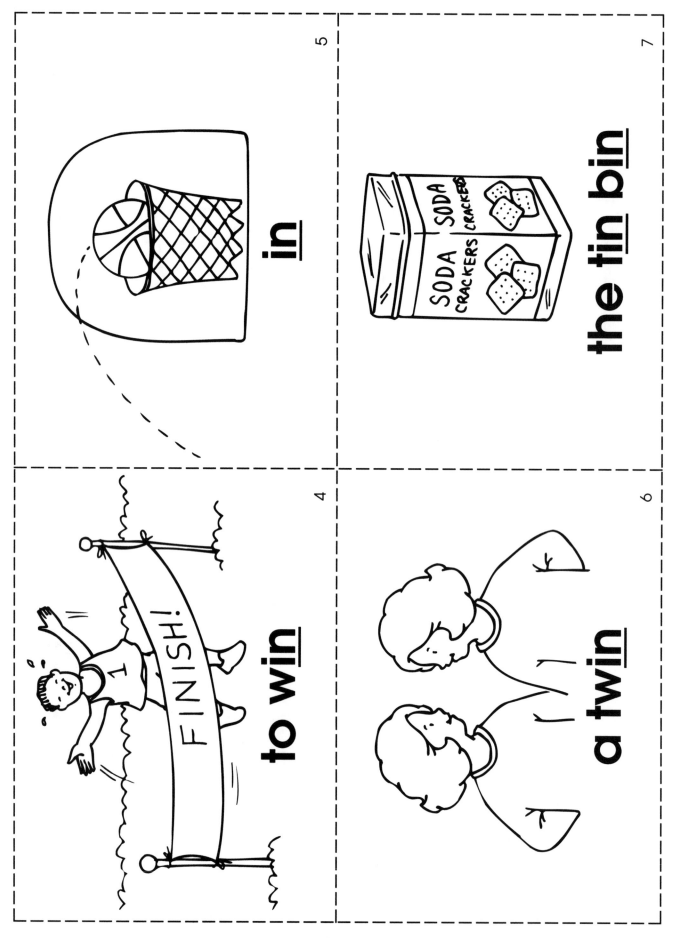

in

the tin bin

to win

a twin

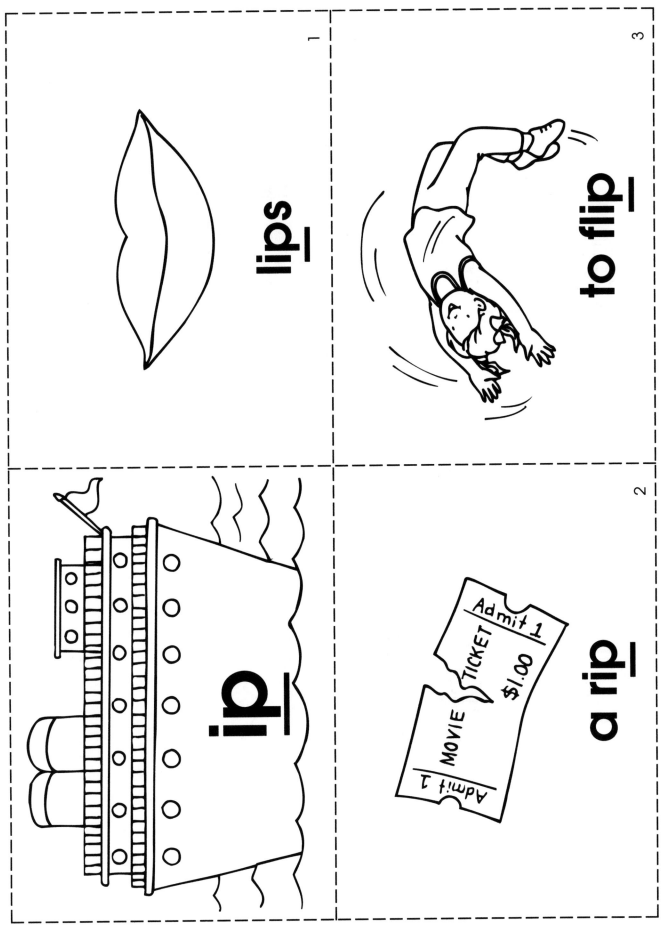

lip_s_

a rip_

to flip_

ip_

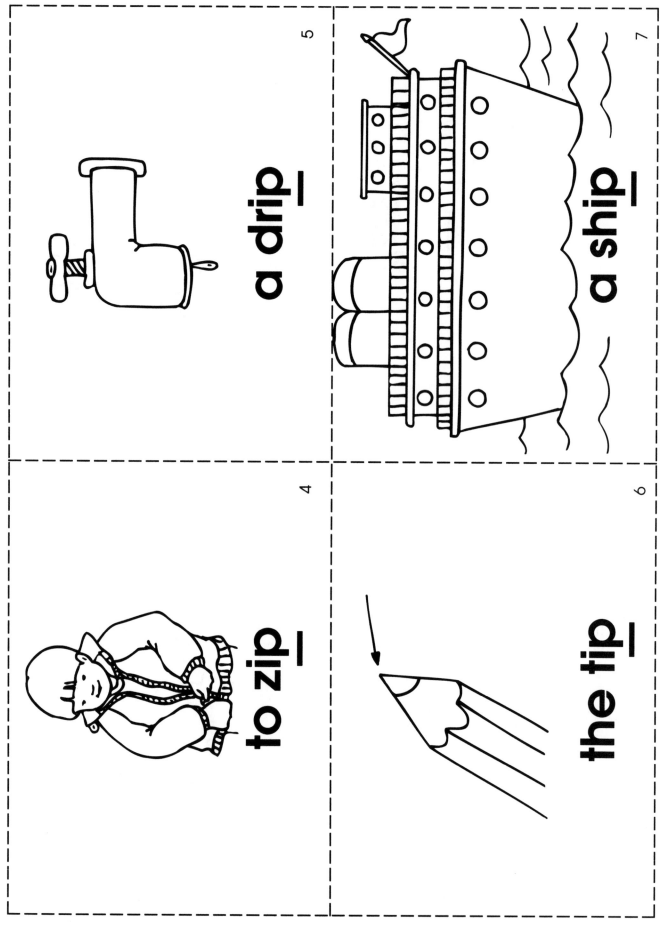

a drip
_

5

a ship
_

7

to zip
_

4

the tip
_

6

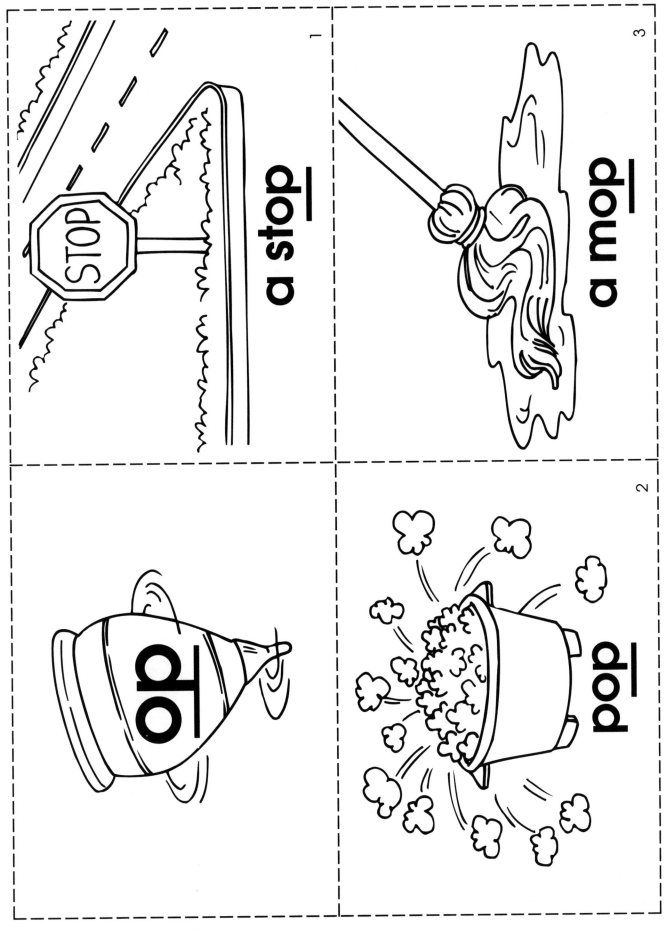

a stop

a mop

pop

up

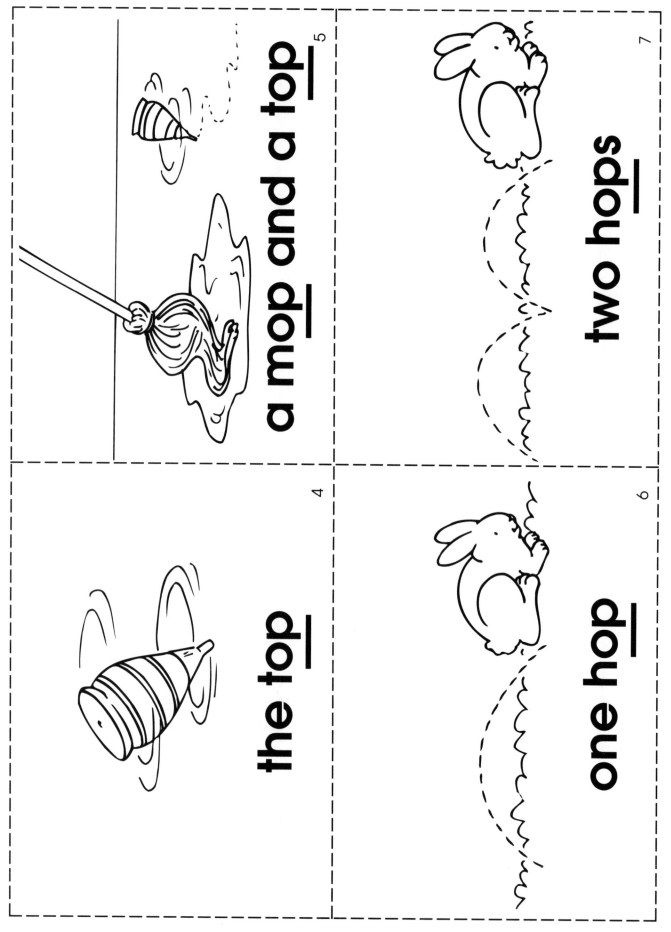

a mop and a top

5

the top

4

two hops

7

one hop

6

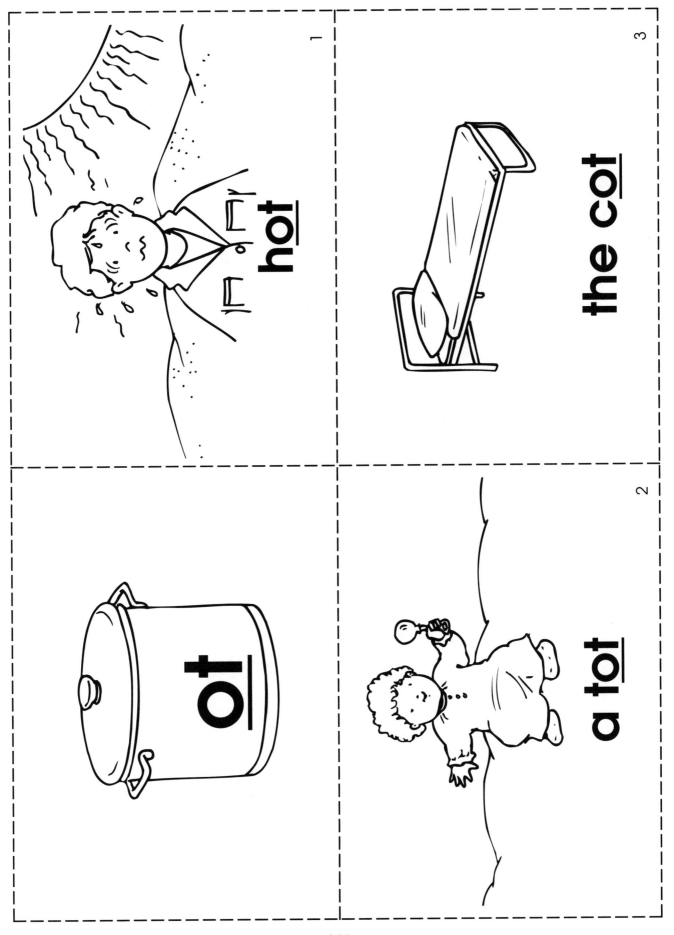

1

hot

3

the cot

ot

2

a tot

291 Reading Connections © 1996 Monday Morning Books, Inc.

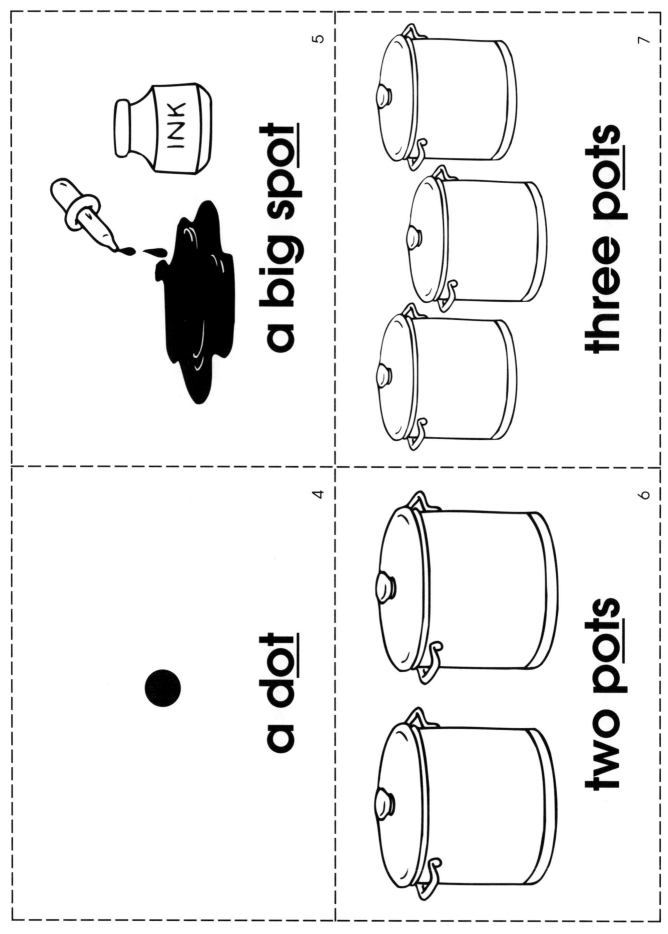

5

a big spot

7

three pots

4

a dot

6

two pots

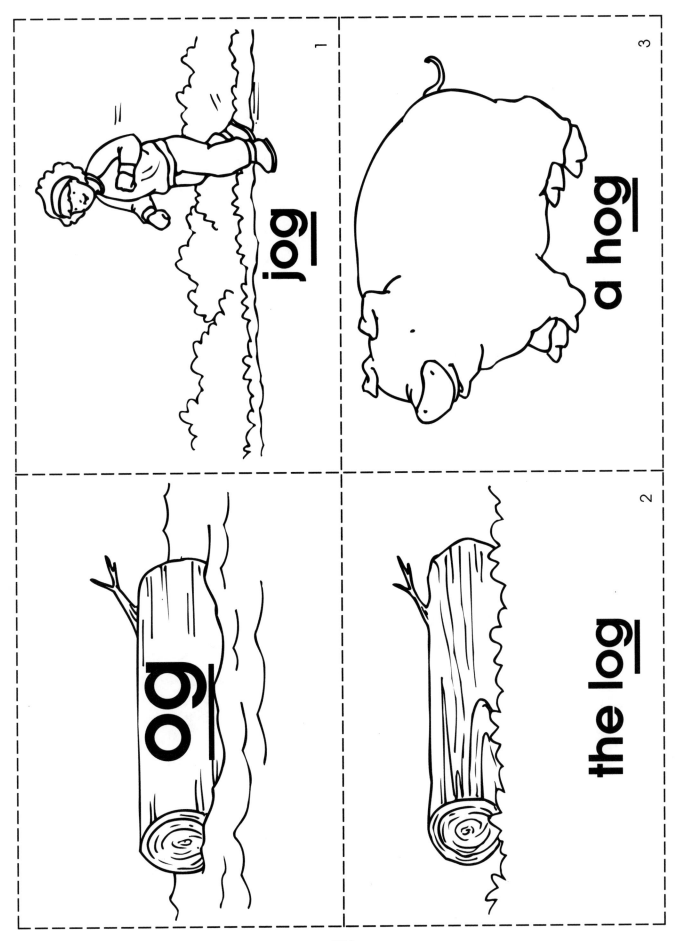

jog

a hog

og

the log

293

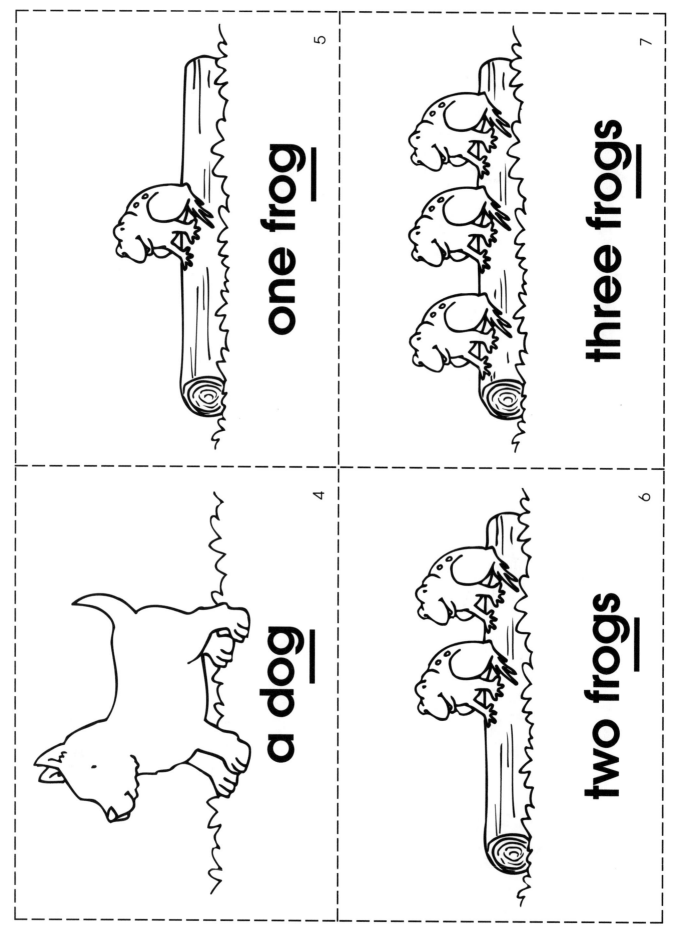

5

one frog

7

three frogs

4

a dog

6

two frogs

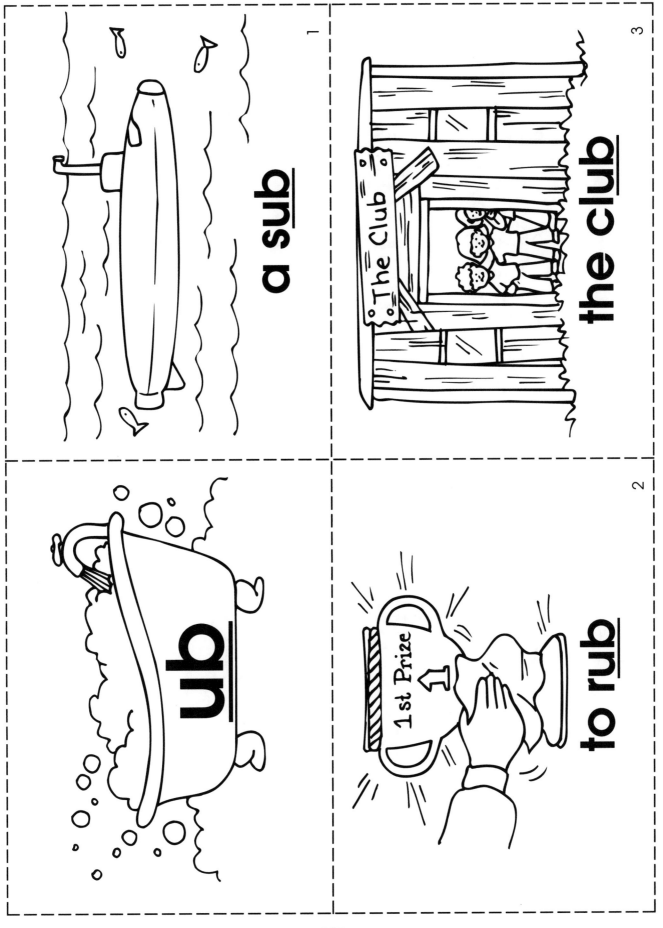

1

a sub

3

the club

ub

2

to rub

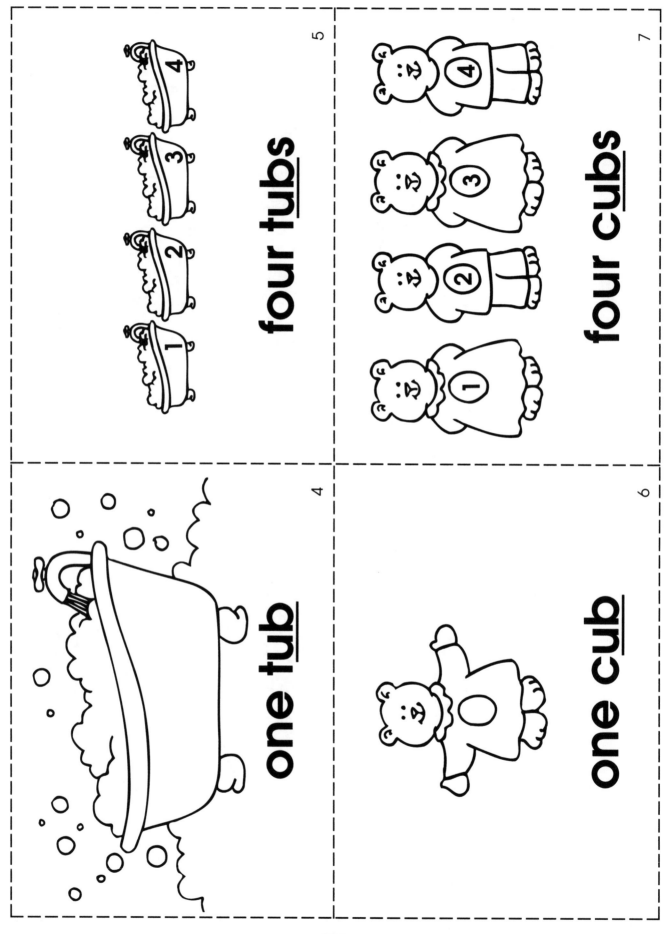

four tubs

5

four cubs

7

one tub

4

one cub

6

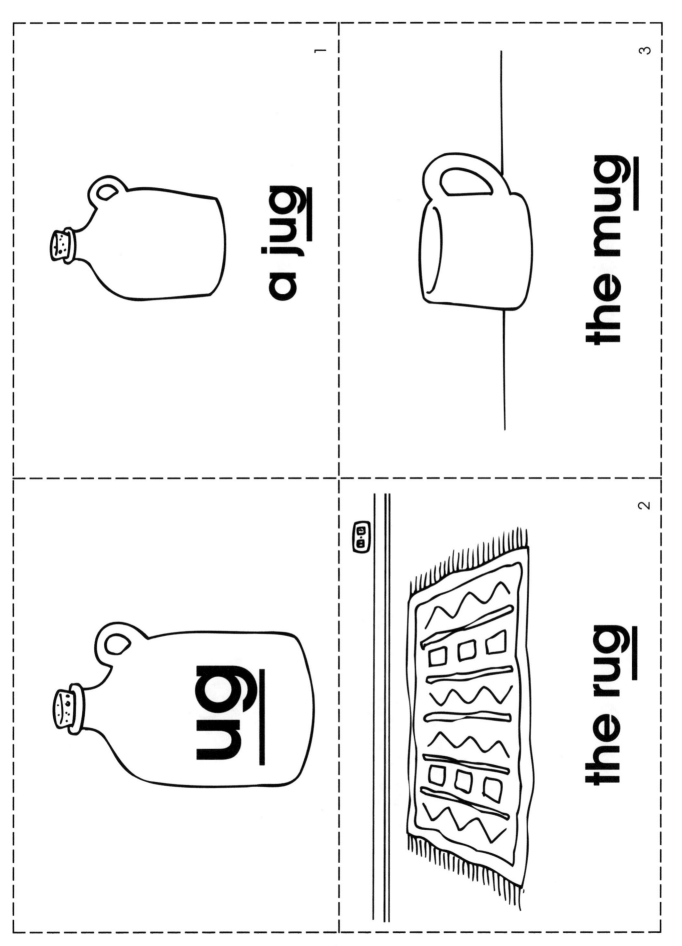

1

a jug

3

the mug

2

the rug

ug

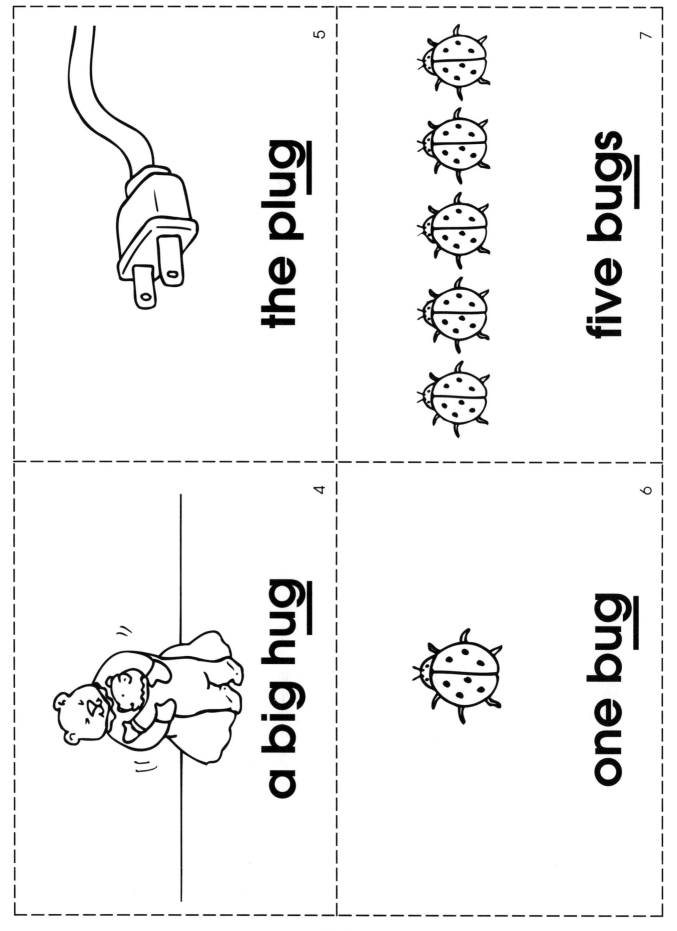

the plug

5

a big hug

4

five bugs

7

one bug

6

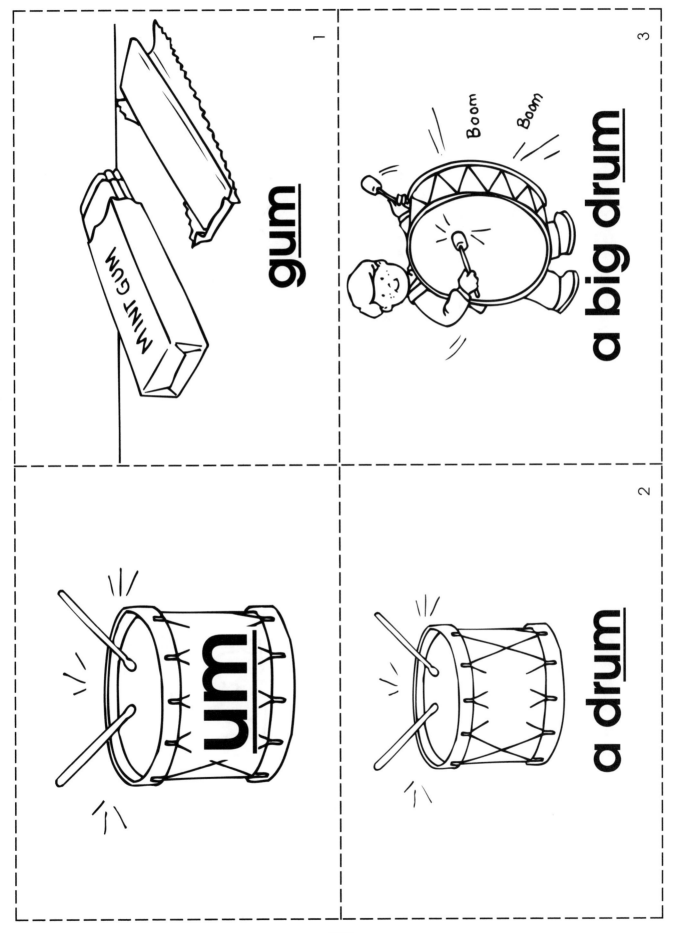

1

gu<u>m</u>

3

Boom

Boom

a big dr<u>um</u>

2

a dr<u>um</u>

<u>um</u>

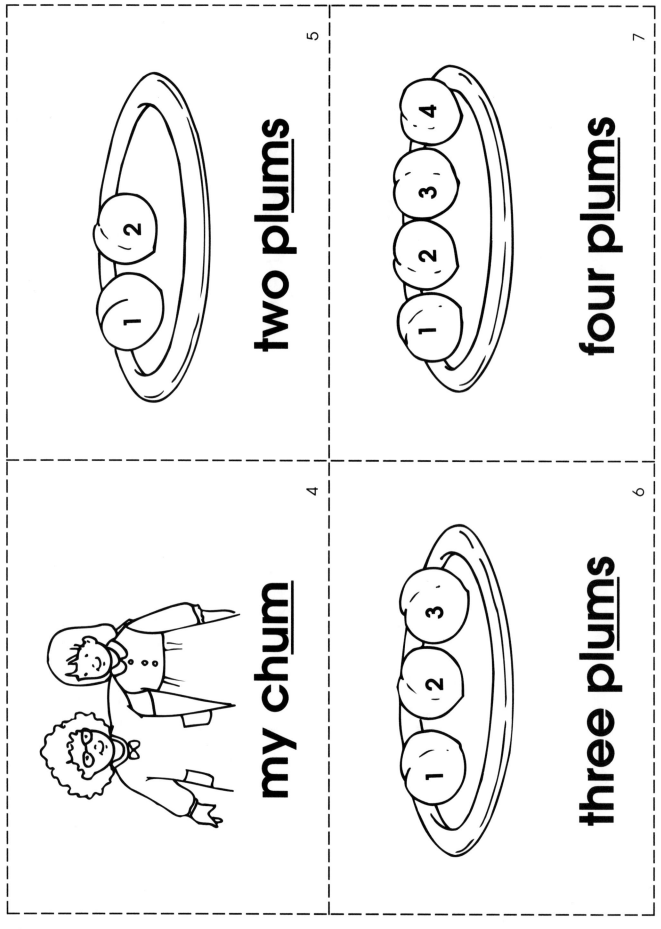

two plums

5

four plums

7

my chum

4

three plums

6

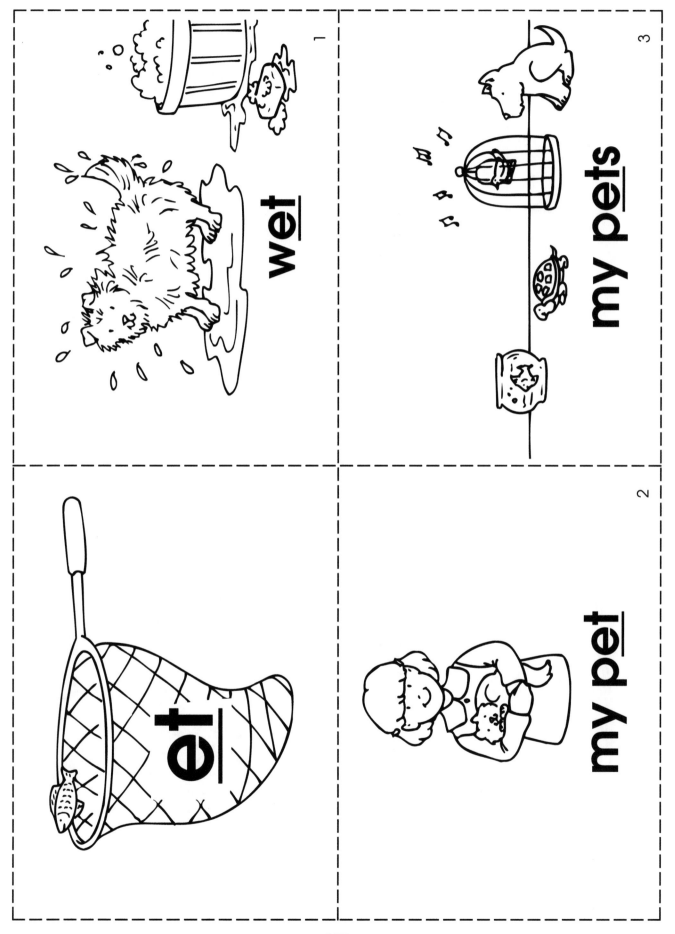

wet

et

my pets

my pet

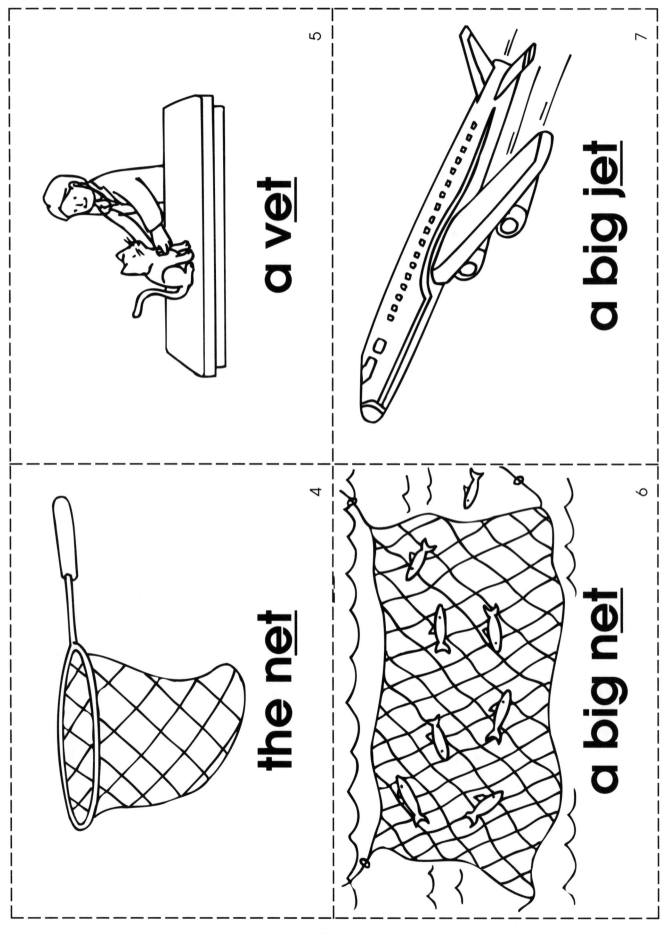

a vet

5

a big jet

7

the net

4

a big net

6

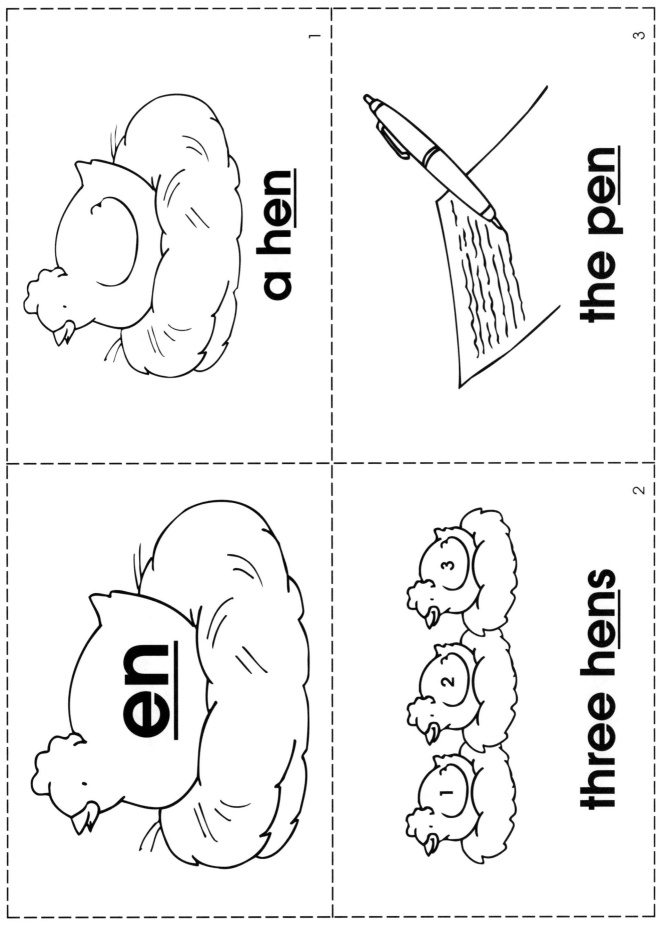

1

a h<u>en</u>

3

the p<u>en</u>

2

<u>en</u>

three h<u>ens</u>

303   Reading Connections © 1996 Monday Morning Books, Inc.

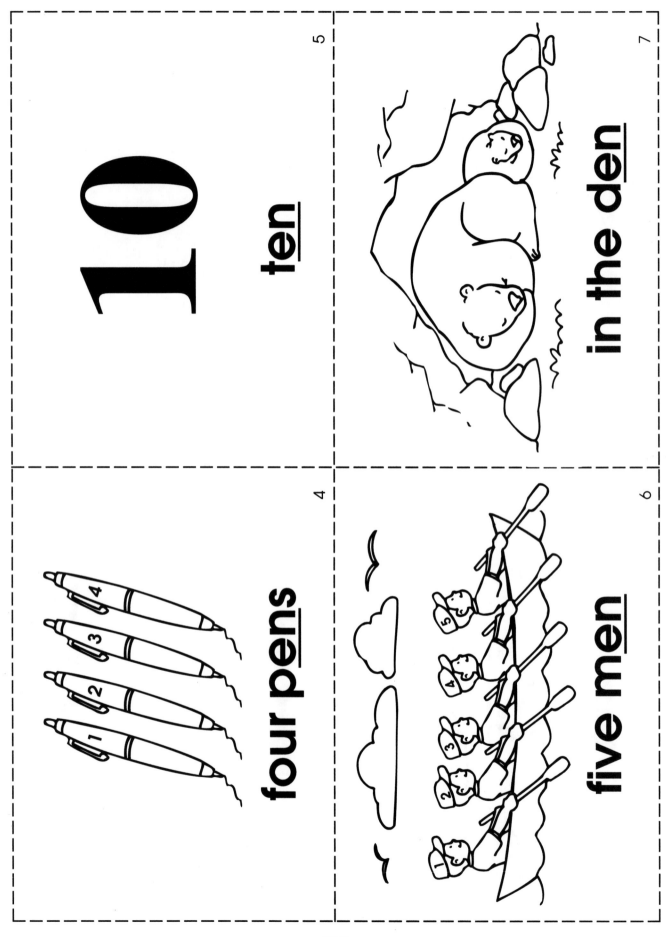

10
ten

in the den

four pens

five men

5

7

4

6

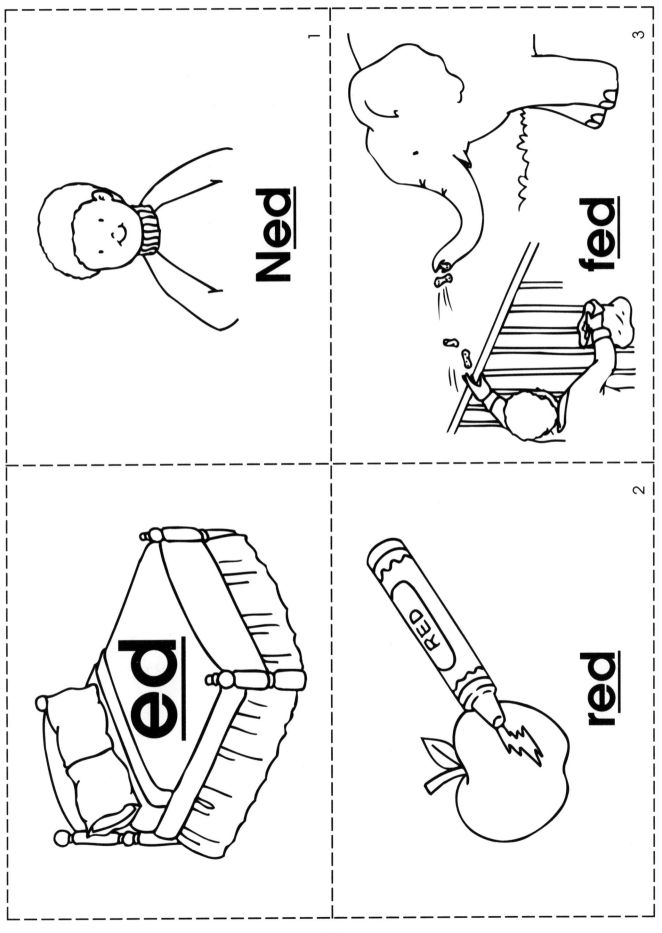

Ned

ed

fed

red

Reading Connections © 1996 Monday Morning Books, Inc.

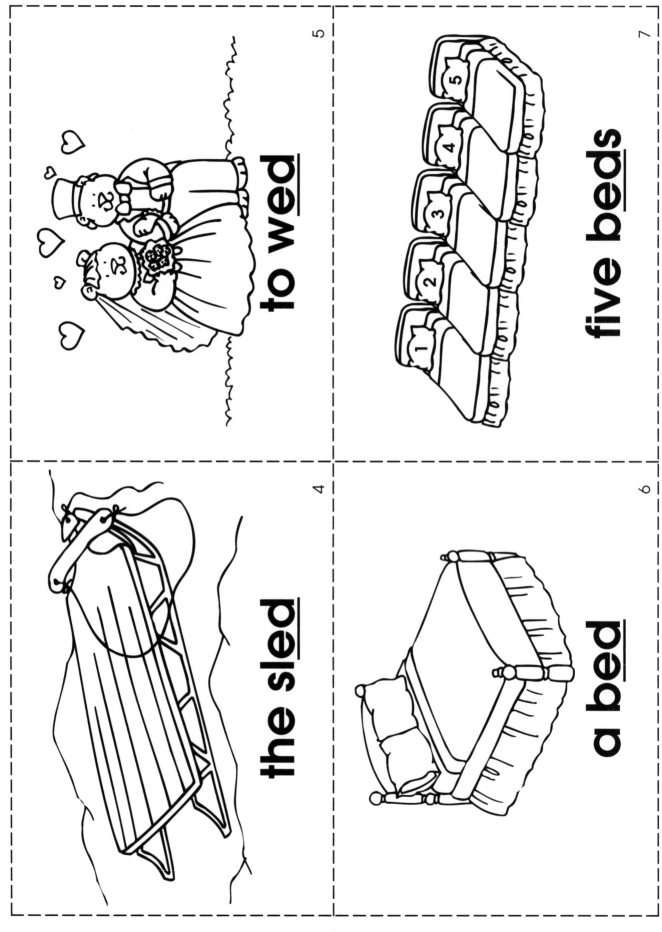

to w**ed**

5

the sl**ed**

4

five b**eds**

7

a b**ed**

6

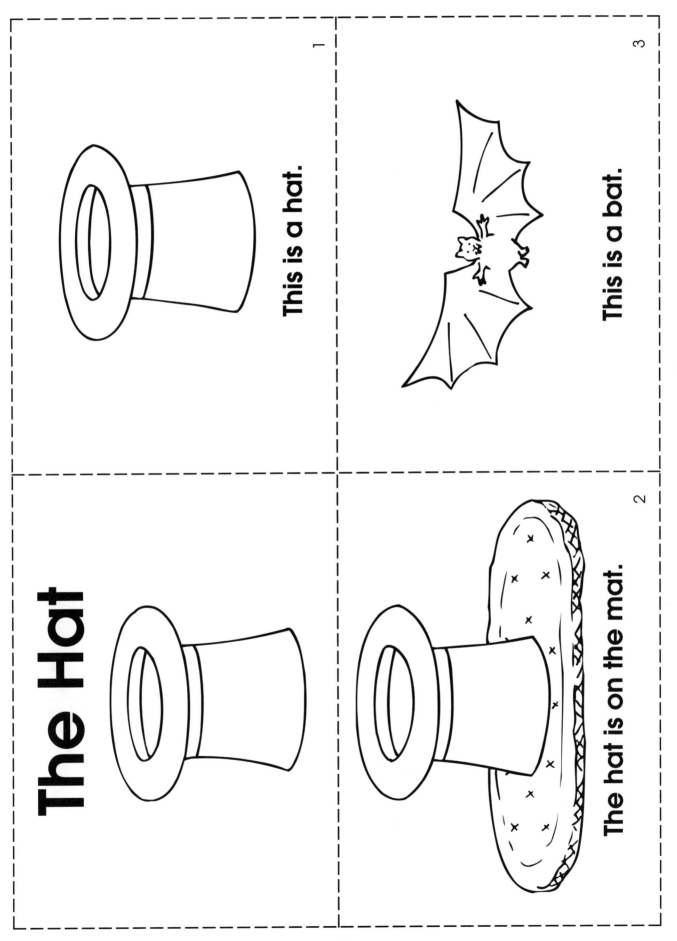

1

This is a hat.

3

This is a bat.

The Hat

2

The hat is on the mat.

5

Look!
A man is on the mat.

7

No!
The bat is on the man!

4

The bat is in the hat.

6

The hat is on the man.
Is the bat in the hat?

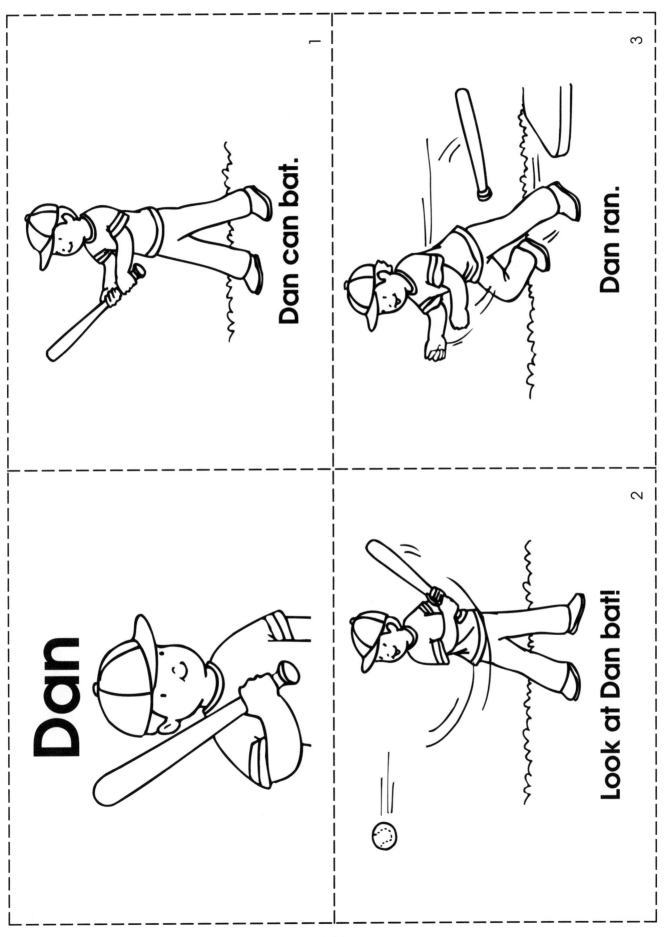

Dan

Dan can bat.

1

Look at Dan bat!

2

Dan ran.

3

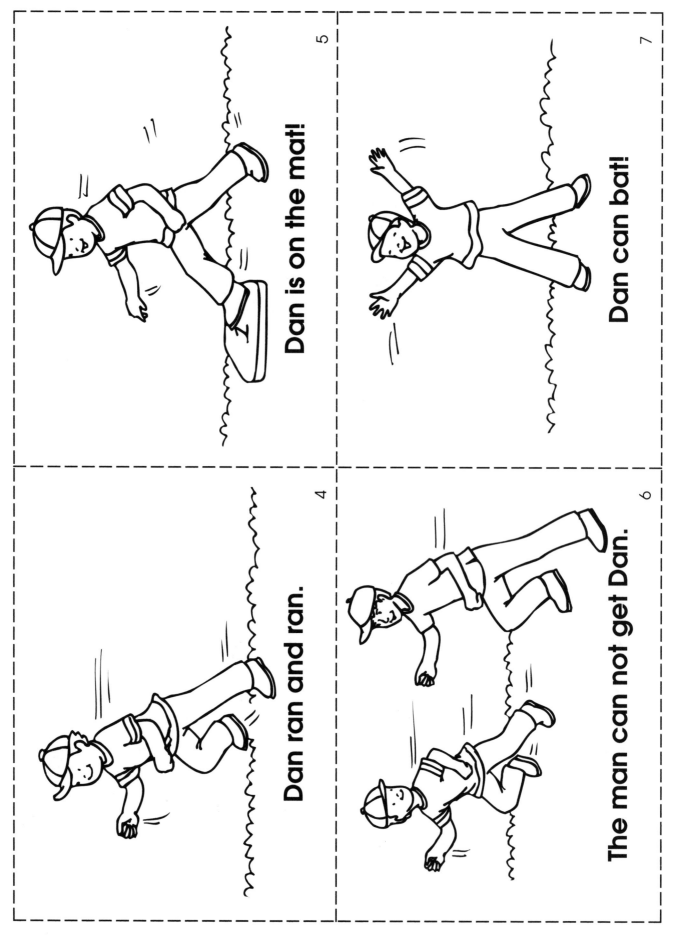

Dan is on the mat!

5

Dan can bat!

7

Dan ran and ran.

4

The man can not get Dan.

6

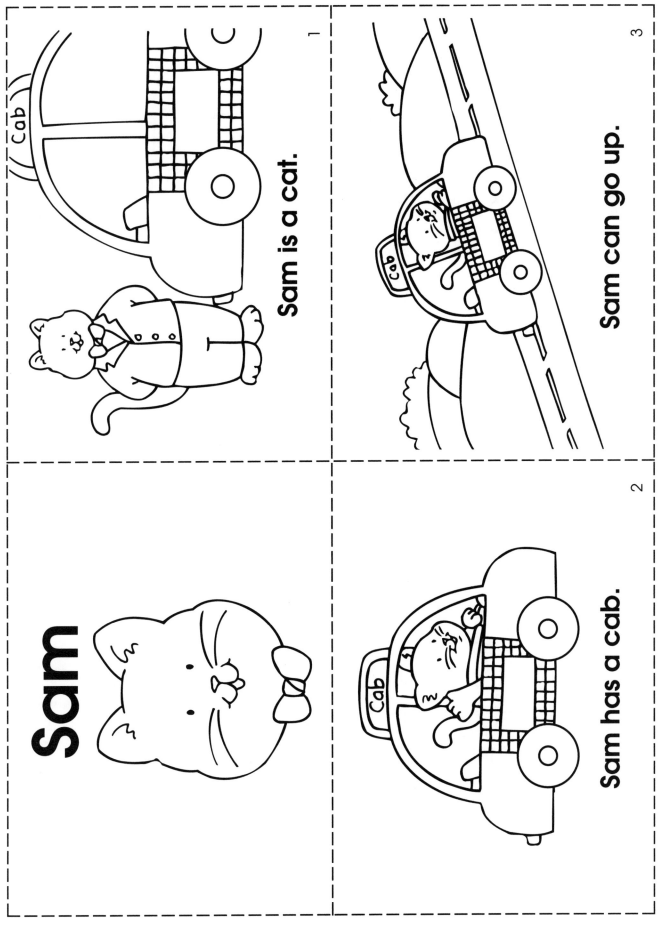

Sam

Sam is a cat.

1

Sam has a cab.

2

Sam can go up.

3

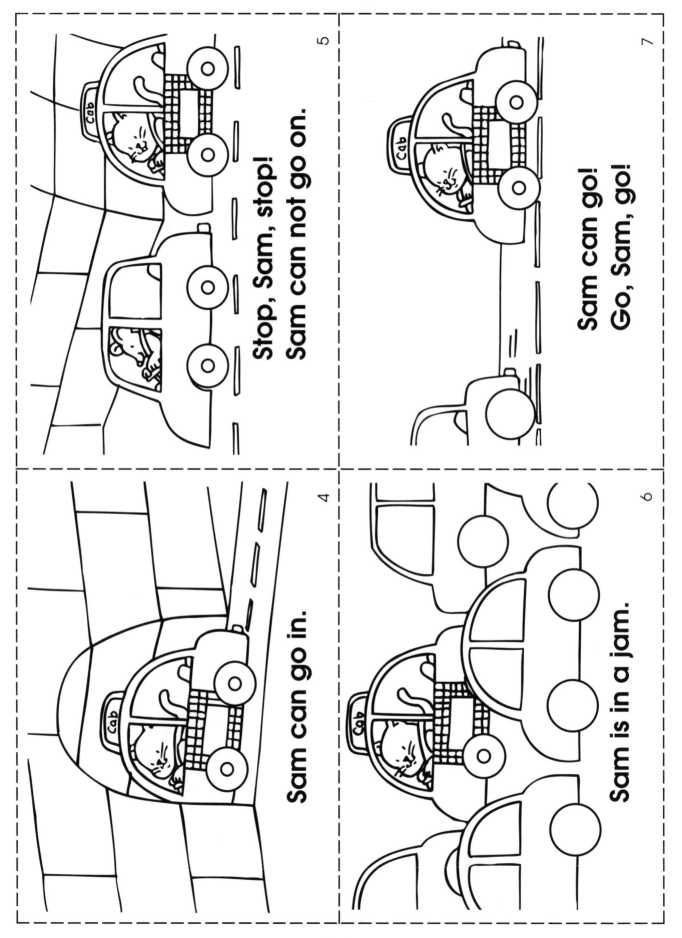

Stop, Sam, stop!
Sam can not go on.

5

Sam can go!
Go, Sam, go!

7

Sam can go in.

4

Sam is in a jam.

6

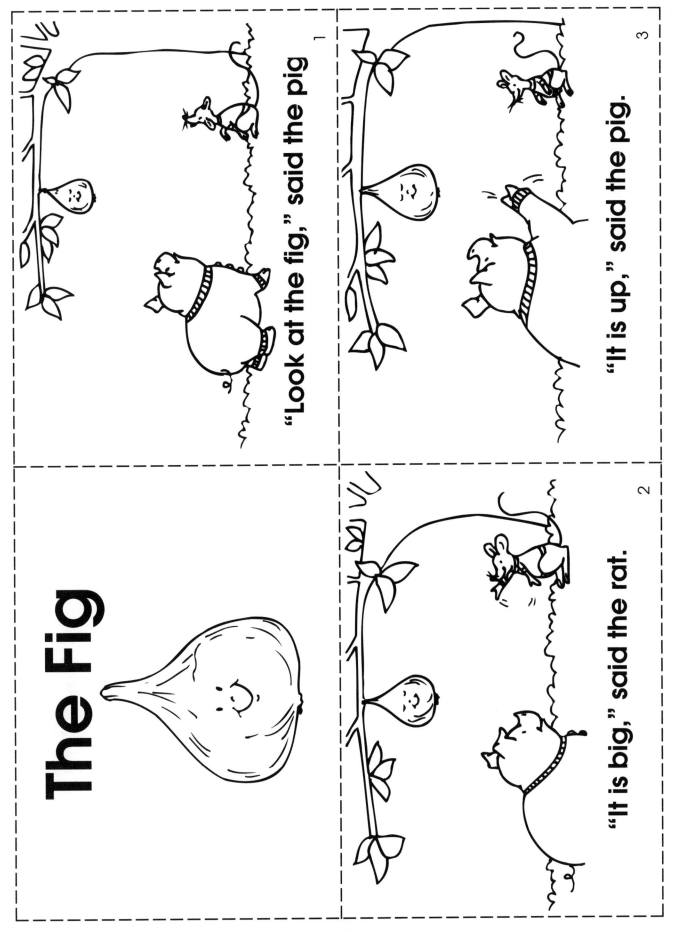

The Fig

"Look at the fig," said the pig

1

"It is big," said the rat.

2

"It is up," said the pig.

3

Reading Connections © 1996 Monday Morning Books, Inc.

"I can jig," said the pig.

5

The pig has the fig!

7

"We are down," said the rat.

4

"I can go up," said the rat.

6

1

"Come in, come in!"
said the spider to the bee.

3

"See me go up."

Spin, Spin!

2

"See me spin."

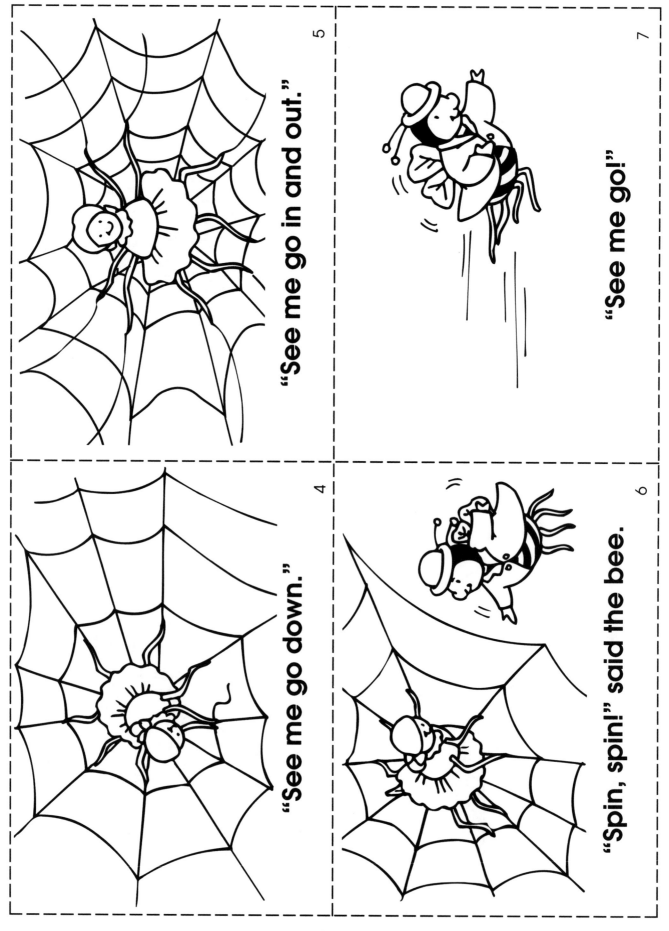

5

"See me go in and out."

7

"See me go!"

4

"See me go down."

6

"Spin, spin!" said the bee.

Skip and Kip

Skip and Kip are good pals.

1

Skip and Kip like to play ball.

2

They like to swim.

3

Reading Connections © 1996 Monday Morning Books, Inc.

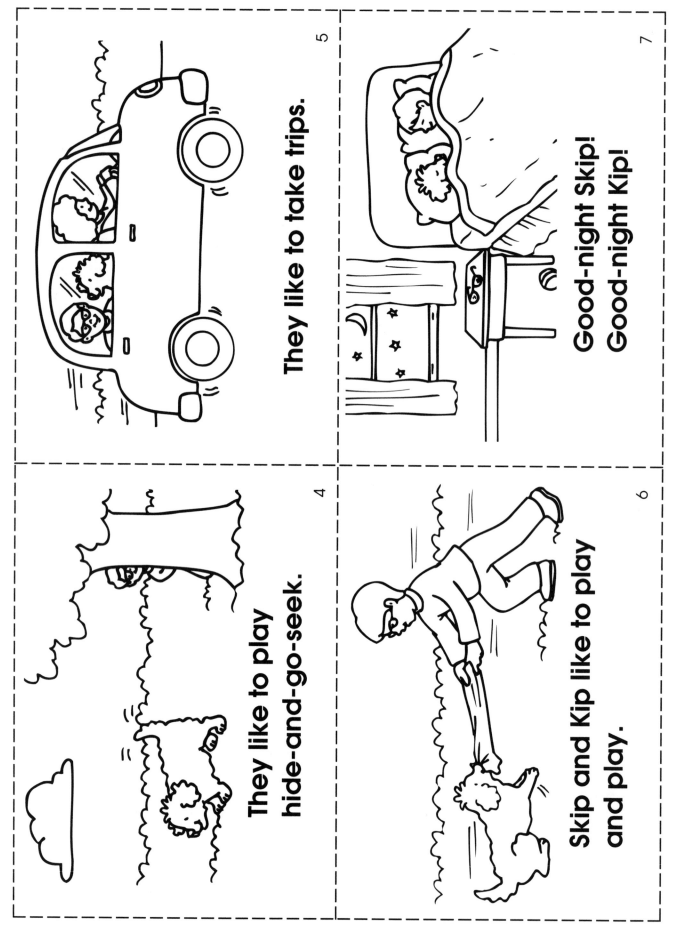

They like to take trips.

5

Good-night Skip!
Good-night Kip!

7

They like to play
hide-and-go-seek.

4

Skip and Kip like to play
and play.

6

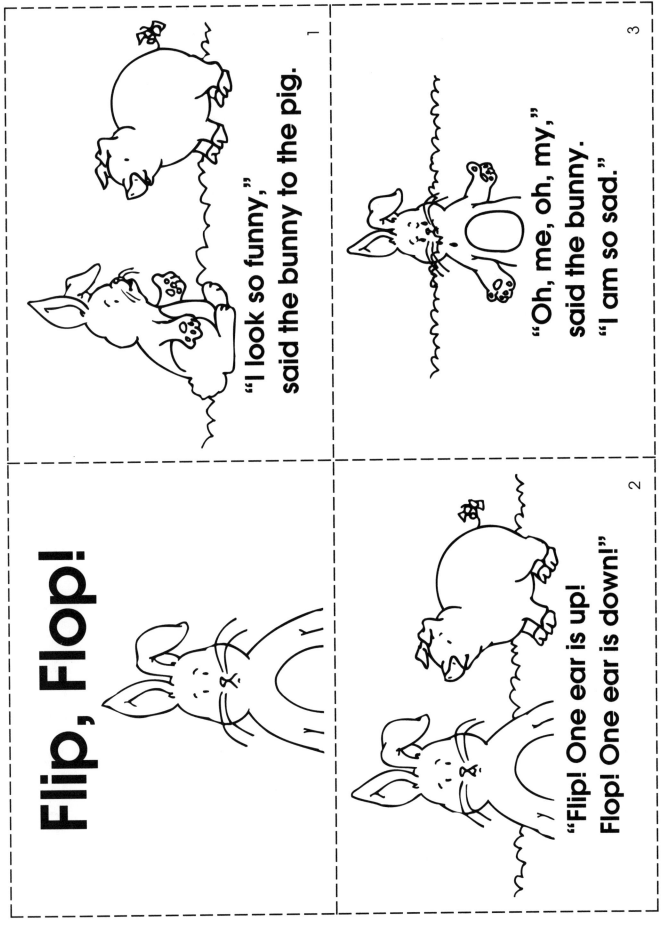

Flip, Flop!

1

"I look so funny,"
said the bunny to the pig.

2

"Flip! One ear is up!
Flop! One ear is down!"

3

"Oh, me, oh, my,"
said the bunny.
"I am so sad."

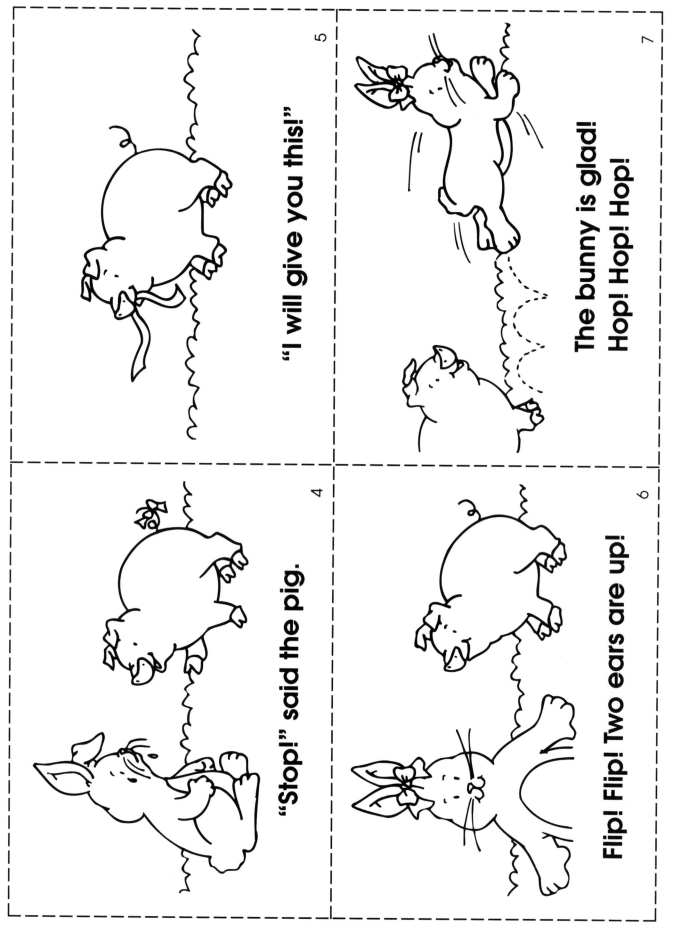

5

"I will give you this!"

7

The bunny is glad!
Hop! Hop! Hop!

4

"Stop!" said the pig.

6

Flip! Flip! Two ears are up!

The Pot

1

"This is the map," said the rat to the cat.

2

The cat saw a dot. "This is the spot," he said.

3

"Stop here. We are at the spot," said the cat.

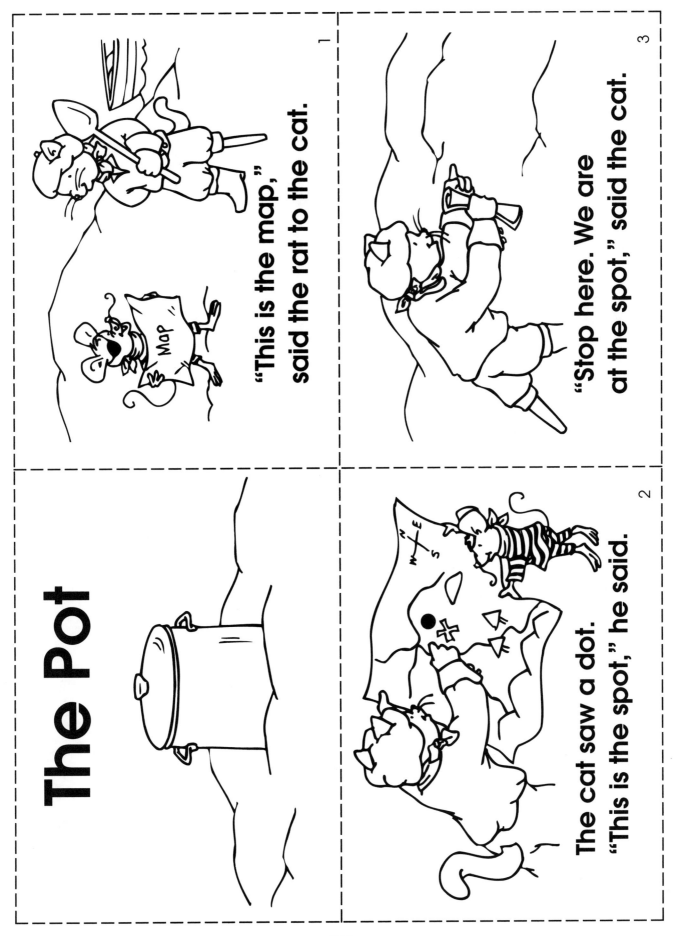

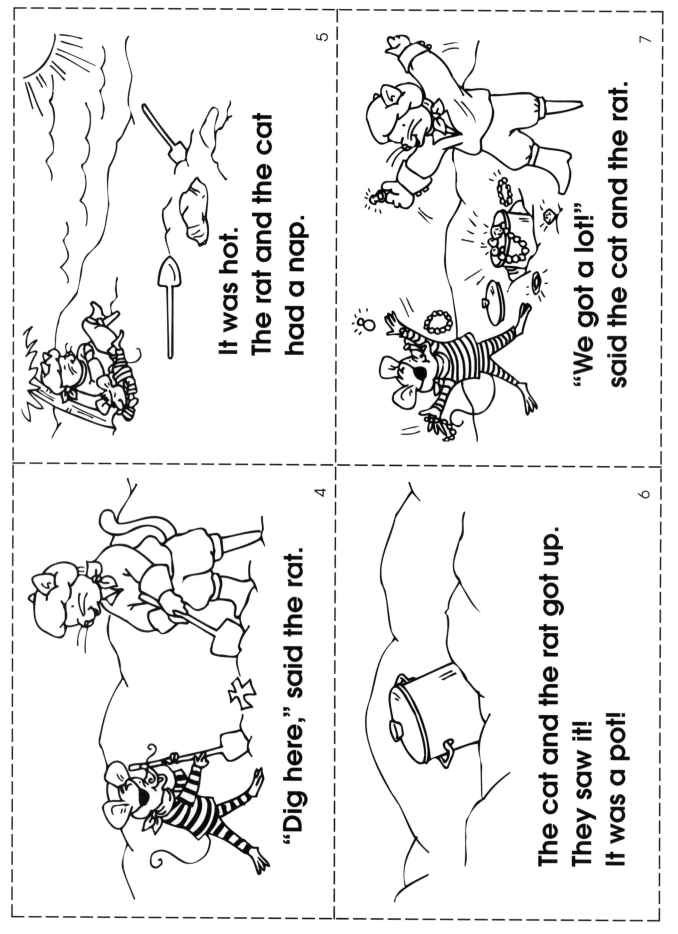

5

It was hot.
The rat and the cat
had a nap.

7

"We got a lot!"
said the cat and the rat.

4

"Dig here," said the rat.

6

The cat and the rat got up.
They saw it!
It was a pot!

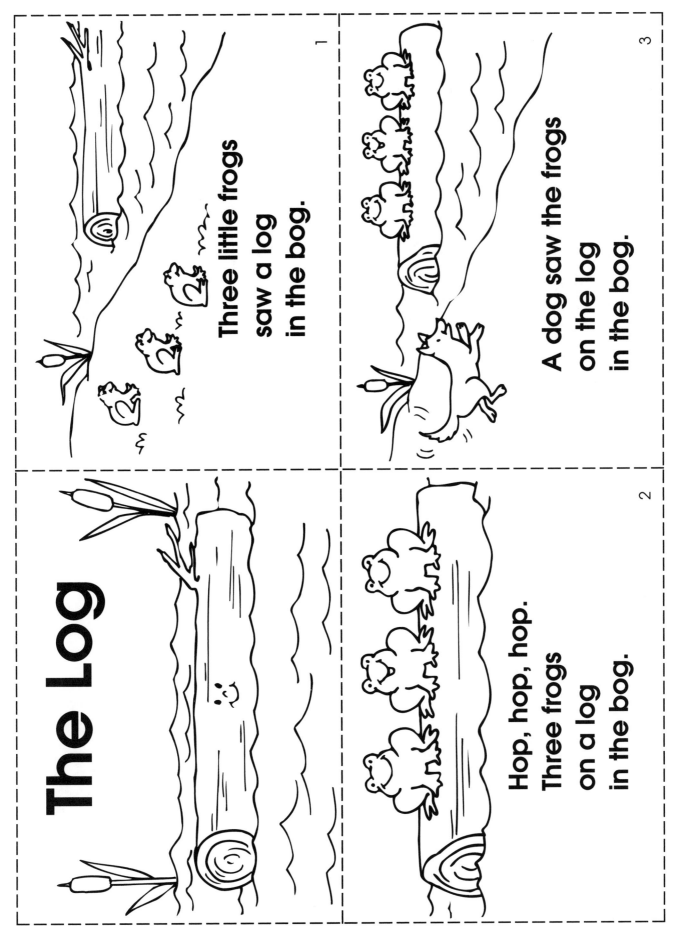

The Log

Three little frogs
saw a log
in the bog.

1

Hop, hop, hop.
Three frogs
on a log
in the bog.

2

A dog saw the frogs
on the log
in the bog.

3

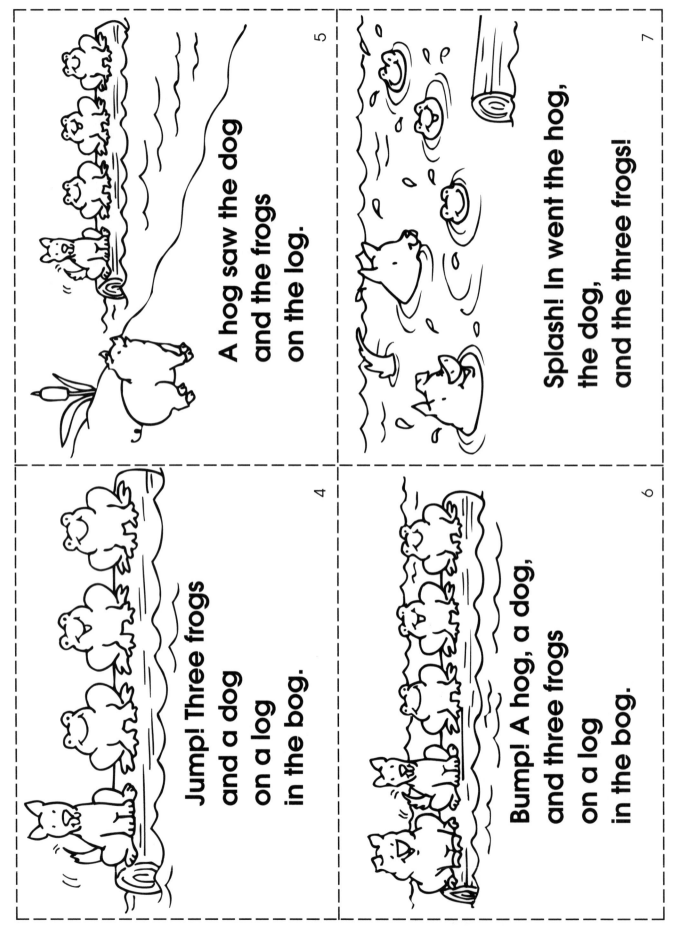

5

A hog saw the dog
and the frogs
on the log.

7

Splash! In went the hog,
the dog,
and the three frogs!

4

Jump! Three frogs
and a dog
on a log
in the bog.

6

Bump! A hog, a dog,
and three frogs
on a log
in the bog.

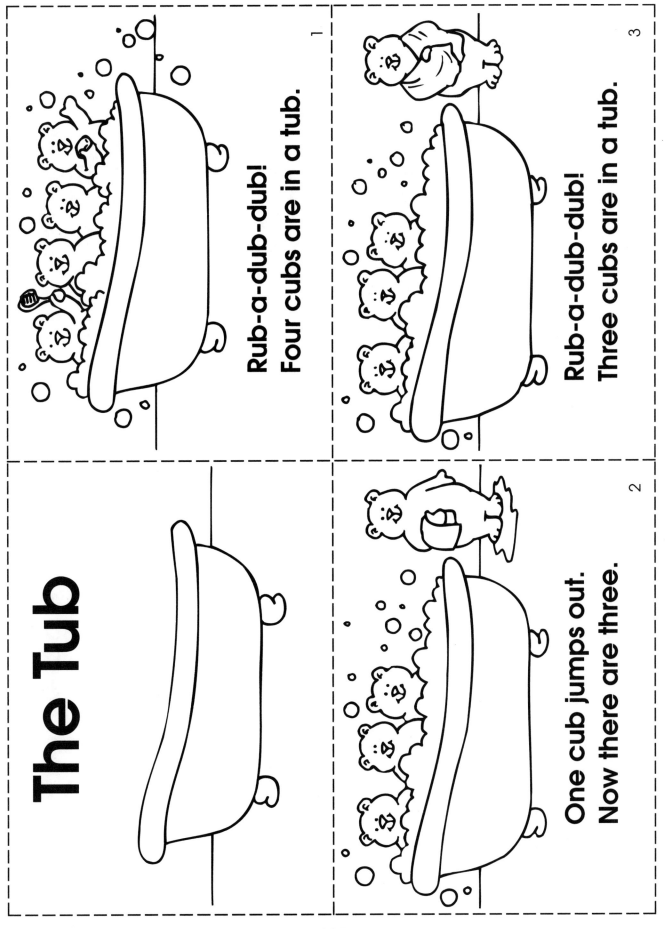

The Tub

Rub-a-dub-dub!
Four cubs are in a tub.

1

One cub jumps out.
Now there are three.

2

Rub-a-dub-dub!
Three cubs are in a tub.

3

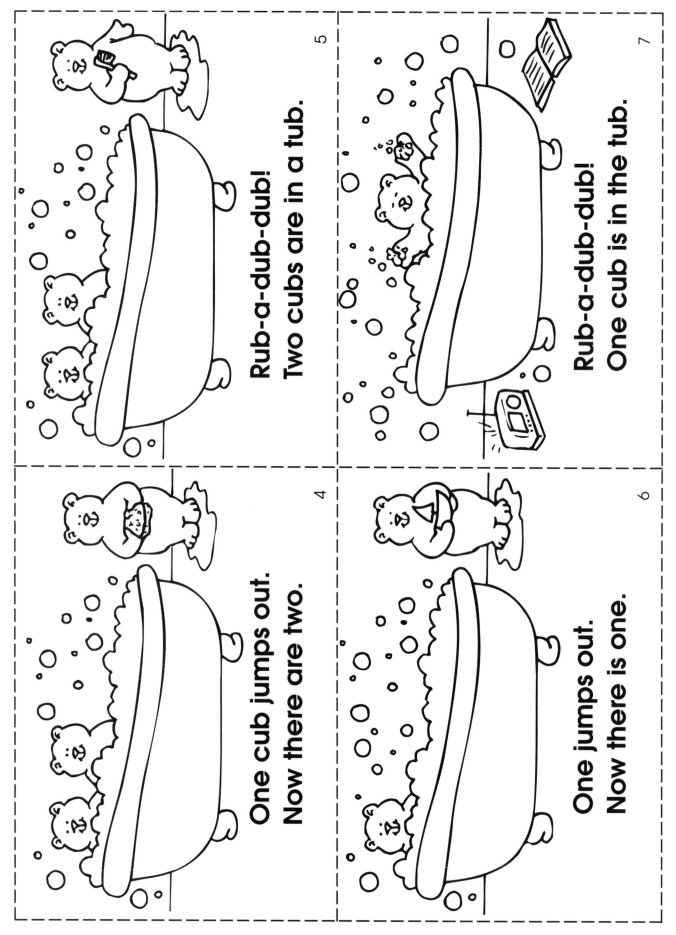

Rub-a-dub-dub!
Two cubs are in a tub.

5

One cub jumps out.
Now there are two.

4

Rub-a-dub-dub!
One cub is in the tub.

7

One jumps out.
Now there is one.

6

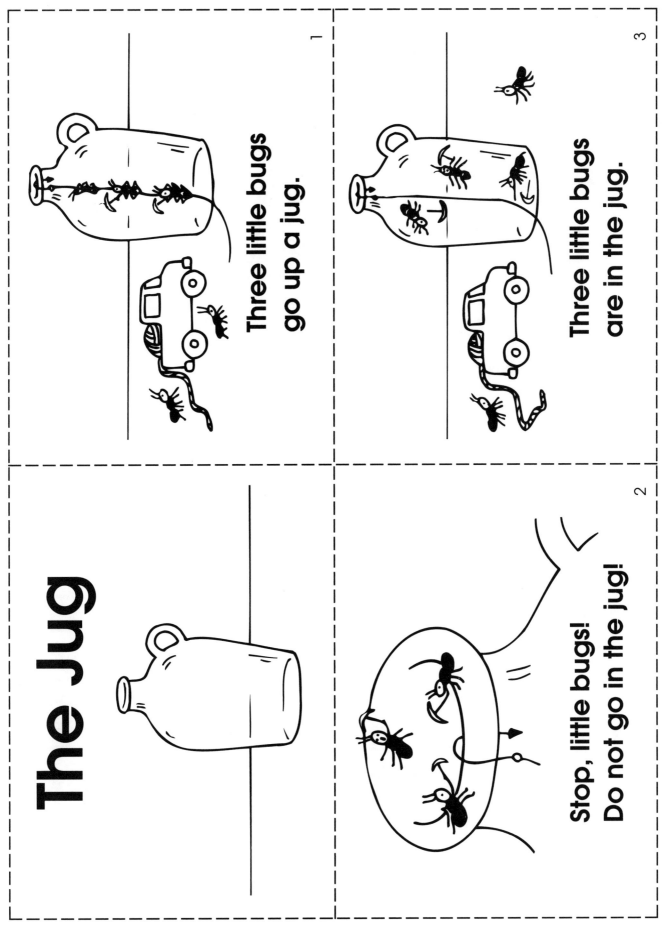

The Jug

Three little bugs
go up a jug.

1

Stop, little bugs!
Do not go in the jug!

2

Three little bugs
are in the jug.

3

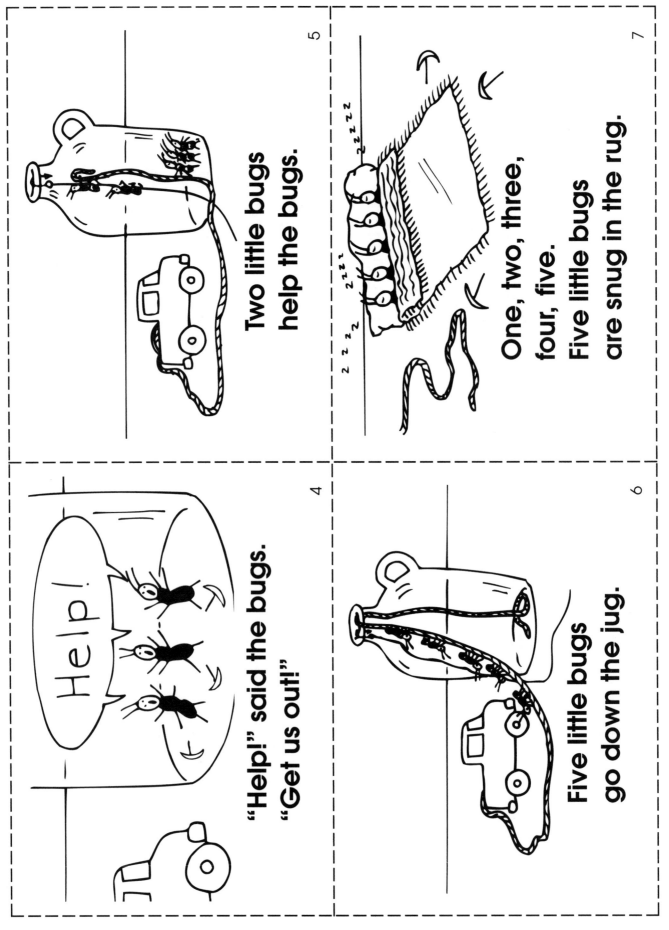

5

Two little bugs
help the bugs.

7

One, two, three,
four, five.
Five little bugs
are snug in the rug.

4

"Help!" said the bugs.
"Get us out!"

6

Five little bugs
go down the jug.

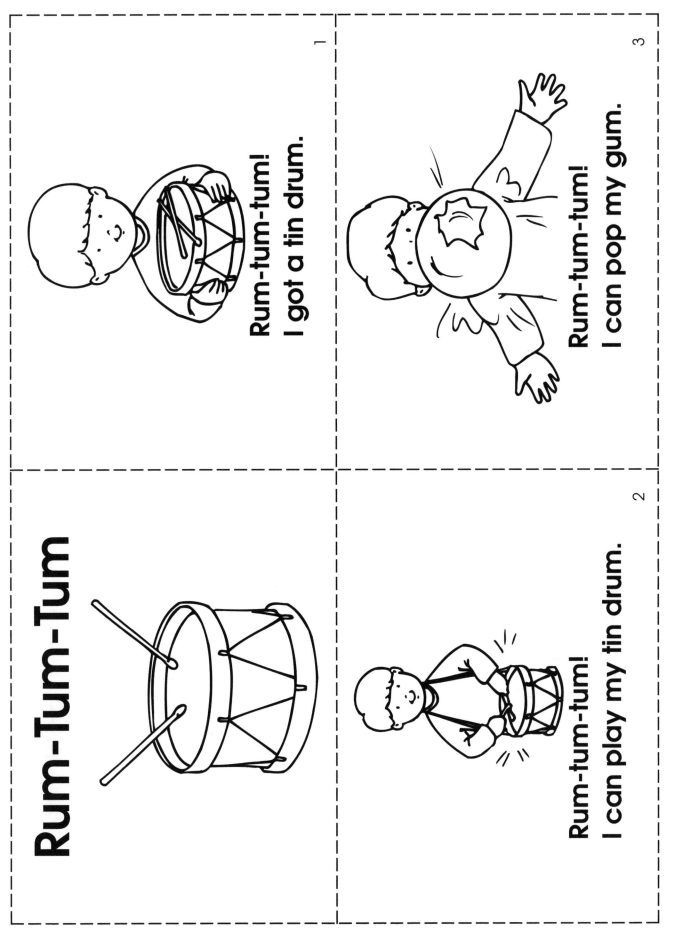

Rum-Tum-Tum

Rum-tum-tum!
I got a tin drum.

1

Rum-tum-tum!
I can play my tin drum.

2

Rum-tum-tum!
I can pop my gum.

3

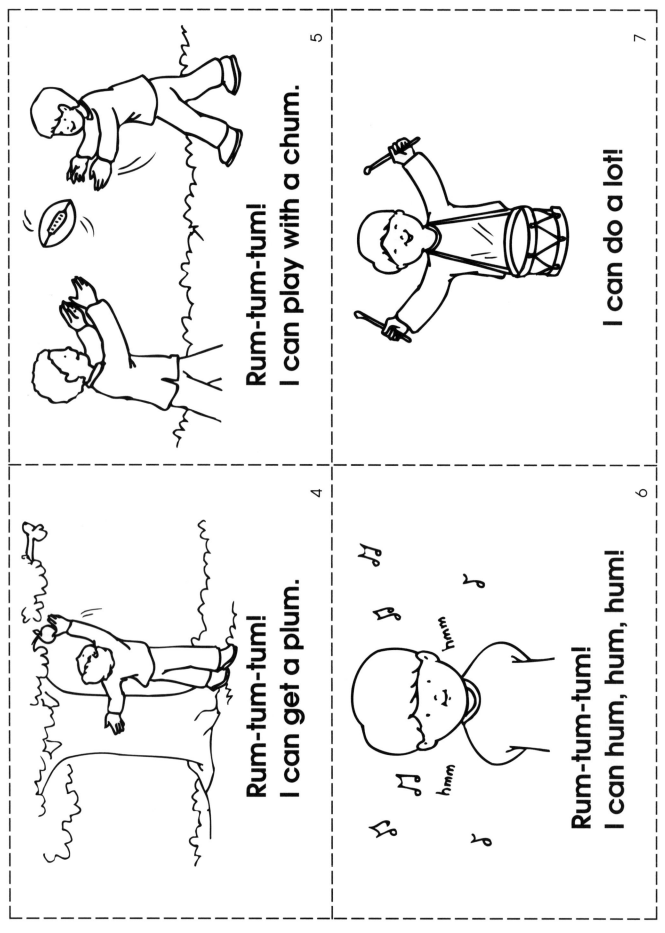

5

Rum-tum-tum!
I can play with a chum.

7

I can do a lot!

4

Rum-tum-tum!
I can get a plum.

6

Rum-tum-tum!
I can hum, hum, hum!

The Pet

1

"Get me eggs," said Mama.
"Here is a goat to give
for the eggs."

2

I met a girl
with a yellow bird.

3

I said, "I will give you a goat
for the bird."

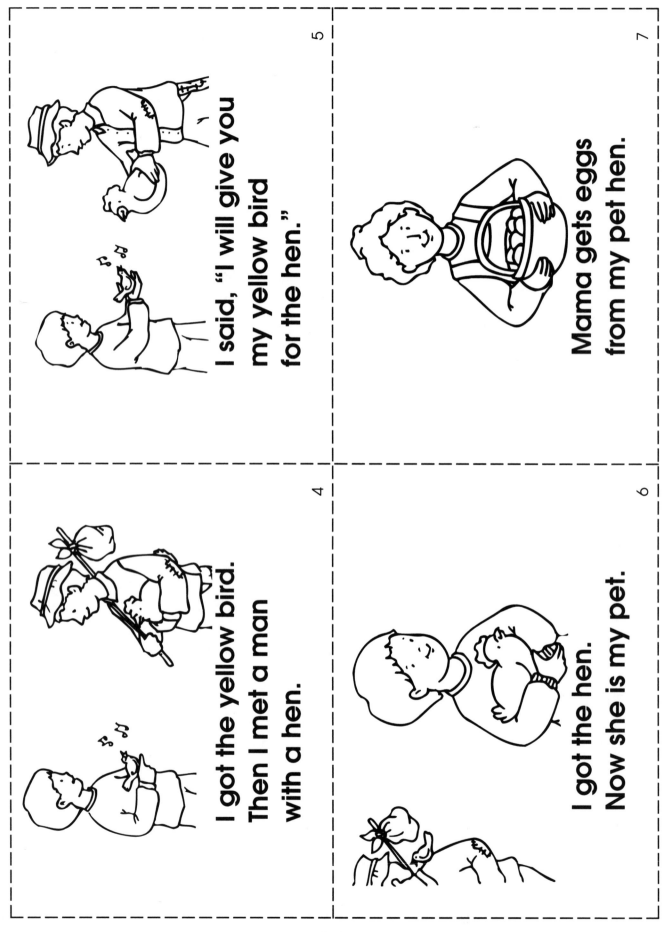

5

I said, "I will give you my yellow bird for the hen."

7

Mama gets eggs from my pet hen.

4

I got the yellow bird. Then I met a man with a hen.

6

I got the hen. Now she is my pet.

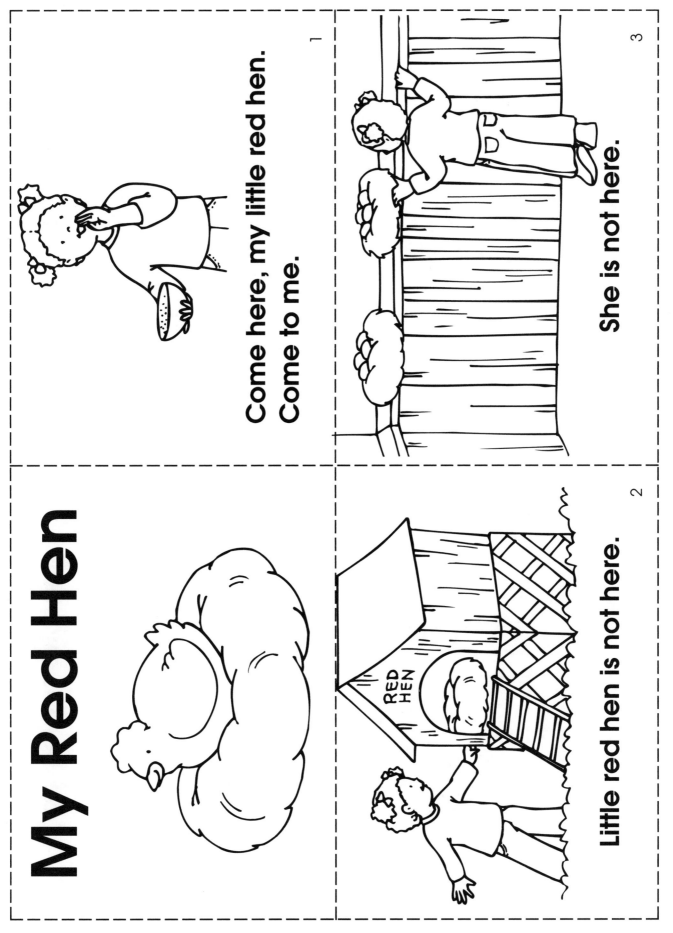

My Red Hen

Come here, my little red hen.
Come to me.

1

Little red hen is not here.

RED HEN

2

She is not here.

3

No hen in the den.

5

Look! Five baby chicks!
One, two, three, four, five!

7

No hen in the pen.

4

Oh, here, is my hen!

6

Ned and His Sled

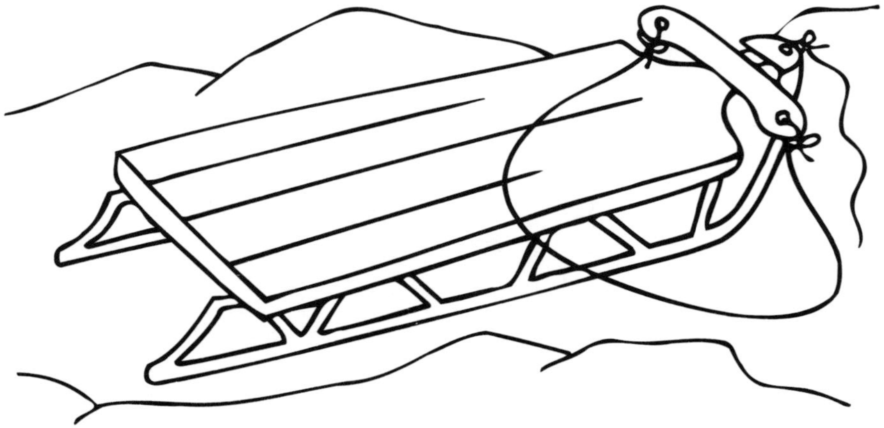

Ned got out his green sled.

"Here I go!" Ned said.

Up go Ned and the sled.

1

2

3

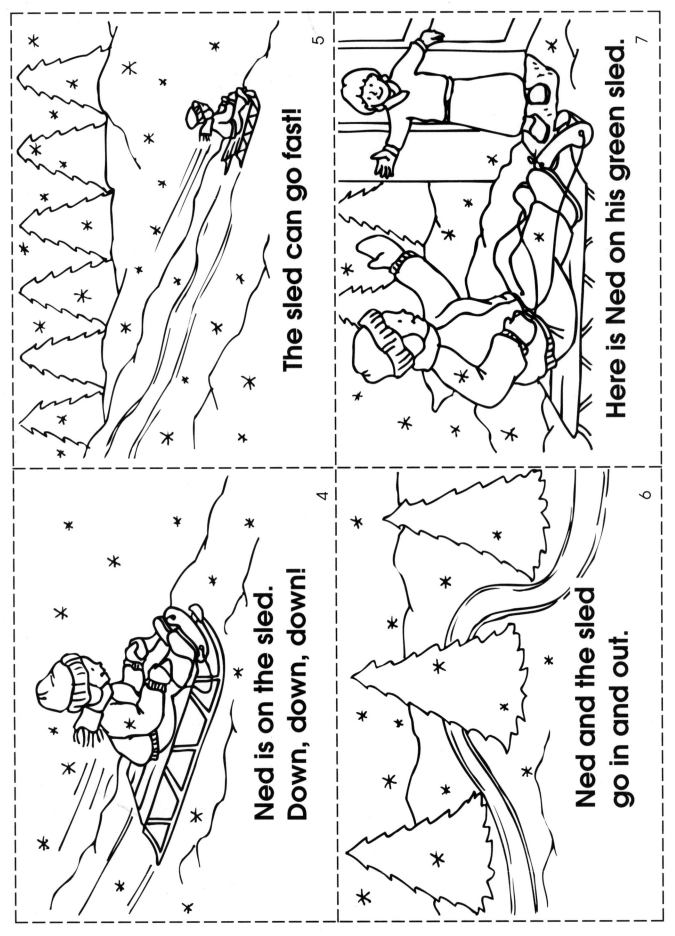

The sled can go fast!

5

Here is Ned on his green sled.

7

Ned is on the sled.
Down, down, down!

4

Ned and the sled
go in and out.

6